About Island Press

Island Press is the only nonprofit organization in the United States whose principal purpose is the publication of books on environmental issues and natural resource management. We provide solutions-oriented information to professionals, public officials, business and community leaders, and concerned citizens who are shaping responses to environmental problems.

In 2005, Island Press celebrates its twenty-first anniversary as the leading provider of timely and practical books that take a multidisciplinary approach to critical environmental concerns. Our growing list of titles reflects our commitment to bringing the best of an expanding body of literature to the environmental community throughout North America and the world.

Support for Island Press is provided by the Agua Fund, The Geraldine R. Dodge Foundation, Doris Duke Charitable Foundation, Ford Foundation, The George Gund Foundation, The William and Flora Hewlett Foundation, Kendeda Sustainability Fund of the Tides Foundation, The Henry Luce Foundation, The John D. and Catherine T. MacArthur Foundation, The Andrew W. Mellon Foundation, The Curtis and Edith Munson Foundation, The New-Land Foundation, The New York Community Trust, Oak Foundation, The Overbrook Foundation, The David and Lucile Packard Foundation, The Winslow Foundation, and other generous donors.

The opinions expressed in this book are those of the author(s) and do not necessarily reflect the views of these foundations.

Owning and Managing Forests

Owning and Managing Forests

A Guide to Legal, Financial, and Practical Matters

Thom J. McEvoy

Foreword by Carl Reidel

ISLAND PRESS

Washington • Covelo • London

Owning and Managing Forests: A Guide to Legal, Financial, and Practical Matters, is a revised, updated edition of *Legal Aspects of Owning and Managing Woodlands*, by Thom J. McEvoy, published by Island Press, 1998.

Library of Congress Cataloging-in-Publication Data

McEvoy, Thomas J.(Thomas James), 1953
Owning and managing forests : a guide to legal, financial, and practical matters / Thom J. McEvoy ; foreword by Carl Reidel.
p. cm.
Includes bibliographical references and index.
ISBN 1–55963–081–7 (cloth : alk. paper). — ISBN 1–55963–082–5 (paper : alk. paper)
1. Forestry law and legislation—United States—Popular works.
2. Forest management—Popular works. I. Title
KF1750.Z9M39 2005
343.73'07649—dc22 2005013823

British Cataloguing-in-Publication data available

Printed on recycled, acid-free paper

Manufactured in the United States of America
10 9 8 7 6 5 4 3 2 1

“It was only after we pondered on these things that we began to wonder who wrote the rules for progress.”

—Aldo Leopold, *A Sand County Almanac*

“Everything should be made as simple as possible, but not simpler.”

—Albert Einstein

Contents

Foreword

As a young forestry student I learned to view a forest only as a physical-biological entity, in hindsight more complex and dynamic than I could then understand. While I was aware of the social and economic aspects of forestry, they didn't seem relevant to my interests in wildlife, trees, and forests. It didn't take long on my first job, however, to realize that my understanding of forestry was sorely inadequate. Experience soon taught that the legal, financial, and social problems of managing the woodlands for which I was responsible were far more challenging than the biological aspects of forestry. Only after some three decades of practicing and teaching forestry have I come to see how inextricably interwoven are the human and natural contexts of forests, and how essential it is to understand those relationships to manage our woodlands for the goals and values we seek.

Most owners of small woodlands know that managing their lands is complicated by problems they did not anticipate when they decided to buy the land or begin active management on a previously ignored or inherited tract. One could find hundreds of books and pamphlets giving advice on such tasks as tree planting, silviculture, harvesting, and forest protection, but little was available to help anticipate and resolve the inevitable legal and financial problems of woodland management. As a result, unwise investments, legal mistakes, and poor financial planning have probably caused more woodland management failures than fires, insects, and inappropriate silviculture combined.

For many woodland owners, this book can make all the difference between success and failure when it comes to legal matters related to owning and managing their lands. Although it is not a substitute for the advice of a professional forester or a qualified attorney, it will make private owners far more savvy consumers of those services. In practical, everyday language Thom McEvoy explains the historical roots, legal principles, and technical details of property ownership and management that will enable woodland owners to ask the right questions of their attorneys, consulting foresters, and everyone they encounter in the complex task of owning and managing land. Knowing the right questions will prepare them to make better choices of partners, forestry and tax consultants, financial advisors, and attorneys, and better able to judge their answers. Little of the information in this book is new, certainly not to a seasoned extension forester like Thom McEvoy. What makes it special and unusually valuable is the way the information is organized and put into both historical and practical perspective, leading the reader to see how decisions in one aspect of management affect others over time. McEvoy explains, for example, how early decisions about methods of ownership and financial management affect long-term goals, tax liability, and estate planning. He sees the legal and financial aspects of woodland management in the same integrated way that modern foresters are coming to understand complex forest ecosystems: everything is connected and interactive.

This book will help the woodland owner to understand and appreciate that the often confusing and seemingly burdensome aspects of the law affecting land ownership are rooted in history as surely as a forest is the result of decades of natural biological succession. And, as we are learning that every aspect of a natural system is critical to the whole, McEvoy leads us to see that our unique rights as private landowners in the United States rest on a complex legal system that balances our rights and obligations with those of the public at large—a system that has evolved and been tested over time. Put simply, the past is always prologue.

This simple truth came home vividly for me a few years ago when I was trying to advise some Russian foresters in Siberia who were charged with transferring state lands to private ownership. I wish I had had this book then, for their questions raised all the subjects that McEvoy so clearly explains: What rights do owners have? How are those rights granted and protected? How is the land marked on the ground? What can people do with the land? Can they change the uses, subdivide it, sell it, give it away to family, inherit it, mortgage it? Can they sell the trees or minerals and keep ownership of the land? Can they exclude others from using it, or use it in ways that destroys wildlife habitat? Who decides? How is government financed to do all this?

I found myself telling the history of the United States and how we created constitutions and such democratic institutions as courts and local governments to carry out those social contracts. I tried to explain how they would have to "invent" a system of surveys, deeds, and titles; town halls and methods of recording deeds and contracts; corporations; a court system; and even lawyers and tax collectors. They were overwhelmed with the realization that they were faced with a task that took the United States several hundred years to develop and refine by building upon centuries of English Common Law!

I reflected recently on that experience in Siberia as I sat beneath a venerable old oak on some land we own along Lake Champlain. That tree has witnessed all those changes in its lifetime. As a seedling it was within the common land of the Abenaki tribe. When a century old, the old oak came within the boundaries of a parcel of private land defined in fee simple under English Common Law. It now stands on a tract of private land governed by the complex laws of our nation, state, and the local town, which both limit and protect the bundle of rights we hold in fee simple. Tracing the history of all the legal and financial claims on this tree is as much a part of understanding woodland management as understanding its ecological history as a red oak. In many ways, it is as daunting a task for us landowners and foresters here in the United States as it for those in Siberia seeking a way to create private land ownership. We are fortunate to now have Thom McEvoy's book to guide us.

Foreword to the Second Edition

This new edition comes at a time when there is even more complexity to the legal and financial aspects of woodland ownership than when it was first published. Thom McEvoy has not only updated the details of how to cope with these practical matters, but has also written a fascinating history of how American private property laws evolved from English Common Law. This added historical depth is not just a good story. Most importantly it helps the reader make sense of the seemingly chaotic legal maze facing woodland owners today by putting it in historical context. He has affirmed the old adage that the past is always prelude. Hopefully that will also challenge woodland owners to think carefully about how best to transfer ownership of the land they have cared for in the past to future generations.

Carl Reidel
Professor of Forestry, Natural Resources,
and Environmental Policy
University of Vermont

Preface and Acknowledgments

I began my career in academics many years ago as a prelaw student at Michigan State University. Fascinated with law, and assured by family and friends that lawyers make a good living, it seemed like the perfect path. That is, until I took a course in forest ecology. Even before the end of my first year in college I had changed disciplines, and four years later—jobless—I did not regret it. Aside from a short stint as a consulting forester struggling to make a living in the aspen forests of northern Michigan, followed by graduate study in forest biology, I have spent my entire career as an extension educator in forestry, a job I love.

About fifteen years ago, I considered going back to school for a J.D. degree. So serious were my plans, I took the LSAT and scored well enough to receive an offer for admission to the law school I wanted to attend. But events and lack of financing conspired against me and I never went. Instead, I audited an undergraduate course in business law at the University of Vermont. It was an excellent course, with one of the best teachers I have ever encountered. I was so inspired by the experience that I began to write and speak about legal aspects of owning and managing woodlands.

In 1986, I was invited to give a presentation to a group of nonresident woodland owners on the subject of selling timber. After the talk, one of participants—a lawyer—came forward to offer his compliments. Although there were several valid criticisms he could have shared, he applauded my unfettered and clear explanations of abstract and often difficult legal concepts. Little did he know it does not take much encouragement from the right sources to launch me headlong into a project. For more than ten years I had wanted to write this book. At first the task was daunting, a good reason to put it off. But I was haunted. The question from colleagues I had not seen in a while became: "So, when is the book coming out?"

An outline for the book began to take shape in the fall of 1995. I shared my ideas with anyone who would listen—woodland owners, foresters, loggers, lawyers, accountants, estate planners, and others. A year later, the outline became the proposal for a twelve-month sabbatical leave from my post as extension forester at the University of Vermont. In the fall of 1996, I circulated a draft table of contents for the book to my extension colleagues around the country and received from them much encouragement and a pile of materials on local regulations and state extension publications dealing with legal aspects of owning land. Some of those materials were very useful.

When I set to writing in December of 1996, the task proved every bit as daunting as I feared. I quickly became bogged down in details, realizing all but the most dedicated readers would fall fast asleep after the first few pages. It took weeks to locate a proper voice and to discover a formula that would allow me to cover a huge subject area in a small book. Throughout, I have taken the position that it is more important to know how to ask the right questions than to have answers to the wrong questions. Detail-oriented people will find the book unsettling; after all, how can anyone explain the complexities of, for instance, land trusts in just a few pages? Generalists will say, "Good, it is about time the emphasis is placed on broad understanding rather than mind-numbing details that make even the most well-accepted, broadly applied set of facts nothing more than fanciful wanderings of the author." In other words, it was pointless to write something that people would not read.

My goal was to write a book that people will read on a subject that is of great importance to woodland owners: understanding the legalities of real property, the rights and responsibilities as well as the opportunities and pitfalls of owning and managing forests. The prospects for future forests, and the importance of thinking like a forest when it comes to long-range planning, are also major themes. My measure of success in this endeavor is the degree to which readers are empowered to become more active forest managers.

I am not a lawyer. Thus, nothing in the text should be construed as legal advice or legal opinion. This book is based on information that is generally known and on my ideas, some of which have been inspired by other cited sources. The ideas are intended to provoke readers to consider strategies and methods to improve the long-term management and care of woodlands, and to seek the advice and guidance of qualified local professionals. Nothing in the book should serve as the sole basis for a reader's actions or inactions. For these reasons, the author and publisher disclaim responsibility or liability for loss that may result from a reader's interpretations or applications of the material in the book.

Many people deserve thanks for their help. Among them are two well-seasoned attorneys who reviewed the manuscript from cover to cover, offering many important and useful suggestions. They wish to remain anonymous "because of potential disagreements with colleagues." Because I know they will see the book, I want to express my gratitude here for their extraordinary efforts. Many thanks to Larry Bruce, a practicing attorney in St. Albans, Vermont, who read the manuscript, made many useful suggestions, and agreed to be acknowledged.

Special thanks go to Doug Hart, a woodland owner in Quechee, Vermont. Doug reviewed chapters throughout the year, and he gave the final manuscript an especially close reading. We communicated exclusively by e-mail, and his many excellent comments and suggestions have made my writing much easier to follow. The illustrations are the work of Marna Grove of Pencil Mill Graphics in Castleton, Vermont. Her creations were a truly collaborative effort, and it was a pleasure—as always—to work with her.

Others who deserve thanks include: Tami Bass, a surveyor in Vermont, for reviewing the chapter on surveys and boundaries and offering some tips on illustrations to help explain blazing; Sarah Tischler, attorney and estate planner, who was of immeasurable assistance in the preparation of the chapter on estate planning; Lloyd Casey, forest taxation specialist with the U.S. Forest Service, who reviewed the chapter on forest taxation and served as my primary source for information on the Taxpayer Relief Act of 1997; and Keith Ross, a forester with the New England Forestry Foundation, for suggesting the section on like-kind exchanges and for providing most of the information presented there. I also want to acknowledge the efforts of other reviewers, each of whom read the entire manuscript and offered comments to improve it: Harry Chandler, Stanley James, Farley Brown, and my extension forestry colleagues Larry Biles and Rick Fletcher. Thanks also to the following people for help with various aspects of the project: Deborah LaRiviere, John McClain, Maria Valverde, and my eight-year-old son, Christopher, who helped organize one of the appendices. Finally, I want to thank my colleagues at the University of Vermont for allowing me a sabbatical leave to complete the project.

I wish to dedicate this book to two important women in my life: my deceased mother, Doris, who always told me I could do anything I put my mind to, even though I eventually learned this was not completely true; and my wife, Hallie, who makes each day a gift. Forever and always. . . .

Preface and Acknowledgments to the Second Edition

When my editor at Island Press asked if I was interested in doing a revision, I said "sure," but then grossly underestimated the amount of time it would take. Now eight months after the first deadline expired, I've learned my lesson about updating and revitalizing an original piece of work, especially one that has rules, regulations, and laws as its central theme. Where it was easy (or relatively so) seven years ago to use generalizations as a tool to ferret out the most relevant applications of laws to the actions of forest owners, I now have to resist the tendency to want to qualify every statement.

This book, however, is more than a facelift of the first edition with new information in virtually every chapter. I have attempted to address the concerns of readers who offered comments on the original work, and added new sections that I scolded myself for omitting from the first book. Nevertheless, for many readers even this new effort is nothing more than a glossing over of important topics, each of which could be easily expanded into a separate book.

The one aspect of forests that has changed most since 1998, when this book was first published, is that forestry communities have finally acknowledged the real yet insidious threats from continued parcelization of forest lands. When forests are the principal source of wealth in a family, parents almost always divide land among children in their wills so that each receives a fair share of the family wealth. Unfortunately, the process of dividing land tends to fragment purpose, making it almost impossible to retain local forest products industries that are essential to maintaining a forest landscape. Tracts that were measured in terms of sections, or bounded by ridges and rivers not that long ago are now divided into parcels of five, ten, or twenty acres; enough land for a home and a place to run the dog, but not enough to support local mills, logging contractors, or untrammeled corridors for wildlife.

If given a choice to obtain one lasting effect on readers who discover this book it would be to encourage them to realize the importance of keeping forest lands intact, and to inspire them to explore the plethora of strategies for passing well-managed lands to future generations. Although many forest owners confess an unwillingness to "rule from the grave," trusting heirs instead to do whatever is necessary, the strategies to pass lands intact are not nearly as exotic today as they were in 1998. Now, leaving forest lands intact is not only an appealing legacy for future generations, but it also an excellent investment; one heirs will attribute to your genius.

Special thanks are due a couple of forestry students who were instrumental to this work: Phil Pare for researching and organizing new information, and Darrel Pendris, who single-handedly developed appendix C—a listing of web resources. I also want to thank the following people for reviewing the final manuscript and offering many helpful suggestions: Alan Calfee, consulting forester in Vermont; Lloyd Casey, retired U.S. Forest Service expert on IRS matters involving forests, and now consulting forester in Pennsylvania; Sara Gentry-Tischler, Esq., an attorney and estate planner in Vermont; and Carl Reidel, professor emeritus at the University of Vermont, for comments on the manuscript and for agreeing to update his foreword to this edition. A very special thanks to Tom Bullock, Esq., an attorney and forest owner in New Jersey, who gave the manuscript a close reading and offered many excellent comments, almost all of which I used.

Finally, I want to dedicate this edition to another important woman in my life, Kara Lynn McEvoy.

Burlington, Vermont
May 24, 2005

Chapter 1

Forestry: Past, Present, and Future

One of the strengths of forests in the United States is the diversity of people who own them. Of the 737 million acres of woodlands in this country, 58 percent are owned by families, individuals, estates, and businesses—a very high percentage by global standards. Private ownership is a strength because different owners have dissimilar ideas about forest resource values and how best to manage lands as well as disparate management schedules and different priorities. This leads to diverse landscapes, and forest diversity promotes healthy forest ecosystems, appealing vistas, and a steady supply of such forest benefits as timber, wildlife, and recreation.

There are about 10 million private woodland owners in the United States, most of whom reside east of the Mississippi River (Birch 1994). With so many different private owners spread across 24 degrees of temperate latitude, one would expect many diverse ecosystems and many goals and needs of owners. All private forest owners have one thing in common, though: at some point during their forest ownership they will encounter legal matters directly related to owning and managing woodlands. For most of them, the encounters will be simple—a sale closing, title search, or timber sale contract. Some will experience encounters with the law that are less simple—boundary disputes, liability, and conflicts of interest. The purpose of this book is to describe the legal nature of forests, from our ideas of private property to the ethics of forestry practice and the difficulties of planning for the future of the forests that we leave to our children.

This is not a definitive guide on how to deal with the simple and not-so-simple legal aspects of owning and managing woodlands, for obvious reasons: laws and forest-use traditions vary from place to place, and the circumstances surrounding one individual almost never apply to another. Because laws help define acceptable and unacceptable behavior, it is the application of law to specific behaviors or circumstances that makes each case different. In many respects, however, laws apply broadly to the experiences encountered by forest owners irrespective of where they live, and that is the emphasis of the chapters that follow.

Owning and managing forest lands is a legal endeavor: from forest acquisition to deeds and boundaries, from timber sales to bequests, a forest owner can do little without confronting laws, rules, regulations, and traditions that define acceptable and unacceptable practices. Aside from a general notion of when legal assistance is necessary, most forest owners do not fully appreciate the extent to which laws and regulations control or influence decisions. Too often a crash course in local laws follows a disagreement, and one can only hope to be on the right side.

The following chapters describe legal matters that are among the most common requests of public agencies that field inquiries from woodland owners. At the top of the list are questions about timber sales and dealings with foresters and loggers. Although the type of information a public forester might offer in a particular instance would probably not qualify as "legal" advice—at least by standards of the legal profession—it is often guidance an owner will listen to and follow. The difference between legal advice and the advice of a public forester is the degree to which information is tailored to a client's request. It is the wise forester who answers specific questions in general terms, with the objective of educating the owner. Specific advice—what to do and what not to do in a particular instance—is dangerous ground for a public servant.

There is no better measure of a democratic society's evolution than the laws by which it lives. The older a society, the more complex its laws become, because legal systems are adaptive, intended to change with society. The U.S. Congress and state legislatures make new laws that, in theory, reflect society's wishes. Decisions rendered in courts through the application of existing laws become "precedents" for subsequent decisions. The specific application of laws, precedents, and the procedures used to argue points of law in court are the main reasons we have lawyers. Not many lawyers, though, specialize in legal matters related to owning and managing woodlands.

Another reason for lawyers is that the technical language of law is Latin—a "dead" language, not in use by society, and thus not apt to change. The law is peppered with Latin words and terms because they can have only one meaning. Ironically, the very thing that assures clarity to lawyers is usually a source of confusion for the layperson. Lawyer jargon, legalese, is virtually incomprehensible unless you have studied law (or Latin). Some skeptics suggest lawyers use legalese to further society's need for lawyers. For the purposes of this book, while it is impossible to describe legal aspects of forests without some legalese, my goal has been to keep its use to a minimum.

The chapters that follow contain descriptions of a wide range of legal issues related to forest ownership and use. Any one of the chapters could be expanded into its own book. For the reader who is well informed in any one of the subject areas, it will be easy to see that I sacrificed subject depth for breadth. Since the legal norms and traditions that affect forest ownership and management decisions are based on experiences and trends, a brief overview of forestry past, present, and future is in order. The history of forest use and society's response to the effects of timber harvesting on the intrinsic values of forests have complicated forest ownership. Although the rules and regulations we live by today often seem excessive and unreasonable, put in the perspective of the past they make more sense.

Forestry Past

A forest is a collection of plants and animals that live in places with adequate rainfall (or nearby sources of water), sufficient soil for nutrients and anchoring, and favorable climatic conditions. More than half the land area of the United States meets the minimum environmental conditions for forests, and about one-third of U.S. soil currently supports forests. The difference between potential forests and existing forests is that potential forests are largely lands that have been cleared for agriculture and for human settlement. A broad swath of land west of the Mississippi River and east of the Rocky Mountains, however, is too dry to support forests, except along rivers and streambeds. West of that region, the presence or absence of forests is mostly related to elevation, aspect, and prior land use. Where there are mountains tall enough to force uplifting and cooling of prevailing winds, there is usually rainfall ample enough to support forests.

Forests are synonymous with trees, their most predominant and obvious inhabitant. It was land clearing for agriculture and the use and exploitation of trees for lumber and charcoal—from the eastern states to the Midwest, then on to the Far West—that led to westward expansion and settlement. With few exceptions, the history of forest use in this country is not pretty. Forests were felled as fast as prevailing technologies would allow, with little or no regard for future generations. In the early nineteenth century, forests seemed limitless, but by the beginning of the next century, almost all easily accessible forests had been harvested at least once. When the end of timber was in sight, the science of forestry was imported from northern Europe.

Modern forestry methods, with the goals of increasing harvesting efficiency and sustaining wood yields, were not widely accepted until after World War II. Government and wood-using industries played a leading role in promoting the cause of good forestry. From the late 1940s until the early 1970s, the message from a rapidly growing forestry community was: "Forests are renewable." Trees were harvested in such a way that new forests were regenerated, or the site was replanted after harvest. The emphasis, however, was on wood yield.

In the mid-1970s, the message shifted to "multiple use," implying forests can be easily managed for more than one resource at a time. Although "multiple purpose" might have better characterized the philosophy, managers were acknowledging competing forest values and beginning to experiment with ways to harvest timber while protecting or enhancing other forest values.

In the mid-1980s, studies of woodland owner attitudes and motivations revealed that many people were more interested in managing lands for wildlife and other intangible values than for timber. Forest owners were not opposed to harvesting timber. Rather, the motivation to harvest increased in direct proportion to the nonmonetary values of a particular action. For instance, an owner opposed to harvesting trees for the sake of income production will harvest to improve access or to create hiking and ski trails. Providing better habitat for wildlife is high on the list for many owners. *Forest stewardship* was the theme du jour, and for the first time managers developed forest-management plans in which timber might be subordinate to other values. Forestry was rapidly evolving from an anthropocentric view of forests to a biocentric view.

Forestry Present

Today, the principles of forest management in this country are less than four generations old—sufficient time to regrow only an insignificant fraction of the presettlement forests. And yet the United States has some of the most productive and well-managed forests in the world. Managers have learned a hard lesson from the past: forests are much more than trees. They are an enchantingly complex association of plants and animals—including humans—that can provide many different combinations of benefits, of which timber is only one.

In the early 1990s, amid a highly divisive debate about forestry's responsibilities to threatened and endangered species, the concepts of *biodiversity* and *ecosystem management* emerged. Although the particulars of ecosystem management are discussed in greater detail in chapter 2, its emphasis is on principles and practices that mimic natural processes and thereby protect the integrity of forest ecosystems. A more appropriate term might be "ecosystem approaches to management," since an ecosystem, by definition, is self-sustaining and does not require management or human intervention. The term management implies human use, and a fundamental agreement of all who have joined the debate is that humans are part of forest ecosystems, and our use of forests must be factored into the picture.

In just the past ten years, forestry practice has experienced a revolution, the emphasis shifting from timber production to protecting forest ecosystems. Although the cause is not clear for this radical departure from traditional forestry, with its emphasis on wood production, a heightened awareness of forest values among the general public, coupled with new science, has changed the way we operate.

Not every manager agrees. There are those who maintain a good forester always considers effects on whole ecosystems. Others charge that traditional forest-management approaches put foresters in the pockets of the wood-using industry, with little regard for nontimber values and the interests of future generations. Although the chances are slim of one side convincing the other it is wrong, both sides appear to want essentially the same thing: productive forests that provide a wide variety of benefits while protecting species and other nonmonetary values that make forests special. The most significant and important aspect of the debate is that it is happening at all. Forestry in the United States is evolving from paramilitaristic origins (possibly due in part to its Teutonic influences), in which authority is never questioned and much is accepted on faith, to a highly multidisciplinary field with few easy answers and many, many questions. A question at the heart of the current debate is: Can we sustain forestry production at current levels and still protect the productive capacity of forests, maintain or improve water quality, provide appealing landscapes and recreation, and provide adequate habitat for a diversity of forest-dwelling plants and animals? The traditionalists say, "That's what good forestry is all about." Others say, "Wood production is subordinate to protecting the long-term integrity and health of the forest. If we take care of the forest, wood will be available but probably not at rates thought reasonable just a few years ago."

The concept of *sustainable forestry* is gradually replacing *sustained yield* as the primary goal of good forest management. If a practice is not sustainable—ecologically, economically, and socially—then the practice should be avoided. Wood yield by itself is no longer an adequate measure of good forestry. For some managers—even those with college textbooks from the mid-1970s—weaned on sustained yield, sustainable forestry is a radically new idea. And forestry is not a science and profession known for quickly and easily embracing new ideas.

The forest industry is changing, too. Through its Sustainable Forestry Initiative (SFI), the American Forest and Paper Association, representing many wood-using companies in the United States, is trying to encourage its members to adopt guidelines intended to protect forest ecosystems. Among the guidelines are new procurement policies aimed at keeping loggers out of the woods when forests are especially susceptible to damage, commitments to quickly regenerate harvested lands, and training programs for loggers. The goal of SFI is to shift emphasis from wood production to long-term forest management. Because many companies are publicly held and have a fiduciary responsibility to shareholders, any change that affects the bottom line is risky. For a risk-adverse industry not known for rapid change, the SFI initiative is a valid attempt to move in the direction of more sustainable forestry. But so long as short-term profitability is a motive—as it is for any company with shareholders—there are limits to which SFI principles and guidelines can be implemented. Only when there is a short-term financial advantage to practicing sustainable methods will the incentive exist to do so.

Forestry Future

Because ecosystems are nested (i.e., smaller ecosystems, such as a population of lichens on the trunk of a tree, are part of larger systems, the largest of which is the earth), protecting ecosystem values requires societal decisions that extend far beyond individual owners, local communities, state legislatures, and Congress (figure 1.1). True ecosystem approaches to forest management must transcend geographic boundaries through multilateral partnerships, requiring an unprecedented level of cooperation across many borders—political, geographical, and disciplinary. Policies to protect ecosystem values may thwart a particular owner's management plans. Herein lies the future forestry debate: How can we protect whole ecosystems without impinging on private property rights? Who makes decisions about which ecosystem values are critical and how we protect them? Who is going to pay for ecosystem management if it

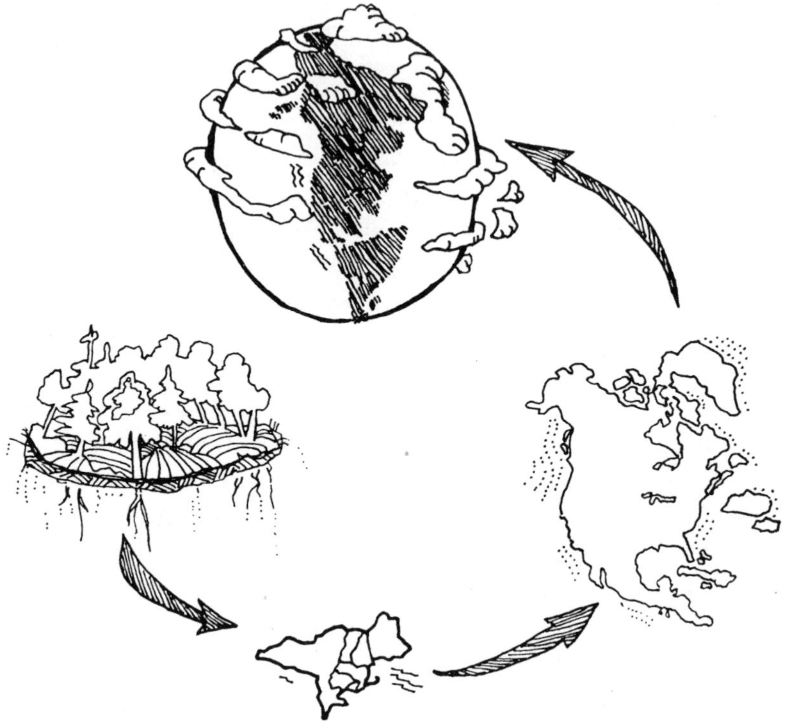

Figure 1.1. An ecosystem can be defined at many different levels, from the lichens growing on the bark of a single tree, to entire landscapes, continents and—ultimately—the earth. The hierarchical effect is what makes ecosystems so complex, enchanting, and challenging.

costs more than traditional methods? There are no easy answers, and some people suggest that questions such as these are the Achilles' heel of ecosystem management. Almost everyone, though, despite where they stand on the issues, agrees that ecosystem approaches to managing forests are here to stay.

While some people are daunted by the prospects of implementing forest ecosystem–friendly policies and practices, others see opportunity. No firm guidelines exist today on the techniques and methods of managing whole ecosystems, but innovative forestry professionals are committed to *adaptive management*, based on the theory that when in doubt, it is better to err on the side of inaction, knowing that practices will change as new science becomes available. Woodland owners are increasingly receptive to new practices, even if it means less immediate income and/or longer investment periods.

An emerging trend in the marketplace may make the wait worthwhile. Consumers in Europe are favoring products that are manufactured in an environmentally sensitive fashion. To give consumers credible product pedigree guarantees, the manufacturing process is monitored and certified by independent, third-party organizations. The certification process extends from raw material to the shelf by maintaining a chain-of-custody. This gives the consumer assurances a product has been manufactured without unacceptable exploitation of people or the earth. Also known as *green certification*, it is an attempt to inform consumers of the environmental and social consequences associated with the products they use. The idea is still relatively new in this country and there is no reliable evidence to suggest consumers in the United States would seek out or pay more for green-certified products. Some manufacturers and retailers, however, are demanding green-certified raw materials or final products, and there is a growing trend to market the earth-friendly aspects of those products. It may be only a matter of time before consumers favor green-certified products over those of unknown origin. As consumer demand for certified products increases, the demand for certified timber will grow. Forest owners who are aware of this trend, and agree to abide by the principles of certification, will be in a good position to supply the demand. Certification of forests and forest products is discussed in greater detail in chapter 7.

Product certification is slowly catching on among primary wood producers, foresters, and woodland owners. A woodland property (or manager of more than one holding, in some circumstances) becomes certified when it is clear to a certifying organization that the owner is adhering to a set of principles that includes ecosystem approaches to management. The standards also include a commitment to sustain wood production, to protect wildlife habitats, forest streams, and scenic landscapes, and to utilize the values of forests in a nonexploitive fashion. Because certified wood is in short supply, a buyer (theoretically) will offer a premium for wood that can be sold to customers as green certified. The idea is similar to a grade stamp on lumber, although the certification has nothing to do with wood quality but only with how the wood was produced.

Most people involved in wood product certification see demand building from the consumer back to the woodland owner. It may take years for this to develop in the United States. The experiences with consumers in Europe, however, suggest interest in green certification will increase among U.S. consumers. For some woodland owners, who are committed to the principles of managing whole ecosystems and are willing to wait for markets, product certification (both the cost of certification and the added expense of longer rotations) may be a sound investment.

Even though society's expectations of woodland owners are changing—from providing forests as a setting or background, to making them everybody's backyard—owning and managing forest lands is still a winning proposition for many families. The future holds promise for all woodland owners, but it is especially promising for those who make long-term commitments to the land, commitments that extend beyond a lifetime. (The special nature of planning for woodlands in the estate is the subject of chapter 9.) It is this need for continuity from one generation to the next that both strengthens families and ensures healthy and productive forests for the future. The days of passive partnerships between woodland owners and the forestry community are over. The future forest will require a much higher level of participation, and preparing woodland owners for the challenge is the goal of this book.

Chapter 2

Private Property

North America and lands that were to become the United States were not vacant in the fifteenth century when European explorers thought they had discovered new trade routes to the riches of the Orient. Sources estimate there were about 1.5 million people living in North America at the time of first contact with Europeans, during the so-called Age of Discovery (late-fifteenth through mid-eighteenth centuries). Although it is now considered quite likely that mariner tribes of northern Europe visited the continent well before Columbus's voyage, there is no evidence of exploitation or attempts to conquer the New World. How then did the lands of a well-established population of indigenous people become the "patents" of European monarchs, granted first to explorers then to the people who settled here? And how were these legally and morally questionable claims eventually consolidated as chattel of the United States of America? Reasonable answers are difficult to tease from the fabric of history at a time when people were emigrating faster than the refinements of civilization, but there are some common threads.

Private real property rights of individuals have evolved over the past seven hundred years from nonexistent to feudal rights, granted only to a limited extent and conditioned on fealty to the lord and his king. Feudal land claims evolved into allodial rights—theoretically sacrosanct, unconditional, and absolute without fealty, rents, or commitments to service. Allodial rights in North America originated from land patents and grants from monarchies that first described—to the "civilized world"—the lands visited by their subjects. But who empowered the monarchies of Europe to claim property rights in the New World?

In January of 1455, Pope Nicholas V, citing divine right, issued the Romanus Pontifex, an edict directing Portugal's King Alfonso V to " . . . claim, conquer, seize and exploit—by right of discovery—any lands to the west." Thus the doctrine of discovery is a product of a Catholic Church that also looked upon non-Christians as "saracens, pagans, infidels and enemies of Christ" (Davenport 1917). Both the *right of discovery* doctrine and the status of non-Christians would figure prominently in the expropriation of lands from indigenous people, and in the chain of authority that is the foundation of private real property rights in the United States, as discussed later in this chapter.

Less than forty years after the Church sanctified the doctrine of discovery, in 1493, Spain was awarded the New World by an edict of Pope Alexander VI. Its claims were based on the voyages and "discoveries" of Christopher Columbus (Newcomb 1992). Since Columbus had assumed he discovered a new route to the "Indies," he called the people he encountered "Indians"; an incorrect appellation that would nevertheless describe indigenous people in the U.S. Constitution almost three hundred years later. After Columbus the Church softened its position on savages, directing "humane" treatment, but only if they agreed to accept the Christian faith. Otherwise, they were considered enemies and a "just cause" for conquest (Thacher 1903).

Peter Martyr, an Italian intellectual, is said to have disabused Columbus of his discoveries, claiming his landfall was far short of the Indies (Boorstin 1983). On a later voyage Columbus allegedly came to the same conclusion, but it was an Italian pilot by the name of Amerigo Vespucci who first promoted the idea that the New World was not the Indies but a land mass between Europe and Asia (Morison 1978). Whether or not Vespucci based his initial observations on a visit to the New World is in dispute, but his descriptions were employed by Martin Waldseemüller, a prominent German cartographer who labeled the New World "America" in his maps of 1507. Although Waldseemüller later had second thoughts about crediting Vespucci, by then thousands of his maps were in use and in 1538 Gerardus Mercator's World Map immortalized Vespucci by assigning the names North and South America to the New World (Wilford 1981).

Following the explorations of Spain were Portugal, England, France, and the Netherlands. England's superior claims to North America were based on the discoveries of John Cabot, an Italian who arrived at the court of Henry VII in 1495 offering to locate a northern passage to the Orient. Two years later the King issued letters of patent to Cabot and his sons, authorizing full power and authority "to seek out, discover and find whatsoever islands, countries, regions or provinces of heathens and infidels, whatsoever they be, and in what part of the world so ever they be, which before this time were unknown to all Christians" (Morison 1971). On the basis of Cabot's voyage in 1498, England made a "legal claim" to North America citing the doctrine of discovery. While England sat on its claim other countries were settling in the Americas and indigenous people were afforded little or no rights.

In 1516, Sir Thomas More argued in his well-known book *Utopia* that "the law of nature" dictates both the rights of civilization to expand into new lands and the obligations of society to use land efficiently. Those who would deny civilization of these rights, and those who refuse to abide by its laws, are enemies. In other words, the failure of indigenous people to make way for colonists who wanted to use their lands was a violation of natural law, and those "lawbreakers" relinquished their rights.

It was impossible, under the conditions of More's Utopia, for non-Christian—and thus uncivilized—people to own land. The doctrine of discovery enables a Christian sovereign to acquire exclusive jurisdiction over new lands discovered by an empowered subject or agent (Parker 1989). If those lands are occupied by savages and heathens—by definition, anyone who is not a Christian—the claim created by discovery is legitimized. In other words, any Indian who was not also a Christian was, by definition, a heathen, incapable of understanding the concept of "rights" and thus incapable of owning land.

During the Age of Discovery England broke ties with the Church, allowing it to ignore Spain's original claims (except for the Caribbean Islands and, for a while, Florida). While France was establishing its rights to land as far west as Lake Michigan, and to strategically significant claims at the mouth of the Mississippi River, by the mid seventeenth century, England had gained a foothold on the eastern seaboard of North America. The crown chartered the Virginia Company to manage its settlements, and in 1618 it developed a "head-right" system to encourage emigration. A head-right guaranteed fifty to a hundred acres to each emigrant who paid for passage. But the Company also offered passage to emigrants who agreed to indenture themselves—to plantation owners, ship captains, English investors, or to the Virginia Company—usually for a period of five to seven years. The concept of head-rights proved so successful that the other colonies followed suit. Thus indentured servants mostly settled the colonies.

England and the other monarchies created a legal claim to the lands of North America based on the doctrine of discovery, first decreed by the Catholic Church almost two hundred years earlier, but indigenous people were not swayed. During the mid seventeenth century, Indians were certain whites had no intention of keeping their word or staying within the bounds of their colonies. It took nearly two hundred years for the population of Europeans and their descendents to equal the presettlement population of indigenous people living in North America, but in that time disease and war had all but decimated Native Americans, now vastly outnumbered.

Colonial charters and grants, such as the head-right system discussed earlier, gave individuals the rights to the soil and to timber with some exceptions, but not the rights to minerals or to establish political boundaries. Lands outside of the colonies, however, were essentially free to those who could clear, settle, and defend them, so long as the lands in question were not part of an existing grant. The best agricultural lands were always settled first, forcing immigrants continually westward.

In 1754, Benjamin Franklin and forty or so other colonists attempted to resolve long-standing and widespread disputes with Indians by an agreement known as the Albany Plan. Considered by some constitutional scholars as a first draft of the U.S. Constitution, the document—principally written by Franklin—was rejected by King George III and a few of the colonies. Significantly, one of the articles in the Albany Plan acknowledged Indian property rights by authorizing the "Grand Council" (thought to be a conceptual precursor of Congress) to " . . . make all purchases from Indians for the Crown (England) of lands not within the boundaries of particular colonies . . . " With this statement (which was probably the deal-breaker for the King and for colonists who were actively at war with Indians), Benjamin Franklin was acknowledging the rightful legal claims of indigenous people to unsettled lands. Failure to ratify the Albany Plan probably precipitated the French and Indian War (1756–1763), weakening Indians further.

From England's perspective, by 1774 the situation was getting out of hand. In that year, the English Parliament passed the Quebec Act, which attempted to lay claim to all lands west of the colonies, as far south as the Ohio River. Any person wishing to settle beyond the Alleghenies required permission from the King. Individuals who viewed the colonies as possessions of England were restricted in their westward movement. Those who were doubtful of the King's claims ignored his edicts, setting the stage for the Revolutionary War. Significantly, the Declaration of Independence was mostly over land and the colonists' claims that the King was meddling in the growth and exploitation of vast new areas.

The first draft of the Constitution was sent to Congress in 1787. It was ratified a year later with no mention of Indian property rights or land claims. The Constitution cleverly subsumed Indians and their lands, granting rights only to those Indians who pay taxes. Some historians argue that the Constitution expropriated Indian lands by right of conquest despite the fact that it is silent on the matter. Others contend that the framers believed it was only a matter of time before Native Americans succumbed to disease—principally small pox, influenza, and other illnesses to which whites had developed immunity—thus resolving the issue of land claims. Regrettably, there are even accounts of Europeans attempting to infect Indians with small pox through gifts of clothing and blankets that had been exposed to the virus. But little was known at the time about transmission of viruses and these appalling attempts at germ warfare were futile. There was, nevertheless, sufficient direct contact to expose Native Americans to diseases that decimated their populations but did not destroy them.

After the Revolutionary War, much of the business of Congress focused on land. With more land than cash, it was easier to pay soldiers with grants of land, located mostly west of the Appalachian Mountains. Each veteran received a grant of 320 acres, and many sold their grants to speculators without ever having seen the land (Ambrose 1996). One of the first acts of the new Congress (Resolution of Congress on Public Lands, 1780) vested in the federal government rights to all lands west of the colonies by trade, purchase, treaty, or conquest. History books have led us to presume that Congress adequately and fairly resolved all aboriginal claims to the lands of Native Americans, but most of North America is conquered land. Land patents and grants at the foundation of even the most primitive abstract of title do not recognize the original claims of Native Americans, and yet rivers, mountains, and vast regions still retain Native American names for those areas.

Thomas Jefferson, an advocate for both the rights of Indians and those who settled Indian lands, is largely credited with espousing sovereignty for private property in the United States when he said—more than two hundred years ago—"Nothing is ours, which another may deprive us of." Property rights advocates argue that Jefferson's words are as true today as then. But most of us forget he lived during a time when the King of England was told by the colonists to mind his own business. Then, a lack of sovereignty meant subjugation and the ownership of property by all "free men" was tangible proof that the American people no longer answered to the King. "To own land and make it productive," according to Jefferson, "is the right of every person."

In the years following the Constitution, there were innumerable attempts by states and by the federal government to appease Indians with treaties, ostensibly for the purposes of obtaining irrefutably legal title to lands. Virtually all of these treaties were violated by white people in areas where settlement preceded government. Ironically, the treaties were probably voidable under the tenets of English common law for having violated the contractual condition of "mutual assent" (Indians understood the concept of territories, but not the legal concept of real private property and associated rights. Contracts are the subject of chapter 6).

Expropriation of Indian lands by the United States was addressed in an 1823 Supreme Court decision that curiously invoked, once again, the doctrine of discovery. It ruled that the

United States holds exclusive title to all untitled lands within its borders (*Johnson's Lessee v. McIntosh*, 1823). The unanimous opinion of the court noted that Christian European nations had assumed dominion over lands during the Age of Discovery. Indians lost their "rights to complete sovereignty, as independent nations" upon discovery (Newcomb 1992). Furthermore, the court determined that "Indian title" includes only the rights of use and occupancy. In other words, unless Indians already hold legal title to land, they are incapable of claiming title—except for use and occupancy as granted by the United States—and thus are not in a position to sell land.

In 1838, the Supreme Court upheld its earlier decision concerning Indian title. But discovery of gold in Georgia precipitated a panicked frenzy among whites to stake claims on Indian lands. President Andrew Jackson, a veteran of many skirmishes with Indians, refused to honor what little rights were left the people who occupied these lands. To avoid further bloodshed, the last survivors of the Cherokee Nation were force-marched at gunpoint eight hundred miles west in the infamous Trail of Tears. Thousands of Native Americans died during this dark period in U.S. history.

Citing Church doctrine established 368 years earlier as a basis for depriving Native Americans of their lands, in a nation founded on the principal of separation of church and state, is the height of hypocrisy. But it was also the end of debate; the courts had settled the issue of Indian lands and those lands are now owned by millions of Americans and others who enjoy property rights that go far beyond "use and occupancy." By 1862, nine acts of Congress dealing specifically with land had been passed, leading the way to real property ownership as we now know it.

Today property claims of indigenous people are mostly ignored or forgotten. Yet our interpretation of private real property rights in the United States is far more liberal than elsewhere. In many European countries, for example, an individual can own land and can benefit from it, but an individual's ability to make decisions about how land is used is severely limited. And in China and most other third-world countries there is no such thing as "private real property." An individual can own crops and trees, but land is publicly owned. Most of the world's population lives on land it does not own. But in the United States we enjoy real property rights that are incomparably more generous than elsewhere.

Americanization of the English Common Law Concept of Private Property

Under English feudal law, all lands—by divine right—were owned by the King. But as society evolved and kingdoms grew, it became more difficult for the King to manage and control his lands. Thus he divided them among favored lords, usually bloodline relatives entrusted to act as the King's agents. Lords further subdivided lands into tracts managed by vassals—the people who planted crops and raised livestock—in exchange for a share of their production and for a commitment to serve in times of war. A lord was granted the privilege of making lands productive, ensuring adequate revenue for the monarch and a steady supply of men willing to defend (or expand) the King's holdings. Generally, a lord's rights under feudal law could be passed within the family by inheritance but not sold. Vassals had no rights, although sons and daughters usually followed a parent's tenure at the pleasure of the lord. The King always retained rights to minerals, timber, and wildlife; extraction or use of these resources was not allowed without the crown's permission.

In time, monarchs discovered other ways to ensure a supply of men for their armies, and gradually property interests were vested in individuals with a limited controlling interest held by the King. Minerals, timber, wildlife, change of use, and the right to tax land were retained by the crown. Known as the "allodial system of property," it is the basis for the common law of land titles in most of the United States. The word *allodial* comes from old French and it implies the right to pass an ownership interest as a bequest.

Early allodial rights (or those rights a current owner could pass within the family) include: the right to possess land and to establish boundaries; the right to control how land is used, whether for crops, timber, pasture, or open-pit mining; the right to enjoy benefits from land, including any income it may be capable of producing, or the intangible benefits from the aesthetics of land; and, the right to give, sell, encumber, or bequeath rights—or a portion of rights—to others.

These rights are necessarily broad and represent the umbilical cord to English common law ideas of allodial property.

Although the Congress was preoccupied with land following the War for Independence, little was changed in terms of the interpretation of property rights. Since land was America's only valuable asset, it was the tool Congress used for change. It paid its debts with land, as noted earlier, and in 1862 President Lincoln collateralized public lands—mostly west of the Mississippi River—to borrow money from European countries to finance the Civil War. In the same year, Justin Morrill, a Congressman from Vermont, convinced Congress to create a nationwide system of universities funded not with cash, but with land. Known even today as the "land-grant system of universities," most state colleges (or at least one in each state) got their first major appropriation in land from this system, and virtually every campus has a Morrill Hall to commemorate Congressman Morrill.

So prevalent were land grants among Americans that for a period following the Revolution land grants were a more common form of currency than gold or paper money. A land grant, written on parchment, frequently folded and dog-eared, might have changed hands to settle a debt many times before landing in the possession of a farmer who filed a claim for title and actually took ownership of the land (figure 2.1). Once claimed, the title to land guaranteed that farmer essentially the same rights available to a prewar colonist. And to this day, our interpretation of private real property rights, based on English common law, is little changed.

The one essential difference between property law in England two hundred years ago and its application in the New World was that American colonists rejected the concept of primogeniture, a hold-over rule from feudal law that restricted transfers of ownership. Under primogeniture, the entire real estate of an English landlord passed to only one heir: his first-born son, or to the closest consanguine male (father, brother, uncle, cousin, and so on). It was not uncommon for an eldest daughter to see her father's lands inherited by a late-born, five-year-old brother (or half-brother). If her father never sired sons the land might go to her uncle. If the uncle predeceased her father, the estate might end up in the hands of a male cousin.

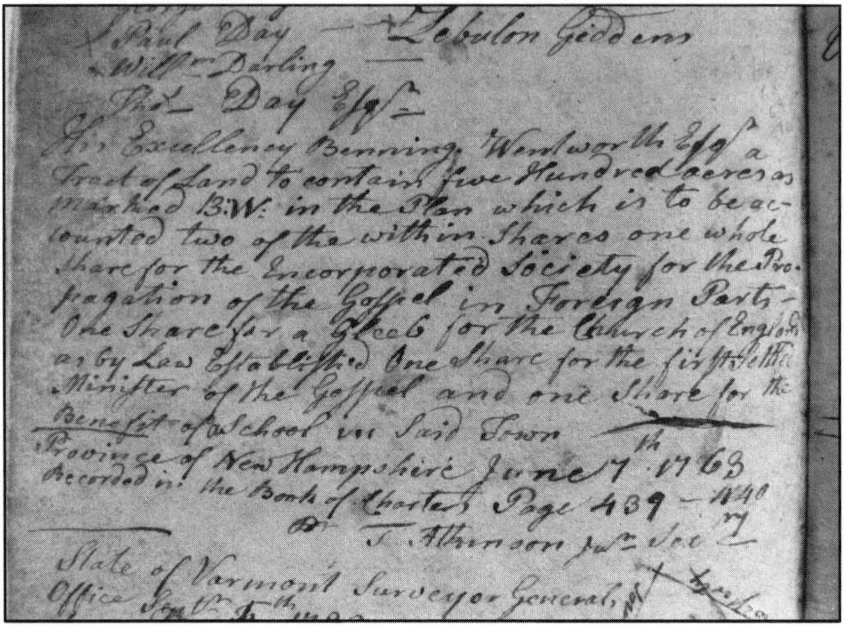
Paul Day — Zebulon Giddens
Willm Darling —
Thos Day Esqr
His Excellency Benning Wentworth Esqr a
Tract of Land to contain five Hundred acres as
marked B:W: in the Plan which is to be ac-
counted two of the within Shares one whole
Share for the Incorporated Society for the Pro-
pagation of the Gospel in Foreign Parts –
One Share for a Glebe for the Church of England
as by Law Established One Share for the first settled
Minister of the Gospel and one Share for the
Benefit of a School in Said Town
Province of New Hampshire June 7th 1763
Recorded in the Book of Charters Page 439 — 1840
T. Atkinson Junr Secry
State of Vermont Surveyor General's
Office Sept [illegible]

Figure 2.1. The original grants for the town of Bolton, Vermont, in 1763.

Primogeniture evolved in feudal times as a way for the King's lands to pass within families of nobility, but since the King was under no obligation to share his interests, the lords had no rights to divide the estates entrusted to them. The concept survived evolution from feudal law because it prevented fragmentation of productive lands and also maintained a relatively easy method of gathering taxes. It did not survive in the American colonies because the emigrants to the new world were mostly families of expatriates, children forced to leave their homelands because only one of their siblings could inherit the family wealth. Given the circumstances, it is not too surprising that primogeniture was left behind and the colonists embraced the rights to transfer ownership to whomever the current owner wishes.

The Bundle of Rights

Real property differs from other personal property in the sense that it is immobile, so the acquisition of land is really the acquisition of rights. The sum of these rights—also known as the *bundle of rights*—defines a person's interests in land. These include: the rights of use, occupancy, cultivation, exploration; the rights to minerals (including the right to extract them); the rights to sell or assign interests in land (such as in the case of selling timber); the rights to license or lease; the rights to develop, to devise, and inherit; the rights to dedicate, give away, and share; the rights to mortgage and exercise a lien, and to trade or exchange land. Notwithstanding this long list of rights, our interpretation of the full bundle of rights is intended to be inclusive. That is to say, even rights that are not specifically described, such as, for instance, the right to dig wells, are implicit. However—and this is a key point, the very substance of the current debate about private property rights—exercise of the bundle of rights is subject to limitations the state may impose for the sake of protecting the public's interests. Private property rights are not absolute. And in the United States, public authorities have reserved essentially the same rights as those originally reserved by the King.

In exchange for the state's willingness to defend an owner's property, it reserves *interests* in those lands, including: the right to tax land; the right to take land for public use with just compensation (also known as *eminent domain*); the right to control use to ensure protection of the public's interests; and—when an owner dies without a will and no known legal heirs—the state has the right of escheat; to take possession of abandoned land.

States also own wildlife on private lands, much as the King reserved rights to game on his lands. A landowner can harvest wildlife, but only with a license from the state and during the proper season. Rules about game licenses vary by state, but the point is that no one but the state owns wild animals until they have been harvested.

It is not too surprising that most of the debate about private property rights is on deciding when the public's interests are at stake, what constitutes a *taking* of rights, and how to figure *just* compensation. For example, does a landowner have the right to install a hazardous waste processing facility? Probably not, but the answer depends on the extent to which the public is protected from any negative impacts that might result from this decision. If the answer is "no," does this constitute a taking of the owner's rights? And if so, what is just compensation for denying these rights?

More likely the situation is reversed: the state offers to buy land for such a facility; if the owner refuses to sell, the state *condemns* the current uses of the land and exercises its right of eminent domain. What is just compensation for a taking in this instance? Not what most would expect because compensation is limited to reimbursing the owner for the value (and future value) of the land's current use. Just compensation for woodlands with a beautiful view approximates the value of land for timber, not the potential loss from selling the land as a future home site.

Federal, state, and local laws can change the way people use their lands, but most often these statutes are intended to protect current uses while avoiding property conversions that might prove costly for the community in the future. It is ironic that people who complain the loudest about erosion of private property rights are the ones who invariably want to retain the option of selling out to a highest bidder, for whatever use, and regardless of the cost to others in the community.

Converting productive farm and forest lands to nonagricultural uses at a rate that threatens the very fabric that supports productive lands would have seemed suicidal to the early colonists. But the prospect of government telling them how to use their lands would have been equally unnerving.

When society extends rights to individuals, it tacitly expects the individual to accept certain responsibilities. It is assumed an owner is not "sleeping on his rights" and that the owner is fully aware and in control of activities on the property at all times. This means that if the owner sells timber to a logger who proceeds to violate the state's Clean Water statutes, the owner is responsible for the violation. (Sharing liability for upholding a state's laws, especially during a timber sale, is discussed in more detail in chapter 6.) As a forest owner you must understand the extent of your liability for the careless actions of others. Personal liability is discussed in chapter 10.

Private Rights versus Public Interests

Deciding when the public's interests are at stake, especially in light of the fact that the costs of ownership—taxes and other expenses—are borne by the individual, is often a divisive and heated debate.

The bottom line is, a forest owner must adhere to the laws, rules, and regulations controlling forest use and avoid doing anything that is apt to have a substantially negative effect on neighbors, the community, or society.

During more than two hundred years of U.S. real property law, broad rights guaranteed by the Constitution and defended by the state have become more narrowly defined. Today, the rights we hold in real property spring from society (Barlowe 1990), and society's interests may be far different from those of an individual. Property owners decry the erosion of their sovereign rights, while environmental groups and others say it is time to shift the debate from rights to responsibilities. The courts are in the middle of the debate, but it appears evident the days of a laissez-faire approach to the rights of private landowners are nearly over.

When a real property owner's rights are lost by government action during his or her tenure, it is called a "taking." The taking of rights is preceded by a condemnation promulgated by a governmental entity that is staking a claim against your rights for the public good. For instance, when the county decides to build a new road that crosses your property, it will condemn the current uses of the land and take it (by right of eminent domain) for the new highway (assuming the owner is unwilling to sell).

Any involuntary loss of real property rights is a taking. The Fifth Amendment of the U.S. Constitution requires the taking government to pay "just compensation." But the authors of that amendment were thinking of eminent domain, where the state takes *all* rights; they failed to consider circumstances where regulations, statutes, and rules might restrict some but not all rights. Also, what constitutes just compensation is rarely agreed to easily, since it usually has nothing to do with fair market value. For example, if hay land is taken for a new road, "just compensation" is apt to equal the capitalized cost of hay to the farmer even though the land could have been developed into housing or some other higher fair market value. The value of hay land is but a fraction of its value for development and herein lays the gripe of many owners whose lands are condemned for public projects.

Recently, the Supreme Court has held (through application of the Fifth Amendment) that if the state's (or community's) actions represent a taking of some of a property owner's rights, the owner should be compensated for those rights—assuming the restrictions, or taking, happened during the owner's tenure and not before, when he or she could have or should have known about the restriction on rights. There must also have been an actual loss of economic value (*Lucas v. South Carolina Coastal Commission*, 1992). The high court's position is that a taking occurs when there is a substantial economic loss through the direct actions of a governmental authority *after* the owner has acquired property.

"Substantial economic loss" in the South Carolina case cited above was more than 90 percent of the purchase price of the property. The South Carolina Coastal Commission had instituted a restrictive law after Lucas acquired his barrier island property but before a devastating hurricane. The law says hurricane-destroyed houses on barrier islands cannot be rebuilt. That law constituted a taking with respect to Lucas because it was instituted after Lucas built on the property, and it had a major effect on fair market value. Although he still owned the land, Lucas could not use it for its intended purpose: a beach house.

How then does the state compensate for a partial loss of rights, and what is a reasonable threshold for loss beyond which the owner should be compensated? When is a taking capricious and when is it necessary or unavoidable? To what extent should society be responsible for the risks associated with the acquisition of any property, whether stocks and bonds or forest land? Forest property in urbanizing areas will be subject to an increasing level of control by municipalities. From zoning to restrictions on forest practices, forest owners can expect to see more control, not less, over how they manage their lands.

In 1995 alone more than one hundred bills containing "partial takings" provisions were introduced in thirty-nine states (Zhang 1996). Already, eighteen states have attempted to protect private property rights from government regulatory takings by enacting laws that change the assessment on these properties, provide compensation for losses, or a combination of both (Zhang 1996). States with updated statutes dealing with this subject include Arizona, Delaware, Florida, Idaho, Indiana, Kansas, Louisiana, Minnesota, Mississippi, Missouri, North Dakota, Tennessee, Texas, Utah, Virginia, Washington, West Virginia, and Wyoming. Information about these statutes can be obtained from the applicable Attorney General's office (appendix B).

Problems with regulatory taking statutes arise when properties are appraised to determine loss. There are as many different approaches to forest land appraisal as there are appraisers, and there are no uniform guidelines with respect to forest values. Most often, loss is calculated as compensation for preventing a current use as described earlier, not for loss of fair market value.

Recent interest among states on the issues of property rights will one day compel Congress to provide guidance and consistency. Property rights advocates are constantly spurring action in Congress. For example, in the late 1990s, the House of Representatives passed a bill that allows compensation for loss if 20 percent or more of the value of the property is taken (and the owner keeps the property). If the loss exceeds 50 percent, the owner is fully compensated. To qualify, the loss must have resulted from the Endangered Species Act, the Clean Water Act (both of which are discussed in more detail below), or agricultural conservation compliance under the Food Security Act. A Senate version establishes a 33 percent threshold for compensation. Neither of these bills is expected to become law in present form, but the debate about property rights will continue. Until Congress acts, courts will validate a taking if there is a public purpose, including a "real and substantial threat to public health." Compensation may be awarded if the taking has caused an "inordinate burden" on the owner.

Before undertaking a forestry project in your woodlands, discover from knowledgeable sources any local rules or regulations that may apply to your activities. A good source for this type of information is your state extension forester (Appendix A). Local government regulation of private forestry practices has increased more than fourfold in the recent years (Martus et al. 1995). Generally, local rules and regulations are easy to comply with even though they may add extra nuisance, mostly for forestry professionals.

Also, if you have concerns about local regulations, become involved in the debate. Remember the prophetic words of West Coast logger Bruce Vincent, "The world is run by those who show up."

Protecting the Public's Interests

You buy land, survey the boundaries, inventory the resources, design access routes, develop a long-term management plan, and pay taxes. Why then should anyone have the right to tell you what to do on your land or how to do it? After all, so long as your activities do not have a negative consequence for neighbors, you have the right to use the land as you see fit. Right? Well not exactly. The public has an interest in your land, and in recent years the U.S. Congress, state legislatures, and local municipalities have passed laws, regulations, and rules that woodland owners must uphold to avoid fines and other penalties. The bundle of rights is not nearly as sacrosanct as it used to be, and from society's perspective owners share certain rights with the public.

Two acts of Congress have had a substantial bearing on forest-management activities: The Endangered Species Act (ESA, 1973) and the Clean Water Act (1977).

The Endangered Species Act

The ESA makes it a crime to take an endangered or threatened plant or animal species. An *endangered species* is one that is threatened with extinction, while a *threatened species* is one that is on the verge of becoming endangered. The act further defines the word *take* as "to harass, harm, pursue, hunt, shoot, wound, kill, trap, capture, collect or attempt to engage in any such conduct." The word *harm* is the most controversial as it relates to forest owners. The U.S. Fish and Wildlife Service (USFWS), responsible for enforcing the ESA, defines harm as "significant habitat modification or degradation [that] actually kills or injures wildlife by significantly impairing essential behavioral patterns, including breeding, feeding, or sheltering." In 1999, five pages of the Federal Register were devoted to defining the word *harm* within the context of ESA. "The purposes of this act are to provide a means whereby the ecosystems upon which endangered species depend may be conserved," is stated as the intent of Congress in its use of the word *harm*.

The ESA also extends to plants, but the responsibility of private owners to protect threatened and endangered plants is not nearly as imposing as their responsibility for wildlife, with one exception—if you have accepted federal funds for work being done on your land, plants have more protection under ESA than if no federal funds or permits are involved.

Because forest-management activities can result in "significant habitat modification," even if ESA does not apply, it is helpful to know if any ESA-listed species use your land. When forest management activities are expected to affect protected wildlife species, a landowner can still proceed with the project by completing a "habitat conservation plan," authorized by an amendment of ESA in 1982. With the habitat conservation plan (HCP) in hand an owner can apply for an "incidental take permit," which affords legal protection in case the project harms a protected species. Biologists with the USFWS are available to help develop the HCP, often resulting in little or no extra cost for the project. For more information on habitat conservation plans visit: http://endangered.fws.gov/hcp/index.html.

Under an HCP agreement the USFWS agrees that a permit holder will not be "surprised" at a future date when extraordinary circumstances requires a renegotiation of the original terms of the contract. Known as the "no surprises" element, the conditions that create "extraordinary circumstances" have been challenged in court following permit revocations that were indeed surprising. In 2003 a federal judge ruled that the no surprises condition is a relevant assurance that an HCP should provide (Murray 2004b). However, there is a possibility the no surprises element will be either substantially modified in the future, especially if new information identities an inordinate risk to the species in question, or the rule could be struck down altogether.

There are 960 species in the United States that are considered endangered or threatened, 431 animals and 529 plants. Most of the animals are aquatic species, and about half the plant species are forest dwellers. The threatened and endangered species of greatest significance to forest owners are birds, mainly in the West, in desert ecosystems, and in the Hawaiian Islands.

If you suspect that threatened or endangered plant or animal species are on your land, you should contact the USFWS, Department of the Interior, Division of Endangered Species, 4401 N.

Fairfax Drive, MS #420, Arlington, Virginia 22203 (703-358-2171) or visit http://endangered.fws.gov on the Internet to verify and to seek guidance on how to protect habitats during management activities. Some owners cringe at the thought of inviting the federal government to inspect their lands. After all, why would anyone knowingly risk having their hands tied behind their backs if a protected species is identified? Unfortunate as it may seem, society has a right to ensure the survival of protected species regardless of the land they occupy. If you own critical habitat, you have a legal and moral obligation to protect the species that live there if they are listed by the USFWS as threatened or endangered. But with a little extra planning and care—and good forest-management practices—it is easy both to use the forest and to protect important habitats.

The U.S. Supreme Court recently strengthened the rights of private individuals to challenge the USFWS in its interpretations of the ESA. Before this ruling, only environmental groups suing for more protection were allowed standing in such lawsuits. In effect, the Supreme Court has extended rights to challenge the act to any person who believes the USFWS has overstepped its bounds. The result is expected to be a substantial increase in litigation involving development interests and environmental groups.

More recently environmental groups have attempted to implicate state and federal agencies that offer assistance to private owners involving practices that may cause a taking of protected species. By providing guidance, financial assistance, or permits, public assistance programs are "vicariously liable" since the action of public officials initiated the chain of events that may have resulted in harm (Murray 2004a).

After more than thirty-two years the ESA is still debated in Congress and the debates are often heated, pitting environmentalists against landowners and natural resource users. Congressional committees regularly review various provisions of the act, especially the processes by which species are listed for protection, delisted, and deciding what constitutes a taking—both of an endangered species and its habitat and of an owner's real property rights. If you have questions or comments, contact either your congressional delegation or the USFWS office that serves your region.

The Clean Water Act

Congress passed the Federal Water Pollution Control Act in 1948. In 1972, the act was amended to include pollution from *nonpoint sources*, such as mud from logging roads, equipment lubricants, chemicals, and other pollutants. Most people think of water pollution as coming from pipes, also known as *point sources*. A nonpoint pollutant is not easily traced to the point of origin, but gets into water as runoff, usually from farm and forest lands.

In 1977 the law was renamed the Clean Water Act (CWA), and it was reauthorized by Congress in 1987. Administered by the Environmental Protection Agency (EPA), the CWA requires states to develop best management practices (BMPs) to protect water quality during timber harvesting. States are also required to develop programs to ensure BMPs are used, and to periodically report to EPA on the status of water quality. Although administered by EPA, enforcement is solely the responsibility of each state, and each state has approached its responsibilities under the CWA differently. A state's BMPs must consider "economic, institutional, and technical factors" so their design and installation is cost effective and reasonable (American Forest and Paper Association 1994). EPA's jurisdiction under the CWA extends to "all waters of the United States, including adjacent wetlands." This broad jurisdiction encompasses every acre of woodland in the country. Congress, in its wisdom, provides an exemption from the permit requirements for discharges that result from "normal farming, silviculture, and ranching activities such as plowing, seeding, cultivating, minor drainage, harvesting for the production of food, fiber and forest products, or upland soil and water conservation practices." In most states this means either (1) the BMPs promulgated at the state level must be followed, or (2) the BMPs are "highly recommended," but if a discharge occurs and the BMPs are not in place, the owner may be subject to fines. Because it is almost impossible to extract timber from most woodland sites without disturbing the soil sufficiently to cause a discharge, it is in the owner's best interests to see to it that the BMPs are followed. Most of the BMPs (notwithstanding state-to-state variations) are common sense, and their use makes timber extraction only marginally more expensive.

The most current debate concerning clean water and forestry activities revolves around the concept of total daily maximum loads (TDMLs). It is a calculation that estimates the maximum amount of soil sedimentation or other pollutant that a stream or lake can hold without decreasing ambient water quality standards. EPA proposed using TDML calculations to monitor the impact of silvicultural activities on water quality. Such a change would require much closer scrutiny of forestry activities, in addition to the expense of water sampling to measure TDMLs. With the risk of expensive and potentially restrictive rules at hand, forestry advocates were able to argue that the effects of good forestry practices on water quality are negligible and thus do not warrant practices that might dampen the public's incentive to manage their lands. With this reasoning the TDML debate was put to rest.

For more information on BMPs, contact your state forester. Also, many local extension foresters have publications that explain a landowner's obligations under the CWA.

Ecosystem Management

Although a discussion of ecosystem management may seem out of place in a chapter dealing with the concept of private property and the public's interests in the rights of private owners, it is most germane to the subject. Managing whole ecosystems will redefine the nature and extent of property rights, and although the debate is still engaged, state and federal forest-management agencies—even forest-using industries—are changing their policies to protect and sustain important ecosystem structures and functions. Ecosystems do not recognize property boundaries, so forest owners need to know the effects ecosystem management practices may have on property rights.

Increased recognition of the interrelatedness of forest organisms and the potentially far-reaching and long-lasting effects of traditional uses of forests has spawned new ways of thinking in recent years. Although not fully embraced by all forestry professionals, some of whom contend that traditional uses correctly implemented can protect and improve forest ecosystems, the term ecosystem management implies three things. First, primary importance is placed on maintaining long-term forest health, not just for human use or even for future generations but for the wellbeing of plants and animals that also occupy and use forests. Humans are nearly coequal users of the forest with the power to control disturbances to lessen the negative consequences and, where possible, duplicate circumstances that mimic natural processes. This is akin to saying that, although we might have the knowledge and power to dominate and fully manipulate woodlands solely for human use, we have a responsibility to protect and provide for all other organisms that rely on forests.

Second, ecosystem management implies that humans accept the responsibility to understand the complexities of forests and to err on the side of inaction rather than risk subtle but irreversible damage attendant upon proceeding in ignorance. Our management strategies, while attempting to mimic natural processes, must change with new science. The days of stocking charts and universal prescriptions narrowly aimed at increasing the volume and commercial value of timber are nearly over. This is not to say forests will no longer supply timber. But it does mean that timber production is subordinate to the long-term health and sustainability of the forest. Fortunately, disturbance—sometimes catastrophic changes brought on by storms, insects, disease, and fire—is the rule in forests rather than the exception. Practicing ecosystem management means designing disturbances in ways that allow us to use resources while protecting landscape integrity.

Third, because ecosystems are recognized at many different levels—from small populations of fungi to whole landscapes—and do not follow geographic or political boundaries, practicing ecosystem management will inevitably modify our traditional ideas about real property rights (see figure 1.1). For example, some migratory songbirds that winter in tropical regions of the Caribbean and the Americas use the forests of North America during the spring and early summer for nesting. We know that relatively undisturbed, old-growth forests are important habitats for many of those species. Practicing ecosystem management to protect nesting opportunities for neotropical songbirds requires guidelines that will probably limit harvesting in certain forest types for a few weeks each year (i.e., during midsummer in the Northern Forest). To some people, that is a small price to ensure the survival of those species. To others, it means an erosion of private property rights.

Since ecosystems vary in size and complexity from the population dynamics of bacteria in a single forest soil to the global interactions of species, including humans, managing whole ecosystems will require an unprecedented level of cooperation among neighboring woodland owners, municipalities, states, and countries. Uncertainty about how this cooperation will occur, especially at local levels, is a primary source of concern for owners, managers, and users of forests. Successful implementation of ecosystem management worldwide will require drastic changes in forestry practice. A short list of things we can expect to see, if ecosystem management is to be implemented on a global scale, includes the following:

- Catalog species at global, continental, regional, and sublevels: Which species are indicators of ecosystem integrity and which species are destined to become extinct regardless of human activities?
- Identify and project human demands for wood and allocate demand to wood-growing areas of the world.
- Speed up the search for wood replacements. Some forest ecosystems that now produce a great deal of wood will produce considerably less than projected demand under an ecosystem management approach. Economical and environmentally friendly substitutes for wood will become essential.
- Clearly establish society's values regarding forests: What are we willing to pay for and what can we afford to give up?
- Redefine silvicultural practices in ways that mimic the natural processes of a particular landscape.
- Rethink timber extraction timing and methods on some sites and employ positive impact forestry practices (McEvoy 2004).
- Increase our willingness to wait longer, to accept more costs for tending forests, and to pay more for wood products.

Some people contend that ecosystem management is a passing fad. Given a few years, a new administration, and substantially higher prices for wood products, we will be back to business as usual. Although it is true our resolve to protect whole ecosystems from excessive and exploitative human uses will wax and wane, most forest managers and academics agree that the lasting effect of ecosystem management will be a change in our thinking about forests, the resources they can provide, and the best ways to use and sustain them. Our concept of private real property will never be the same.

Carbon Credits and Environmental Mitigation

Although forests are private real property they provide many benefits to society. Also known as *positive externalities*, these public benefits include things like: clean air and water, scenic vistas, habitats for wildlife and millions of other organisms, and many other economically intangible values. Any significant value that is difficult or impossible to evaluate in terms of dollars and cents, is referred to as an *intangible value*. The visual impact of forests in a landscape is a perfect example of an externality of woodlands whose value is intangible. An entire community and society at large benefit from forests in the landscape, but the people who own and manage those forests are not compensated for providing these benefits to others.

Couple society's failure to pay for the positive externalities of forests with the expense of owning land, rarely compensated during any single owner's tenure from revenues associated with tangible benefits like timber, and it is easy to see why one of the biggest threats to forests is parcelization—the continual division of land into smaller and smaller units, usually for housing or some other developed use.

Loss of forests and the effects of industrialization on earth's ecosystems were the subjects of discussion in 1997 at a global conference on the environment in Kyoto, Japan. The principles discussed and agreed to by participants at the conference, representing almost every country in the world, were codified into thirty pages of articles describing ways that developed countries can join a concerted effort to clean up the earth's atmosphere, waters, and soils. It is known as the Kyoto Accord, and the United States is one of only a few developed countries that have yet to ratify the document. Why? Because as the wealthiest of developed countries, we use a disproportionately large share of the earth's resources—including fossil fuels—and thus will bear most of the cost of clean up.

Among a plethora of great ideas outlined in the Kyoto Accord is the concept of *carbon credits*. Since the release of carbon from the burning of fossil fuels is one of the principal causes for global warming, the idea behind carbon credits is to have those who use carbon-based fuels pay the cost of extracting carbon from the atmosphere. How is atmospheric carbon extracted? During photosynthesis in forests and in other ecosystems, which converts light energy into chemical energy.

Carbon dioxide, or CO_2, is known as a "greenhouse gas" which means that, although it is colorless and odorless, it tends to blanket the globe, trapping atmospheric heat by reflecting infrared radiation back to earth. CO_2 concentrations and atmospheric temperature trends are self-perpetuating: a warmer atmosphere means a warmer ocean forcing more CO_2 into the atmosphere, causing more warming. There is a direct relationship between the amount of atmospheric CO_2 and temperature. Although scientists are not sure which is the driving factor—CO_2 concentrations or temperatures—the long-term trends move in the same direction.

Just one hundred years ago data from ice cores show that atmospheric concentrations of CO_2 were about 290 parts per million (ppm). Direct measurements today indicate that atmospheric CO_2 is about 370 ppm and climbing rapidly, far beyond the range of natural variability at other times in the past. Scientists estimate earth's climate will continue to warm until 2100, even if we were to use far less carbon. A warmer earth means a warmer ocean, which takes up more volume. Under the direst predictions, a swollen ocean will inundate 10 to 20 percent of the earth's land area over the next hundred years.

If there is no slaking our thirst for petroleum and coal—and no other viable energy alternatives—then we need to figure ways to absorb more carbon from the atmosphere. This is where the concept of carbon credits and forests come in.

When carbon is not in the atmosphere, or dissolved in the oceans, it is locked up in minerals, glaciers, fossil fuels, and in plants and animals. Carbon that is either mineralized or tied up in organic compounds is said to be *sequestered.* Since trees use atmospheric CO_2 during photosynthesis, converting it into complex sugars such as cellulose, woodland owners that grow trees are also sequestering carbon. The Kyoto Accord proposes to "tax" companies for carbon they release, but the tax is in the form of helping to promote ways to scrub carbon from the atmosphere. Tree planting in areas that have been deforested and managing existing forests so as to maximize photosynthesis, are two carbon sequestration strategies the Kyoto Accord proposes to develop. Thus, a company responsible for pumping a million tons of carbon into the atmosphere would pay the cost of establishing or managing sufficient forest to use this extra carbon.

Woodland owners who are willing to dedicate forest lands to sequestering atmospheric carbon would lease their forests to a worldwide carbon bank. By exercising a carbon *easement* (essentially a promise to dedicate stands to the cause of a cleaner atmosphere; easements are discussed in greater detail in chapter 3), the owner would sell carbon credits to the bank. Companies that use fossil fuels would then buy carbon credits—or pay for technologies to lower carbon emissions—or a combination of the two.

Sounds like the perfect plan, but will it work? In principle it is an excellent idea, but in practice it is highly doubtful that forests—even very well-tended forests—will have anything more than a minor impact on anthropogenic carbon. Why? Because the developed world is pumping greenhouse gasses into the atmosphere at rates that are many times the ability of earth's forests to sequester. Yes, forests do convert CO_2 into wood fiber. But recent studies of forest carbon budgets are demonstrating that most forests use only slightly more carbon than they produce, in the form of leaves, twigs, and other organic products that are recycled.

The Kyoto Accord has the right idea, but it is highly doubtful a world carbon bank could afford to pay more than a token amount for the carbon-scrubbing value of most forests in the United States. Nevertheless, some state governments—such as Alaska in 2003—are exploring the advantages and disadvantages of encouraging carbon sources and sinks to work together. As we learn more about carbon budgets in forests, there may be opportunities for woodland owners willing to take a more long-term view on management to convert the intangible value of carbon sequestration into a tangible value of carbon credits.

Another evolving alternative for woodland owners who are willing to commit their lands to long-term management strategies is known as *environmental mitigation*. The concept works almost exactly the same as carbon credits but applies mostly to detrimental landscape changes. For example, an environmentally conscious developer may need to fill in some wetlands to obtain access to lands that are otherwise suitable for development. In order to mitigate the effects of wetland loss, the developer will usually acquire, either as an outright purchase or as an easement (discussed in chapter 3), an equal number of acres that are permanently set aside to provide wetland values approximately equal to those lost through development.

The concept of environmental mitigation is much further along than that of carbon credits and there are many developers who are very willing to mitigate habitat losses provided there are easy opportunities for them to do so. Many states already have programs that amount to a market place for "trading" environmental detriments with mitigations that are long-term solutions. Woodland owners with lands they are willing to set aside for the purposes of mitigating changes elsewhere should contact their state forester (see appendix A). Wetlands are probably greatest in demand, making it possible to trade an easement in these lands to offset the impacts of habitat losses elsewhere.

Both environmental mitigation and carbon credits rely on legal methods that allow a forest owner to trade a long-term commitment—one that stays with the land irrespective of future owners—for a current value, usually cash. These methods involve separating the bundle of rights in land and thus changing the nature of ownership for all subsequent owners. Dedicating forest lands to a long-term environmental purpose is always a worthy cause. But the legal methods to achieve these ends, discussed in the chapter that follows, should not be taken lightly.

Chapter 3

Acquiring and Owning Forest Lands

When you acquire forest lands, you acquire whatever rights the seller or donor (in the case of a gift or inheritance) had in the land. Or you acquire only those rights he or she is willing to convey. For example, the owners may want to retain some of the rights for themselves (retaining mineral rights used to be very common in some parts of the country). The seller or donor may also want to protect against a future owner's attempt to exercise rights the current owner deems inappropriate, such as the right of development. Separating the bundle of rights is tricky business and requires the efforts of an attorney who specializes in property law. When an owner grants a separation of rights to another person or legal entity or, upon sale, retains some rights, this is known as an *easement*. Easements are discussed later in this chapter.

Before acquiring forest land, be absolutely certain of the rights that go with it. For most land transactions, it is essential to have a local attorney verify the title to a tract of land and to identify any potential problems that may exist from past relationships among owners or from previous transactions. The actual *title* is nothing more than words that describe the extent of a person's rights. A *deed* is a document that describes the physical location of the property and the extent of an owner's rights. Whenever land changes hands, the buyer (or the buyer's attorney) must examine the tract's title to be sure the current owner has all the rights the buyer wants to purchase and that there are no undisclosed claims (easements or other claims) on the current owner's title. Although a lawyer's opinion on the title to land is not always required, it is usually a good idea to have a local lawyer assist in transactions involving land. When a buyer is borrowing funds to purchase land, the bank or other lending institution will usually require both a lawyer's opinion on the title as well as title insurance to protect against claims in the future. Real estate title is discussed further in the next section. Here, I want to discuss briefly the nature of a person's estate—the legal extent of an individual's interest in land—to help explain why the history of a tract's title is so important.

A title to a tract of land can be *original* or *derivative*. An original title is usually assumed to be vested in the government or the state and is acquired through discovery, conquest, or occupancy. In the eastern United States, the concept of original title is antiquated, but there are vast areas in the West and in Alaska where much of the land is under original title. A derivative title is vested in individuals and can be passed by sale, gift, or bequest. A contract to convey title, or an option to acquire title when certain conditions have been met, will create a *title by devise*, compelling the seller to pass his interests in the land at some future date as specified in the contract. (Title to real estate is discussed in more detail in the next section.)

The extent of ownership, or the conditions under which one has a claim of rights and the duration over which those rights belong to a person, is known as the *estate* of the owner. There are two primary forms of estate, defined by the presence or absence of imposed time limits:

1. A freehold estate has no fixed time limits on the current owner's rights, and the rights can be passed without time limits to another person. Most land is owned as a freehold estate. It represents the greatest extent of rights available to a property owner and it is the least restrictive form of ownership.

2. A less than freehold estate is a situation in which the person who holds the estate retains rights for a specified time period. For example, a lease creates a less than freehold estate.

Aside from the obvious differences between these two forms of estate, a freehold estate usually encompasses the full bundle of rights, and a less than freehold estate encompasses something less than the full bundle. A long-term lease to tap conifers for the production of naval stores is a less than freehold estate. The person holding the lease (the lessee) has the right of access and the right to gather sap, and no other rights. Usually this type of estate has an expiration date after which the lessee must relinquish all rights. Another example of a less than freehold estate is a property from which mineral rights have been separated.

A property can encompass more than one estate. For example, an owner of a freehold estate can create a less than freehold estate vested in another person, as in the example above involving a lease for naval stores production.

Under the concept of freehold and less than freehold estate, there are seven different forms of estate that define the extent of an estate holder's rights, arranged below from the most inclusive and extensive bundle of rights to more restrictive estates in which the person has rights but not necessarily by virtue of ownership.

1. An *estate in fee simple* (or just fee or fee simple absolute) encompasses the most extensive bundle of rights available to an owner. Most tracts of land in the United States are held as estates in fee simple. Unless the current owner places restrictions on the title, the buyer (or the beneficiary or heir) can assume he or she is acquiring a freehold estate in fee simple.

2. A *life estate* can be an estate in fee simple, but the current owner's rights expire when he or she dies. The essential point is that a life estate cannot be passed on to heirs.

3. An *estate in remainder* encompasses all of the rights that were available to a decedent before he or she passed away. These may include all the rights of a fee estate, partial rights, or no rights at all if someone else can prove a better claim. An estate in remainder may be freehold or less than freehold.

4. An *estate in reversion* means the current owner's rights have expired and the estate "reverts" to someone else. For example, when a long-term lease expires, the estate created by the lease reverts to the person who granted the lease.

5. An *estate from year to year* (or month to month) is a less than freehold estate that usually exists for a year or less. If an owner

(the lessor) were to lease hunting rights one year at a time, it would create (for the lessee) an estate from year to year. Unless a termination date is specified, the lessor must notify the lessee that the lease has ended.

6. An *estate at will* is a less than freehold estate that can be terminated at any time by the person granting the rights or by the person holding the rights. For instance, an agreement granting a neighbor the right to pick strawberries on your land may be an estate at will for the neighbor, because you can revoke those rights at any time. An estate from year to year becomes an estate at will if the lessor is silent as to the ending of the lease and no termination date was specified.
7. An *estate at sufferance* is a less than freehold estate in which the conditions by which the rights were originally granted expire, but the person granted the rights continues to use them "at the sufferance of the owner." For example, a long-term lease expires and neither the lessor nor the lessee bothers to renew it. The lessee continues to pay rent and the lessor, by his or her actions, accepts the conditions.

The law also recognizes two different types of conditional estates. An estate in fee simple *determinable* is a conditional estate that exists for a duration as long as certain conditions are maintained. The conditions are usually prefaced with the words *so long as, while, or during the period that.* If conditions change, or a period expires, the estate reverts to the original grantor or his heirs. An example might be a gift of forest land, *so long as it is used for educational purposes.* The land can never be sold for any other uses, and the estate is also conditioned on the forest being used for educational purposes. Such a fee simple determinable estate ends automatically when the property is no longer used for its intended purpose.

Another conditional estate is an estate in fee simple *on condition subsequent.* Words like *if, provided that, or on the condition that* indicate the allowed conditional uses of property. Condition subsequent differs from fee simple determinable in that the words make no reference to duration. They also differ in another major way. An estate in fee simple determinable reverts to the original grantor automatically when the conditions are not met or a specified period ends; an estate in fee simple on condition subsequent must be reclaimed by the original grantor or the grantor's heirs for the rights of the current owner to end.

Title to Real Estate

A title to real estate is an abstract concept. You cannot hold a title in your hands, yet it is very real and significant because it expresses a person's legal rights to land—rights as evidenced by a deed, a survey, or some other legal documentation, such as a contract or a bill of sale. A person acquires forest land by obtaining legal title to it, one that no other person can challenge. The process of passing title is called *alienation.* A current owner must alienate the title to pass it to a new owner, and that title defines the extent of an owner's estate in that property.

The laws surrounding private ownership of real estate are exhaustive and often confusing, and they vary from state to state. Law students devote an enormous portion of their time to the study of real property law, but not all lawyers make a practice of handling title issues. Anytime you anticipate changing the title to your land, or you are presented with a claim against a title you hold, seek advice from a competent local attorney. Among attorneys, the finesse with which a title is passed is the legacy by which their future peers will judge them.

A tract's title history is analogous to an animal's bloodlines to a breeder. Both the purchaser of real estate and the person shopping for particular traits in an animal look to the past to ensure they are getting exactly what they are paying for and there are no problems that may crop up in the future (due to error conveying title in the past or—for a breeder—a mismatch of bloodlines). An error in a tract's title, or an ambiguity caused by marriage, bequest or gift, or a title acquired by fraudulent means will create a *clouded title.* A clouded title must be cleared up before a prospective buyer takes possession. If it is not, the new owner faces the possibility of having the claim challenged by an earlier, legally valid claim. The courts will recognize the earliest legal claim on a tract's title, which may be from the grandchildren of the person who incorrectly alienated title in the past—the person you purchased the land from. For this reason, it is essential to have an attorney or title company search the title of the tract you are acquiring and to suggest legal methods to clear up any clouds on the title. The process of searching land titles is described in chapter 4, principally to describe the process, not to make experts of buyers who refuse to pay attorney fees.

Usually a portion of attorney fees is applied toward the cost of title insurance. The purpose of title insurance is to help cover losses associated with a superior title claim. It is not a guarantee that the property will remain in your name. Notwithstanding, even in states where title insurance is not required, it is money well spent to protect against losses from title claims of others. Title insurance is a one-time fee paid at the time title changes hands.

As discussed earlier, most real estate titles are derivative, which means their history over the past few generations is traced by the legal alienation of rights by former owners. These rights are vested in a new owner, who has then *acquired* title. Alienation is usually voluntary through a legal conveyance of deed, such as when property is sold or willed. Sometimes, however, title is acquired by involuntary alienation without the current owner's consent. Involuntary alienation results from actions such as the following:

- *Eminent domain.* A (local, state, or federal) government's right to take land for the public good.
- *Escheat.* The state's right to claim land of a decedent who has died without a will and no legal heirs.
- *Judicial sale.* A court-ordered and supervised process whereby property is sold to satisfy a judicially established debt on which the property holder has defaulted.
- *Adverse possession* or *partition.* Any action where an owner's claim to property is passed to another against his or her will by action of a court or through some other process whereby another individual stakes a claim against an owner's property. Divorce proceedings can result in a partition, when jointly owned property is divided or awarded to one of the spouses.

An adverse possession can also create an original title vested in the person who claims ownership by right of occupancy and use of another's property for a statutorily defined period of time (which varies from state to state, but seven years is common). Acquisition of title by adverse possession must demonstrate open use of the property in a manner contrary to the best interests of the titleholder. Evidence of an adverse possession usually must include the requirement that the person making the claim has been responsible for paying property taxes on the tract in question. For example, a caretaker living on the property cannot make a claim by reason of adverse possession unless it is clear the owner has relinquished his or her rights. A squatter living on your land has no rights to acquire title by adverse possession unless all of the above conditions are met. Adverse possession applies only to private lands, and it is the only method available—short of future conquests—to create an original real estate title.

Deeds

A deed is a legal document used to convey a person's interests in land. A deed must be a written legal description of the property so the location of the tract and the rights that go with it are clear to everyone (including future generations). The current owner, or grantor, must have a legal capacity to convey clear title, and the receiver, or grantee, can be any legal entity (person or company)—even minors have a legal capacity to acquire title. The deed, as a form of contract, must also have the following:

- A clause that actually conveys title from grantor to grantee.
- A clause demonstrating that consideration has been paid by the grantee for the rights the grantor is about to convey. The consideration clause is usually a nominal statement, such as "For the sum of one dollar and other valuable consideration . . . " (However, in some areas a statement of full consideration is required.)
- The legally witnessed and publicly acknowledged (witnessed by a notary) signature of the grantor. Unlike other types of contracts, it is not necessary for the grantee to sign the deed.

After the deed has been executed, it must be delivered to and unconditionally accepted by the grantee for it to be valid. To effect a legally valid deed, the delivery must also be unconditional and voluntary. Delivery cannot be conditional on future events or circumstances, and it must be clear that it is the grantor's intent to immediately convey title to the grantee. Usually, if the grantor's signature has been notarized, it is assumed delivery is voluntary and immediate and that the grantee has accepted the deed without conditions. Once the deed is delivered, it is usually recorded in the town or county where the property is located. Even if the deed is lost before it is recorded, however, the grantee still holds title to the property (at least with respect to the grantor's conveyance, or passing, of title to the grantee).

The important and very significant purpose of recording a deed is to publicly acknowledge the grantor's conveyance and to establish the grantee's claim to the property, since priority is given to the earliest legally valid claims to title. An unrecorded deed is invalid with respect to earlier recorded claims by other parties against the same property. For example, a grantor conveys title to forest land while a timber sale is in progress. On the day the deed is delivered, the grantee tries to stop the sale. When the grantee goes to record the deed he or she discovers the timber buyer recorded the timber sale contract months ago, creating a claim (a title by devise) that precedes the grantee's. Who owns the timber? The timber buyer—at least to the extent it is defined in the recorded contract.

A title search preceding the transaction would have discovered the contract. If there was no record of the contract, who legally owns the timber after the grantee has recorded the deed? The grantee! The timber buyer must seek recourse from the grantor (former land owner) and cease harvesting once he has been given legal notice of the grantee's claim. A properly recorded deed will take precedence over an earlier deed that has been delivered but not recorded. An unrecorded deed is invalid against subsequent claims that have been properly recorded. Since town and county records are open to the public, the only way to keep track of and discover valid claims to property is to record with the municipality legal documents that create claims.

Deeds and other legal instruments (such as a long-term timber sale contract in the example above) are recorded chronologically by reference to volume and page of the town or county's property records. An alphabetical card file (or electronic database in more sophisticated and better-funded municipalities), cross-indexed with the names of grantors, lien and mortgage holders, grantees, and others who have had a legal association with the property, provides the person searching a title with the first reference to a property in question (figure 3.1). The system varies from place to place, but the ability to cross-reference names and claims is essential. A title search of the grantor in the example above will yield a notation (or card) in the timber buyer's name (being the grantee). The notation will give the volume and page number where the timber sale contract is

Figure 3.1. Deeds, surveys, contracts, and other real property documents are filed with the town or county and can be located by a cross-reference of the names of grantors and grantees. Some communities use a card file index or database to locate the volume and page of the documents in question. Today, most systems are computerized databases.

recorded. Any other claims against the grantor's title will be located in the card file in sequential order, beginning with the first claim (which takes precedence over all subsequent claims). The grantor's original title will be cross-referenced to the name of the person from whom he or she acquired title and the volume and page where that title is located. In this way an abstract of title can be methodically searched back to a grantor so far removed from the current grantor as to ensure no outstanding legal claims to the tract's title.

In most states, statute defines the minimum period over which a title must be searched. Unless there are ambiguities because of boundaries or easements granted in the past, the search usually extends over the past thirty to sixty years—about three generations. Searching property titles in public records is discussed in chapter 4.

Types of Deeds

There are many different types of deeds, defined by the purpose for which title is being conveyed. The four most common deeds involving forest land transactions are the following:

1. *Warranty deed.* The grantor accepts liability for defending the claim he or she conveys to the grantee. It is the best deed a grantee can accept because it is, in effect, a guarantee that the title is good and clear. A warranty deed will include an affidavit of the grantor claiming that the title is clear and marketable. The grantor will also give assurances to the grantee that there are no encumbrances on the title other than those listed in the deed. Finally, the grantor is obligated to cooperate in the future if it is necessary to execute other documents to clear up any clouds on the title, a process known as *perfecting title.*

2. *Mortgage deed.* The grantor (mortgage purchaser) acknowledges the claim of a lender (as grantee) and pledges to conserve the value of the property and to accept financial liability to the lender—as secured by the property—at least to the extent of the mortgage balance. The mortgage deed (in some states it is called a "deed of trust") is a means of putting the lender's interests first if the property is sold or claimed by adverse possession. Banks,

however, are often reluctant to loan money for the purchase of forest land unless the fair market value of the land (usually for development) greatly exceeds the loan amount and the borrower has other sources of income to repay the loan. When a mortgage is treated as a lien against the deed, the ownership interest of the buyer is witnessed by a deed of trust.

3. *Quitclaim deed.* The grantor agrees to convey only the interests he or she might have in a property. Because the grantor's claims may be questionable, he or she does not warrant the title in any way. The quitclaim deed, as the name implies, is often used to eliminate confusion about claims resulting from marriage, divorce, name changes, or other circumstances—such as a poorly marked boundary—where there is (or might be in the future) ambiguity about who owns what.

4. *Gift deed.* Similar to a quitclaim deed and used to convey title by gift. A gift deed can be invalidated, however, if the grantor is making the gift to avoid creditors, including the federal and state government, if the gift is made in anticipation of death and solely for the purpose of avoiding estate tax liability. (Estate taxation and tax avoidance strategies are discussed in chapters 8 and 9.)

Other, less common, deeds include an executor's deed, a tax deed, and a sheriff's deed. In each instance, title is being alienated by a legally appointed grantor who has been given the right to convey title by action of the court.

Easements

An easement grants rights to land without actually owning the land. In other words, it is a legal document that passes some of the rights to land without giving up all rights. An easement is usually permanent or very long-term. It is the most common method of separating the bundle of rights, especially for the purposes of protecting land from development. The title that holds an easement, or the property that benefits from it, is called the *grantee*, and the title that gives up the easement is the *grantor*.

The grantor of an easement conveys rights to a grantee usually for very specific purposes, such as for a driveway or for drainage. An easement, though, is usually not temporary. It stays with the land and is passed on to future owners of both titles. The grantee of an easement, if he or she happens to be an *abutter* sharing a boundary with a grantor, should have a reference in the deed regarding the terms of the easement. When the grantee's property is adjacent to the parcel with the easement, it is called an *easement appurtenant.* In this case, the grantee's property is the *dominant estate* and the property of the easement's grantor is called the *servient estate.* The dominant estate benefits from the detriment of the servient estate.

When an easement holder has a right to use land that is not adjacent, it is called an *easement in gross.* For example, an easement granted to a municipality for sewer lines that cross your property, or to a power company for high-tension lines, are examples of easements in gross. Another example is when development rights are sold or given to another legal entity, such as a land trust. (Easements as they apply to land trusts are discussed in more detail in chapter 9.) When an easement is given or sold to a land trust for the purpose of forever protecting land from development, it is also known as a *transfer of development rights* (TDR). An easement in gross involves only one property and it is almost always granted for public benefit.

The conditions of easements in a property title are also known as *covenants.* A covenant is a promise—in the case of an easement, a promise to honor and protect the terms as originally set forth. An owner who acquires land with covenants accepts the promises of a former owner and agrees to honor the terms as though the promises were his own. A deed may also include other covenants made by the grantor, such as a covenant that the title is free from encumbrances. When a covenant creates restrictions on the titleholder, however, it is known as a *deed restriction.* Any condition referenced in the deed that limits in any way the titleholder's use and enjoyment of the full bundle of rights is a deed restriction. For example, a requirement that a deed holder maintain the color scheme of a house because of its historical significance is an example of a deed restriction imposed by a municipality.

A *prescriptive easement* can evolve from the continuous, open use of another's property. For example, an abutter's driveway cutting across a neighboring property (to avoid a stream or for some other reason) may become a prescriptive easement if the use is obvious and continuous, without interruption for a number of years (anywhere from five years in most states to sixty in Texas). If a beneficial owner can prove that a prescriptive easement exists, a new owner of the servient property will not be able to deny continued use of the intruding driveway.

Owners of servient properties can avoid prescriptive easements by periodic inspections and maintenance of boundaries, and the purported owner of a prescriptive easement can perfect the easement by initiating a *quiet title action*—a court proceeding to prove that the conditions of a prescriptive easement have been met. If so, the court's judgment is recorded as an easement appurtenant, also known as a *deeded right-of-way.*

In some states, the law allows for *easements by necessity*, especially in circumstances where a property is landlocked. Depending on purpose, the easement may only be temporary, such as in states that permit access to landlocked parcels for agricultural and forestry purposes. However, if the owner of a servient property is not willing to allow access, the owner of a landlocked piece may need to pursue a quiet title action.

An easement for conservation purposes is an easement in gross and it is the most common method of relinquishing development rights on farm and forest lands. When the grantee of the easement is an IRS-qualified, nonprofit organization dedicated to holding land for conservation purposes, the original grantor may take advantage of IRS rules that can result in substantial tax savings. The tax advantages, however, are available only when the easement is made for conservation purposes and in perpetuity. This type of restriction is often used to limit development on farm and forest lands. It does not restrict locally acceptable forest-management practices and—aside from the conservation easement—the land can be sold, willed, or given as an estate in fee simple absolute. This type of easement does not require the landowner to open farm and forest lands for public access; one of the most common misconceptions about conservation easements. (The nature of easements for conservation purposes and tax benefits are discussed in chapter 9.)

By their nature easements are often viewed as restrictive and hostile. It is true a property title that has given up easements is an *imperfect* title, but it does not mean the title is defective or any less marketable. In fact, easements can be used as a highly effective forest management tool. For example, the same forest owner who transfers development rights to a local land trust can also require the trust to continue managing forest stands according to prescriptions laid out by the current title holder. By an easement in gross the forest owner clearly spells out how forest lands are to be managed for habitat, timber, scenic vistas, and other values. Most land trusts have management guidelines they follow, but there is nothing to prevent an owner from imposing his or her own ideas about how lands are to be managed. So long as the vision is not too drastically different from that of the trust—and the owner is willing to pay the extra expense of creating a more complicated easement—the land trust will usually comply.

Another example of an easement in gross that is apt to be much more common in the future is one that allows current timber owners to extract value from standing timber without cutting it. In exchange for an easement in timber rights, a public or private funding authority (like a bank) allows the current titleholders to obtain fair market value for timber. Depending on the exact nature of the easement, the payment could be either a loan against equity the current owner's have in timber, an outright sale of timber, plus whatever extra value timber is expected to grow (according to the funding authority's guidelines) less management costs and rent, or a long-term timber lease. Note these alternatives are different from an outright, unconditional sale of timber rights, which is not uncommon in areas surrounded by timber-using industries. In fact, mineral rights and timber rights were probably the two most common types of easements before the advent of land trusts willing to accept—and protect—development rights. For those woodland owners who are presented with an opportunity to extract value from timber without cutting it, the way to avoid surprises is to understand the motivations of the entity offering cash in exchange for timber.

Methods of Holding Property

There are five principal methods of holding property, but not all five are recognized in all states. The differences among methods have to do with the number of different people (or legal entities) involved and their relationship to one another (figure 3.2).

When a property is held in *severalty* it means there is only one owner, separate from all others, either an individual or a corporation.

Tenants in common involve ownership by two or more people, each of whom is entitled to an undivided possession of rights even

Figure 3.2. Property can be held many different ways. Knowing the best method to hold assets with others is an important consideration for an owner of forest land.

though the total ownership involves the sum of separate interests. Without specific mention of proportional interests, it is assumed the interests are equal. Also, it is usually assumed the interests of the owners apply to the entire property even though separate interests can be defined. A tenant in common can sell or lease his or her interests in land to another, and can will his or her interest to heirs. Often a decedent's estate will pass to heirs, who become tenants in common. An heir wishing to sell interests to the other heirs would usually do so with a quitclaim deed.

A noncorporate *partnership* is most apt to be owned by tenants in common. A partner generally cannot sell his or her interests at any time unless provisions in the partnership agreement prescribe otherwise.

Joint tenants, or *joint tenants with rights of survivorship* (JTROS), is an ownership by more than one person where possession of property and interests are shared equally through one title of a freehold estate (no time limits). This is a common way for married couples to own property (in many states where common law is recognized), although there can be more than two joint tenants. The separate interests of the parties cannot be willed, and when there are survivors, the property of a joint tenancy is not probated. When one joint tenant dies, his or her interests pass automatically to the other joint tenants. In some states, a joint tenant can sell his or her share of the interests without consent of the other parties, but the person who acquires title does so as a tenant in common with the other joint tenants. If the shared interests of joint tenants are to be sold, the parties must act together. Notwithstanding, a joint tenant with rights of survivorship usually cannot sell his or her interest to a third party. Without an agreement, a court order is necessary to split up the rights of joint tenants.

A *tenancy by the entirety*, not recognized in all states, is only available to married couples. It is as though the couple were one person, thus there is no such thing as equal shares, and one party cannot sell (or will) interests in the property without full consent and cooperation of the other. Tenancy by the entirety implies rights of survivorship, and the surviving spouse will hold title in severalty. In the event of divorce where the property must be divided for settlement, the title can be vested—by stipulation of the parties or by action of the court—as joint tenants or as tenants in common.

In some states (Arizona, California, Idaho, Louisiana, Nevada, New Mexico, Texas, Washington, and Wisconsin), property acquired jointly by spouses during the marriage is treated as *community property*. Any property brought to the marriage, or acquired by gift or inheritance after the marriage, is separate property (held in severalty by one spouse or the other). The property must be maintained by separate funds and not by commingled funds of the spouses. Community property is assumed to be shared equally and can be willed to other parties, who become tenants in common with the surviving spouse.

Contrary to community property, in some states *marital rights* are recognized. These are rights (usually a percentage of the entire estate) that extend to a spouse regardless of the independent actions of the other spouse. For instance, when a husband dies with property held in severalty, the wife has dower rights that may supersede a bequest of the property to someone other than the wife. Curtesy is the same rights extended to the husband. If either spouse predeceases the other, all marital rights die with them.

Owning Land with Other People

Most private nonindustrial forest land is owned by married couples. In many instances, however, individuals or couples pool resources and purchase land with others. They do this by forming either a corporation, a partnership, or a limited liability company (LLC).

Corporations

A corporation is an ownership in severalty. Thus it is a legal entity that has the same rights and obligations of a person. Corporations evolved as a means to protect individuals from liability and to enable widely shared ownership. For example, publicly held corporations can raise capital for the business by selling shares. A *share* in a corporation is an equity-interest in the assets of company. A *shareholder* is entitled to a proportional share of the profits of the company, but when debt exceeds asset values and the stock price goes to zero, the shareholder is not liable for debts in excess of asset value.

There are a few different forms of incorporation that vary depending on the purpose of the business, but generally the variations come with these features: limited personal liability, centralized management, and continuity of existence or the ability to outlive the owners. The IRS likes to view a corporation as the equivalent of a taxpayer without a body. When the corporation makes money, it is taxed just like any other taxpayer. But when the after-tax profits are passed to shareholders, the income is taxed a second time.

Double taxation was the cost of limited liability until Congress allowed variations (described below) that eliminate double taxation, primarily for small businesses and nonprofit companies. Individuals incorporate the assets of a forest holding to create a single legal entity. There are some advantages to holding forest assets as a corporation, especially if the holdings are extensive and several people share an interest in the land.

The six criteria used by IRS to define a corporate entity are as follows:

1. An association of individuals that have a stake in the corporation, also known as shareholders
2. Profit motive
3. A centralized and collaborative management structure, usually involving a board of directors who make day-to-day decisions
4. Longevity that exceeds the lifespan of shareholders; in a sense, a corporation has its own "life"
5. The ability of shareholders to transfer their interests to others without restrictions by the corporation
6. Limited liability for shareholders that may result from actions of the corporation

The biggest advantages of a corporation are that shareholders can come and go, and although they share in the profits (and losses), they are protected from liability. Incorporating forest holdings among family members is sometimes used as a strategy to lower the value of a person's estate to avoid estate taxes (see chapter 9). Of the primary profit-oriented methods of incorporating recognized by the IRS, Subchapter S (Sub S) is most commonly used by individuals and families. The major advantage of a Sub S is that profits or losses go directly to the shareholders' tax returns. Thus, profits are taxed only once and losses can offset income from other sources. On the other hand, profits earned but reinvested are still taxable to shareholders, who then must come up with the cash to pay taxes due. Setting up a Sub S corporation is fairly easy but requires the advice, guidance, and skill of an attorney with this type of experience. Also, under current law a Sub S corporation can have no more than one hundred shareholders, only one class of stock, and the corporation has no rights to control ownership. For these reasons, a straight Sub S corporation may not fit the long-term needs of most forest-owning families.

A variation of the Sub S corporation that is especially well-suited to family woodland enterprises is the *closely held* S corporation. The primary advantage of a closely held corporation is that it can control membership so shares stay within the family. A distinct disadvantage, however, is that under current law the maximum number of shareholders is thirty, a size that is easily exceeded after only a few generations. An S corporation, closely held or otherwise, that breaks the rules (from the perspective of the IRS) is likely to be viewed as a regular corporation, with the threat of back taxes and penalties.

The advantages and disadvantages of Sub S corporations are discussed further in chapter 9. For those readers looking for more information on corporate structures, there is plenty of further reading in the small-business reference section of most bookstores.

Partnerships

A partnership is a noncorporate association of two or more people—usually as tenants in common—who are personally liable for the actions of the partnership. There are two types of partnership: *general* and *limited*. In a general partnership, individuals are equally (or proportionally) involved in the day-to-day operation, sharing in profits and losses. They are jointly and severally liable for the separate acts of each of the partners and for the collective acts of the partnership.

In a limited partnership, there are two kinds of partners: the general partner(s), who controls the operation, and the limited partner(s), with no management authority and only limited liability for debts and other claims against the partnership (Shumate 1995). A limited partner is often the source of capital for an operation, sharing in the profits and losses (with the advantage of writing off the losses against other sources of income at tax time).

A partnership of two married couples creates a tenants in common ownership with respect to the couples, even though the husband and wife are joint tenants with respect to their combined share of the partnership.

Family partnerships are a common way for parents to maintain control of a forest property (as general partners), while dispersing the assets to children, who become limited partners (creating a family partnership as an estate-planning tool is discussed in more detail in chapter 9). In recent years, the IRS has given much closer scrutiny to family partnerships set up ostensibly for the purposes of avoiding taxes.

Limited Liability Companies

Forming a variation of an S corporation was an excellent alternative for woodland owning families looking to protect personal assets from liability. That is, until fairly recently when a new form of organization, known as a *limited liability company* (LLC) or a *limited liability partnership* (LLP), became widely available. Although the LLC concept has been in existence for more than a hundred years (first in Germany then throughout Europe spreading in the 1900s to Latin America, and then north), it has only been within the last few years that every state in the United States has developed a statute that allows this form of organization. Vermont was one of the last states to adopt an LLC code in 1996.

An LLC combines the most favorable aspects of a partnership (eliminating double taxation) with the best characteristics of a corporation (limited liability). But here is the hitch: an IRS-acceptable

LLC structure assumes that at least two of these four conditions of a corporation are *not* true:

1. Limited liability for the owners
2. Centralized management
3. No restrictions on ownership interests (anyone can hold stock)
4. Continuity of existence

An LLC is taxed in the same manner as a partnership (i.e., profits and losses are passed through to individual tax payers) if it lacks at least two of the above conditions. Although circumstances vary from one business to another, most often organizers are willing to sacrifice Items 3 and 4. Why? Because an LLC by nature is intended to protect owners from liability (Item 1 is true), and there is usually (but not necessarily always) a centralized management (Item 2 is true). However, most LLC owners—like partners—want to restrict ownership and decision making (Item 3 is false); and despite the advantages of a business that can exist irrespective of the founding owners (like a corporation), to meet IRS conditions Item 4 must also be false. An LLC business cannot have a continuity of existence. Thus it must have either a finite existence or exist at the will of its members.

Assuming IRS conditions are met, the LLC is composed of two parts: one public, the other private. The public part, called *Articles of Organization*, is filed by the founder(s) with the secretary of state. In their simplest form the articles are no more complicated than short answers to a series of questions, one of which has to do with management. Is the LLC to be managed by *members*, or by *managers* who may or may not also be members? A member in LLC parlance is the same as a shareholder in a corporation.

Another question has to do with the issue of *continuity of existence*. The founder(s) must choose whether the company has a fixed *term*, or it exists *at-will* of the members. Other questions have to do with the business name (followed by the abbreviation "LLC" or "LC" or "LP" for limited partnership, which tells the world how the business is organized), and contact information. In answer to the question of term, generally, a woodland owning family would chose a fixed-term of fairly long duration for reasons that will be discuss in chapter 9.

The second—private—part of an LLC is the *operating agreement.* It sets forth in detail the purpose of the LLC, who its members are, and all the conditions of the company. In addition to regulating the affairs of the company and the conduct of business, the operating agreement also addresses governance. It describes how members will handle the *expiration* of a term (presumably by specifying a new term), and how managers or the member-management team will operate. The operating agreement is a proprietary document of the LLC. It is not filed with the secretary of State, but each member should have a copy.

In addition to the obvious advantages of an LLC, another is that they are easy to set up. Although the process in most states is designed so that almost anyone can create an LLC, for most it is money well-spent to seek the guidance of an attorney who has experience with LLCs. For those woodland owners who intend to transfer assets to the LLC, legal guidance is absolutely necessary. For example, there may be time limitations on property transfers to avoid property transfer tax on real estate. The attorney may also advise transferring land to a trust rather than directly to the LLC.

Using LLCs as a way to pass lands within the family is discussed in much greater detail in chapter 9.

Trusts

A *trust* is an agreement or contract where the legal and beneficial interests in property are separated according to the terms set forth. Legal interests encompass the rights to change the status of the property and to fulfill any obligations the property might require. For example, a person who holds a legal interest in property has the right to sell it, or to use it as collateral for loan or to give it away, so long as those specific rights are not disallowed in the trust agreement. A beneficial interest, on the other hand, encompasses only the right to benefit from the property without any control over how the property is used to create benefit.

The concept of trusts evolved from English common law. In the early sixteenth century property owners would transfer title to a third party while retaining all the benefits associated with ownership. In this way they avoided creditors, taxes, and any call to arms in times of war. Obviously a landowner would only develop such a relationship with a trusted person, and with written terms that limited the third-party's ability to sell or dispose of the land. It is easy to see how the term *trust* evolved. Another definition of a trust is: property (or wealth) that is held by a *fiduciary* for the primary benefit of another. A fiduciary is a person (or an entity, like a bank or a law firm) with a legal duty to act exclusively for the benefit of someone else.

In a trust, the fiduciary is known as the *trustee*. The person who creates the trust (or, more correctly, funds or endows the trust) is called the *trustor*, *settlor*, or *grantor*, and the person who benefits from the trust is known as the *beneficiary*.

It used to be that trusts were the exclusive realm of the rich and famous; only wealthy people needed to know about trusts. But such is not the case anymore. Trusts have a variety of uses, one or more of which can benefit almost anyone. They are especially helpful to people who care about the future and this is why woodland owners need to know about them.

One of the most intriguing aspects of current trust law, a twist that makes trusts a favorite among those who want to shelter wealth from taxation, is that the three parties of a trust can be one and the same person. An individual can, at once, be the trustor, trustee, and beneficiary. A trust of this kind, usually involving the assets of a husband and wife, can double the gift and estate tax exemption available to taxpayers (discussed in chapter 8). Under ordinary circumstances, husbands and wives are viewed by the IRS as one entity. But when it comes to trusts, and funding trusts, the IRS allows a married couple to operate as individuals.

Some people use trusts simply to avoid the probate process. Such *simple* trusts may not have any tax benefits, but assets that are controlled by a trust are not usually part of the probated estate. Such an estate can usually be settled in six months or less, while probate takes a minimum of six months, and sometimes two years or longer. Using trusts as an estate planning tool is discussed in chapter 9.

Another advantage of trusts is privacy. Probate is a very public process that reveals for public scrutiny the decedent's assets and liabilities. Assets held in trust, however, are not listed as part of the probated estate.

The frightening thing about trusts for most people is transferring ownership of assets to the trust. Remember, the trust is a separation of legal and beneficial interests controlled by a document. The trust must own the property, but the trust document explains how the assets are to be held, who makes legal decisions about them, and who benefits. The concept of trusts is easy to understand, but the nuances of developing and funding them can be quite complex. An attorney with experience in trust law should be involved in the formation of any trust, regardless of its purpose.

Although the concept of trusts is not difficult to understand, there are many legal trip-wires to negotiate to ensure the trust serves its intended purpose. Even a simple trust requires the expertise of an attorney who is familiar with trust law, and any variations of trust law that may exist in your state. Since the primary benefit of a trust often comes into play after the person who set it up dies, it is especially important that it does what it is intended to do. This is especially true for trusts that are irrevocable.

Purchasing Woodlands

There are three ways to acquire forest land: by purchase, by gift, or by inheritance. Most of the 10 million private forest holdings in the United States have been acquired by purchase, but increasingly, lands are being passed through inheritance. Because the average age of forest owners is increasing, and owners are holding their lands longer, the trend toward inheritance is expected to continue. Unless heirs want the land, however, an inheritance may result in a quick sale to help settle the estate. Gifts of forest land are fairly rare, but aging forest owners will often consider the possibilities of giving land to children to help lower the estate value. (Leaving forest land to heirs and making gifts of land to family members are discussed as estate-planning strategies in chapter 9.)

Today, most forest land buyers do so primarily because the land is associated with a house they want to buy or with a parcel on which to build. Many buyers, though, look to acquire forest land for the sake of long-term management of forest resources. Acquiring forest lands by purchase requires good planning and careful evaluation of many details. What follows is a brief discussion of what to look for in forest land, ideas on how to pay for it, and important questions to ask the seller.

The best buy in forest land (assuming timber production is one of the buyer's objectives) is a relatively young forest that will reach maturity within the next ten to fifteen years. Why? Because the timber has not reached merchantable size and thus its contribution to the appraised value of the land is negligible (figure 3.3). For patient buyers, the forest inventory will go from almost nothing to substantial merchantable volumes within a relatively short period. It is also easier for a trained eye to see productive potential in young stands. Older, larger stands can mask poor productivity with larger trunks. A buyer with an eye to timber potential will look for tall, pole-size trees supporting healthy crowns in easily accessible stands. Some buyers are tempted to buy land with saleable timber, hoping to sell the timber and pay back the bank (or the parent). This may seem like an excellent strategy, but it is not. After all, who wants to live with heavily cutover lands for the twenty to forty years or more that it will take for the timber to grow back?

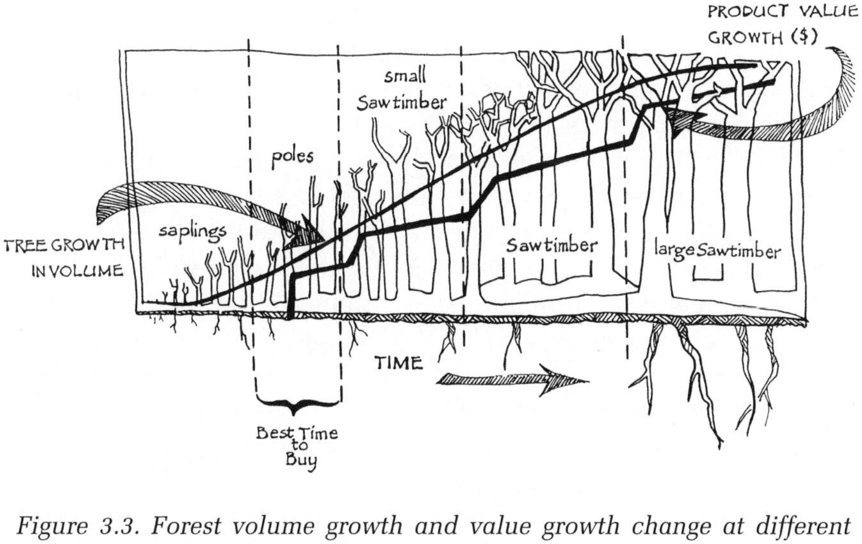

Figure 3.3. Forest volume growth and value growth change at different rates as stands get older. The best time to buy forest land is just before trees reach merchantable size.

Another important consideration is access. Does the land front directly on roads, or is access gained via easements through surrounding lands? How good are the roads, and are there any access restrictions? Are there any rights-of-way on the land, and what are the prospects for future public and private claims for access? What about the extent and condition of roads on the property? Are they well designed and maintained? Are there any erosion problems? Do streams run through the property? What about stream crossings and the condition of bridges and culverts? Is there a source of sand and gravel on the property? Roads need periodic upkeep, and a local free source of gravel will seem like a gold mine.

Some other important questions have to do with boundaries. Are the property boundaries clearly established and marked? Are they accepted and recognized by neighbors or are disputes brewing?

Something else to consider: Is there a good, accessible building site on the property, if you should decide to build a house? Will the soil allow a conventional septic system, or will it require special (and expensive) designs? Is good-quality water available at a reasonable well-depth near the house site? Are any zoning restrictions in place that will limit your ability to build? Are there any sources of contamination in the aquifer you are apt to tap into? Generally, look uphill for sources of pollutants—it may be necessary to obtain the opinion of a geologist.

Also, before making an offer to purchase, be sure no toxic dump sites are on the property. Look near barns and toolsheds for areas where no vegetation grows, or where the vegetation is sparse and distinctly different from surrounding areas. Dig around and ask questions, because when you buy property you also buy any dumps that are on or in it and any future liabilities arising from them. The purchase agreement should include an opinion about former activities that might have produced hazardous wastes. Before the closing, arrange to have all drums, fluid containers, and other noninert materials removed from the site, and have the seller sign an affidavit stating there are no toxic dumps on the property.

How are you going to pay for the land? Most banks are reluctant to loan money for forest land unless it offers an express and obvious profit-oriented business opportunity. The exception to this is when the land is to be used for a primary residence; otherwise, expect to put up collateral for a bank mortgage and to pay a higher interest rate over a shorter loan period than for a primary residence. Sellers are often willing to help finance the purchase of their forest land, usually with a *land contract* or a *contract for deed.* Both are creative methods of owner financing, where the seller retains title to the property but agrees to convey title to a buyer on or before a specified date, or when certain conditions have been met. The land contract and contract for deed, however, create a title by devise for the buyer, because they witness the buyer's first interest in the tract's title when the contract terms are fulfilled. Financing in this type of arrangement is set up to be affordable for the buyer, but with the stipulation that the entire balance due is paid before the end of the loan amortization period. Known as a *balloon note,* the loan is amortized over a long period—to make monthly payments affordable. But the note comes due, or balloons, on a date well before the end of the loan amortization period. The buyer must locate another source of financing at that time or make new arrangements with the seller. For example: a couple agrees to purchase 160 acres of forest land from a seller who is willing to finance the purchase with a note that balloons in five years. The purchase price is $80,000, and the couple puts $10,000 down and finances the balance, $70,000, with the seller at 7.5 percent amortized over fifty years. Monthly payments are $448.16, but the sixtieth payment is $69,242—the balance of principal due. The couple must refinance or otherwise pay the balance at the end of five years.

Finally, there is the question of how much to pay for woodlands. Your offer should be based on the going price for forest land in the region and on how you intend to use the land. A local consulting forester can help suggest a fair price. The more land you buy, generally the lower the price per acre. The land probably will be priced as though it were to be developed, which is substantially more expensive than if the land is to be used strictly for forest values. If you intend to maintain the land as forest, you may be able to persuade the seller to sell (or give) the development rights to a local land trust, or you may agree to pay fair market value and sell or give the rights after you own the land. (The sale or donation of development rights is discussed in chapter 9.)

Chapter 4

Surveys and Boundaries

Many forest owners have no idea where boundaries are located, especially in the original thirteen states. In these states, parcel locations use a survey system based on landscape features, vegetation (which can change over the course of a single generation), and surveyor-placed monuments. Known as metes and bounds, and described in greater detail below, the primary problem with this system is that every parcel has its own reference, which may or may not agree with the references of surrounding tracts. It is easy to see how confusion about property lines can arise with metes and bounds. In fact, boundary ambiguities are one of the primary causes of title imperfections in the region.

West of the Allegheny Mountains and in areas of the country that were not widely settled before the Revolutionary War, lands are surveyed based on a system enacted by the U.S. Congress in 1785. This system relies on *benchmarks* (references) common to all properties and defines parcels that are exclusively rectangular. Appropriately named the rectangular system, or Government Survey, it was adopted by Congress because once a point defined by the intersection of north-south, east-west lines is established (the benchmark), it is as though an imaginary grid were laid over the land defining every possible parcel, even though the corners of any particular parcel are not marked. Such a system enabled Congress to quickly lay claim to vast tracts of land and to grant claims to Revolutionary War veterans. Because the orientation of tract lines is always north-south, east-west, and corners are approximately 90 degrees, locating and marking a parcel is fairly easy. The rectangular system is described in greater detail below.

The boundary of a property is more than just the perimeter. It also serves as a dividing line between parcels. People who share a boundary are known as *abutters*. If they agree on a boundary, there are no problems. If they disagree, a survey by a licensed surveyor is the only way to resolve the dispute. A survey, besides establishing boundaries on a map, also provides a legal and (you hope) defensible description of a parcel and its location relative to other ownerships. A copy of the survey is recorded in the municipality as part of the description of the title to a parcel. The earliest recorded, error-free survey takes precedence over all subsequent surveys. In the eastern states, a surveyor of a difficult parcel is apt to spend almost as much time title searching in the public records as reckoning lines and corners in the field.

Metes and Bounds

Colonists needed a quick way to claim land. Accuracy was not important as long as earlier claims were respected. A valid claim needed obvious markings in the field and a description of the marks recorded in public records. Landmarks and natural boundaries, such as ridge lines, rivers, and lakes, were often used to define a property boundary. Where there were no prominent landscape features to note, a settler created his own boundary marks using blazes on tree trunks, or by making rock piles and stone walls. Often the distances between points were paced or unmeasured, and the bearing of lines only vague references to a feature in a particular direction. Among those early surveyors who used a compass, some made measurements based on true north, others based on magnetic north—an automatic error of up to 12 degrees in some parts of the country. Magnetic north is also known to wander from one decade to the next. Modern instruments correct for the declination of true north from magnetic north.

Interpreting a metes and bounds survey (the term comes from metes for measures of distances and bounds for limitations, such as a stream or another property line) is similar to following the directions of a treasure hunt (figure 4.1). The inaccuracies, inconsistencies, and ambiguities of the past have become the bane of present-

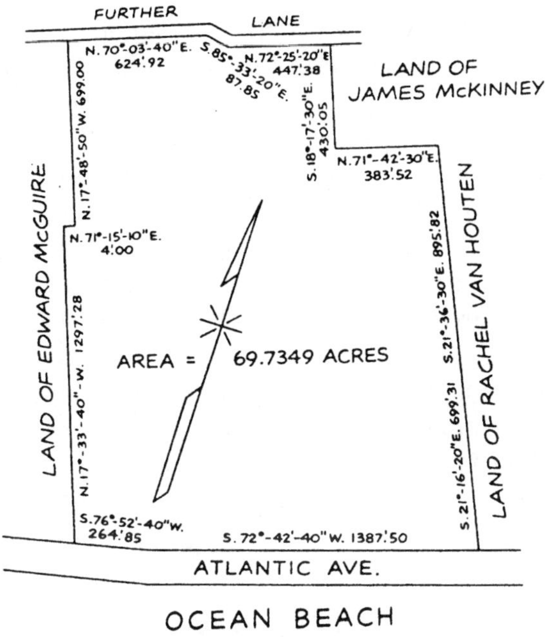

Figure 4.1. A survey map showing the metes and bounds. (Used with permission of Thomson Learning.)

day surveyors. Of the two—metes and bounds—the latter is the controlling factor. In other words, metes are used simply as guides to locate a property's *bounds,* or boundaries. Thus the system depends on accurate public records.

A modern metes and bounds survey has the following features: a distinct and easily located starting point, definite corners or places where the line changes direction, the bounds noting ownership of surrounding parcels, accurate distances between corners or points, and bearings to the next major point or corner back to where the survey closes at the beginning. A surveyor will also estimate the total acreage within the boundaries and provide an estimate of the error of closure—where the beginning and the ending are supposed to meet exactly. Precisely measured angles and distances applied to legally valid and reasonably accurate earlier surveys are the methods by which surveyors today create clear, obvious, and irrefutably accurate surveys. Even modern surveys, however, are not without error. The difficulties of measuring distances and angles over uneven terrain coupled with small, seemingly insignificant measurement errors over the entire course of a survey can make the beginning and ending points impossible to close. The surveyor's goal is to create as small an error of closure as possible. Generally, the more accurate a survey need be, the smaller the error of closure and the more expensive the survey.

Since the bounds of a survey take precedence over metes, accurate public records are essential. The earliest recorded, accurate, and legal boundary will prevail over any subsequent boundary that differs from an earlier survey. Thus if a former property title holder ignored the legal boundaries of others—which was not uncommon—then filed a survey to document his claims, it does not necessarily create a superior title. So long as a surveyor can prove that there is an earlier record (predating the incorrect survey) that faithfully represents the most correct boundary, the earlier survey will prevail.

Rectangular Survey System

The rectangular system, or government survey, is used in thirty states, mostly west of the Allegheny Mountains. It is not used in states of the original thirteen colonies, in northern New England, nor is it valid in West Virginia, Kentucky, Tennessee, or Texas. As discussed earlier in this chapter, the rectangular system was devised as a means to quickly lay claim to public lands after the Revolutionary War, and to facilitate subdivision of those lands for a fast-growing and westward-moving population.

Although rectangular survey systems, based mostly on parcel size rather than location, had been used in the New England states during colonial times, the government survey—based on parcel location—was developed by Andrew Ellicott, an astronomer and mathematician who taught celestial navigation to Captain Meriwether Lewis of Lewis and Clark fame. Ellicott was commissioned by Congress to establish a north-south benchmark from which the government survey would begin. That line, appropriately commemorated as the Ellicott Line, now serves as the eastern border of Ohio.

Beginning at the Ellicott Line, the country is divided into north-south running lines, called prime meridians or principal meridians. A prime meridian is intersected by east-west running baselines, creating coordinates that become the primary references for all land around those points. In between prime meridians are guide meridians, spaced every twenty-four miles, and in between baselines are standard parallels, also spaced every twenty-four miles (figure 4.2). Guide meridians are used to adjust for the curvature of the earth, since parallel north-south lines will eventually converge at the earth's poles, and the area in the grid will get smaller and smaller.

Each twenty-four-mile by twenty-four-mile block is subdivided into townships that measure six miles on a side. Townships are arranged in east-west rows that extend north and south of a baseline. A north-south column of townships extending east and west of a prime meridian is called a "range" (see figure 4.2). The first township

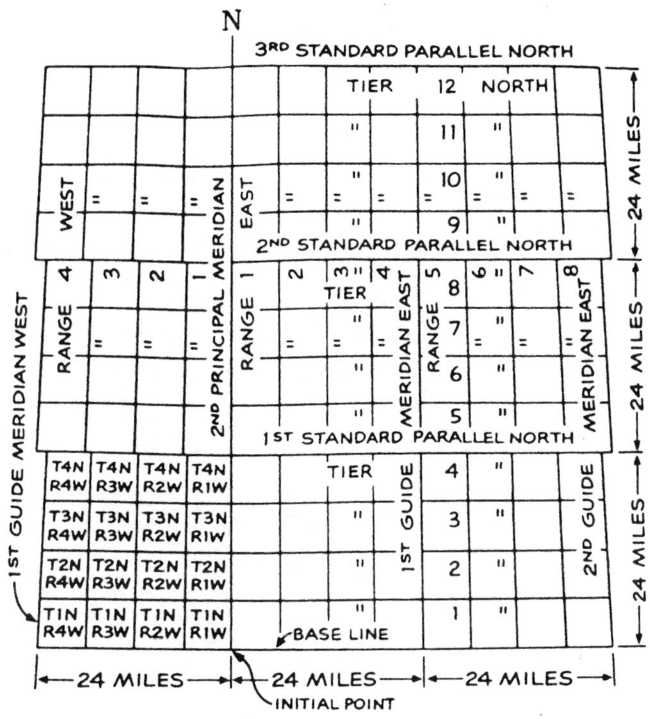

Figure 4.2. The rectangular survey system is based on the intersection of a principal meridian and a baseline. At 24-mile intervals from the principal meridian, a guide meridian is located to correct for curvature of the earth. The resulting grid is further divided into townships, which measure 6 miles on a side. (Used with permission of Thomson Learning.)

north of a baseline is called "township 1 north," abbreviated T.1N. The first range west of a prime meridian is called "range 1 west," abbreviated R.1W. In this way, every township is referenced by its east-west row number and north-south range relative to the intersection of a prime meridian with a baseline.

Townships are further subdivided into thirty-six *sections*, each one mile square (figure 4.3). Note that sections are numbered beginning in the northeast corner of a township. Each section is exactly 640 acres, and all subdivisions of a section refer to the half- or quarter-section where a parcel is located. Further subdivisions have similar references, so it is easy to place a rectangular parcel of almost any size in a section of a township (figure 4.4). The pattern of subdivision is also regular, so a half section is 320 acres and a quarter section is 160 acres. Further subdivisions are eighty, forty, twenty, ten, and five acres, and the sides of each par-

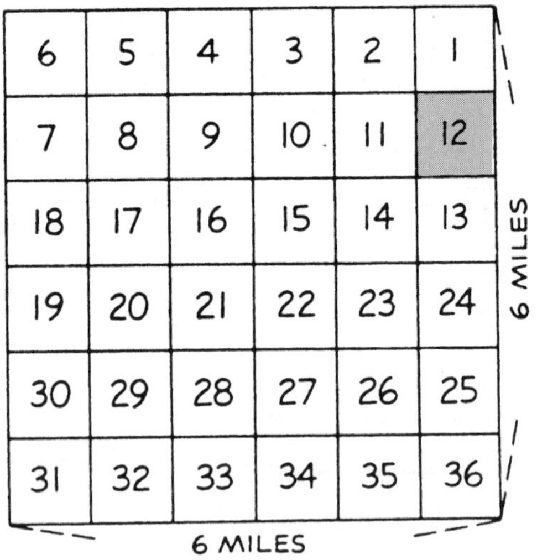

Figures 4.3. Each township is identified by it coordinates relative to the intersection of the principal meridian and the baseline. A tract, township, or tier is defined by east-west lines, and the position east or west of the principal meridian is known as the range. Each township measures 6 miles on a side and is composed of thirty-six sections. Each section is 640 acres. (Used with permission of Thomson Learning.)

cel are proportionally less, which makes surveying parcels in the field relatively easy.

Because parcels are rectangular, with lines consistently bounding in cardinal directions, knowing the location also tells you something about the size of the parcel and the length of each of its boundaries. Thus a parcel's location is also its legal description in the deed. In many counties where rectangular surveying is used, parcels are mapped relative to one another, with each owner identified, and the information is published in a booklet called a *plat* or *tract book.* The plat book is the equivalent of tax maps under the metes and bounds system.

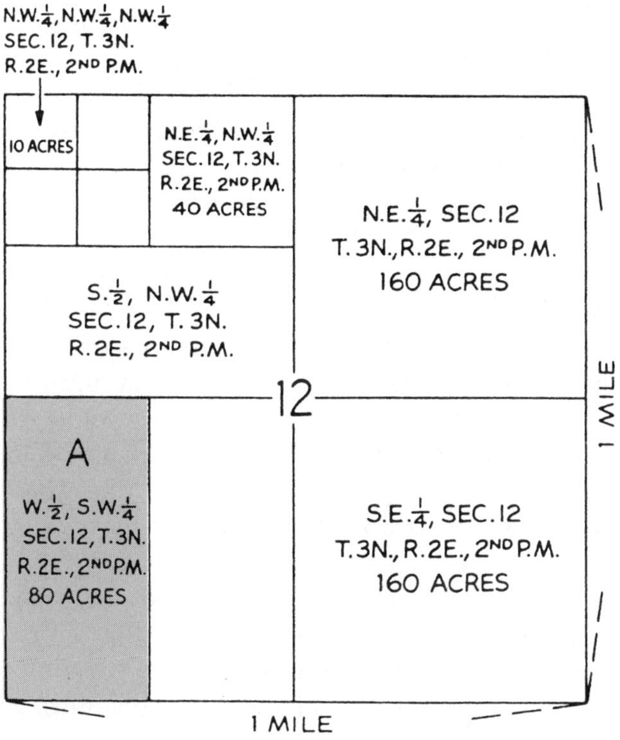

Figure 4.4. This is Section 12, Township 3 North, Range 2 East of the principal meridian. When a section is subdivided, the resulting parcels are rectangular. A parcel's location within the section also provides a legal description for the property, and the size of the parcel. For instance, a half section is 320 acres. (Used with permission of Thomson Learning.)

Searching Title in Public Records

The only way to verify the title to a property is through a title search. Generally, a title search precedes a title transfer of any or all interests in a property. The purpose of the search—as a means of verifying title—is to ascertain the following information: Is the current owner of record the actual owner and does that owner have full rights to convey title? Is the property's legal description complete, accurate and uncontested? Are there any others who hold ownership interests, or who might have a claim that is superior to that of the current owner? Are all taxes paid? Did any former owner borrow against the value of the property, and if so, were the loans paid? Are their any legal claims, also known as *liens*, against the property? Is the property a servient or dominant estate to any others (see chapter 3), and are those easements clear? Were all earlier conveyances handled properly thus ensuring no outstanding claims? The goal of searching title is ultimately to protect the interests of a prospective grantee, especially when the grantee is a purchaser. The product of a title search is an abstract of title or an opinion on title, representing a summary of all legal actions involving the property in question.

In metes and bounds states, property titles are more difficult to search than in midwest and western states that were surveyed using the rectangular system. In states that use the rectangular system, property records are maintained at county clerk offices and virtually all of the records reside in electronic files. Since the emergence of computers, the services of title companies have grown in these states. For a very reasonable fee, usually in the range of one to two hundred dollars, a title company will provide an abstract of any property title extending back through a period that varies from state to state, but usually encompassing one or two generations. Unless there are ambiguities because of boundary disputes, unresolved liens, or easements, a valid abstract of title usually extends over the past thirty to sixty years. As noted earlier, an abstract of title is a history of the chain of ownership that may or may not uncover hidden problems that can cloud a title. For example, an outstanding lien for unpaid taxes, or an unpaid mortgage, can create a clouded title.

The term *title* is actually a legal record that determines rightful ownership interests to property. Deeds are written documents used to convey an interest in land. Legal title is verified by deeds and other documents that can affect the rights of ownership. In most instances, rightful ownership is not in question and an abstract of title will prove it. But occasionally there are claims against property, about which the current owner may or may not know, which make ownership interests questionable.

Counties in rectangular survey states usually also print a physical copy of its property survey records in a plat book. It is often a reduced photocopy of its tax maps, sometimes superimposed on aerial photos that show the location of every parcel in the county and lists the names and addresses of all owners of record. Seasoned timber buyers in these states are no strangers to plat books, the perfect tool to connect any particular tract of timber with the owner of record. Where plat books are available, forest owners with salable timber receive so many postal solicitations to sell timber that they tend to look upon these letters as junk mail. Also, those who use plat books need to remember that the plat is not an abstract of title, and the book is not current since land records change daily.

In states that use the metes and bounds survey system, land records are maintained at the county level or in towns, which are geographic provinces of roughly six by six miles (encompassing within its boundaries a distance most residents could easily travel in a day, round trip on horseback) but with far more irregular boundaries than the similarly sized townships recognized in the rectangular system. The primary difference between properties surveyed by the rectangular system and metes and bounds is that in the former, all parcels are surveyed relative to a common base line. In metes and bounds states, every parcel has its own reference point, which often does not agree with the reference points of surrounding properties. For this reason, boundary discrepancies are the most common form of dispute between property holders in these states; so much so, that it is a wise buyer who takes the time to search the property title and verify boundaries.

Land records in some metes and bounds states have been computerized as well but not nearly as extensively as rectangular survey records, for obvious reasons. The former are much more complicated and thus more expensive to digitize. Nevertheless, counties and towns in urbanizing areas, or in other localities where property values are high, can afford computerization more than rural towns that still use card file systems originated by the colonists. The card file, introduced in chapter 3, is an index of property records that allows searching by the names of owners, claimants, abutters, easement holders, and others that have a legal interest in a property. The card file is then cross-referenced with a chronological listing—by volume and page—of every recorded transaction involving the property in question. The cost of recording documents that establish a legal claim in property is usually five to twenty dollars per page, money well spent if there is any chance a claim might be challenged.

Searching public records to verify ownership in a metes and bounds state is fairly easy with the help of a cooperative clerk. For example, a timber buyer with an owner's name in hand can search the card file that lists the volume and page of the most recent action involving the owner in question. The owner's original title will be cross-referenced to the name of the person from whom he or she acquired title and the volume and page where that deed is located. If the owner obtained a mortgage to purchase land, a search will discover a mortgage deed, or a deed of trust in some states. If the owner obtained the land by inheritance and then purchased the inheritances of brothers and sisters, the search will discover quit-claim deeds for each family member that sold his or her interests to the owner in question. If the owner's land is enrolled in any tax abatement programs that create a lien (usually in favor of the state should a title holder violate program conditions), the search will discover the lien. Page recordings in public records are chronological but the index, or card file, is arranged in alphabetical order.

If a financial decision will hinge on the outcome of a title search, it is money well spent to hire the services of a title searching company or a local attorney. Despite the increasingly obvious path into the past that a property title follows, there are many ways to make mistakes. For this reason, title insurance companies will only write policies on abstracts they believe are accurate.

Establishing Boundaries in the Field

A surveyor's job is to verify accuracy of the current title and to correct any ambiguities by researching earlier titles to the same parcel and to abutting parcels. The surveyor will also locate and mark corners in the field and provide the owner with a certified map that shows the parcel's survey and boundaries relative to surrounding parcels. Marking boundary lines in the field is not usually the surveyor's job unless there is a prior arrangement with the owner. Corners are marked by iron pins driven into the ground (or by a hole drilled into rock ledge, with or without a pin) so as to make it virtually impossible to move or alter. Even so, it is common practice to hide a corner pin and reference its actual location by triangulating from two or more surrounding landmarks (figure 4.5). This prevents tampering, which is illegal. State law in most places makes it unlawful for anyone other than a licensed surveyor to tamper with or set boundary markers.

When the boundaries of a woodlands survey are marked, the line between two corners is blazed. A surveyor makes a blaze by removing a small patch of bark from trees on or near the property line (figure 4.6). The top and bottom of the blaze are angled, and the exposed bare wood is scored along the same angle to make it as

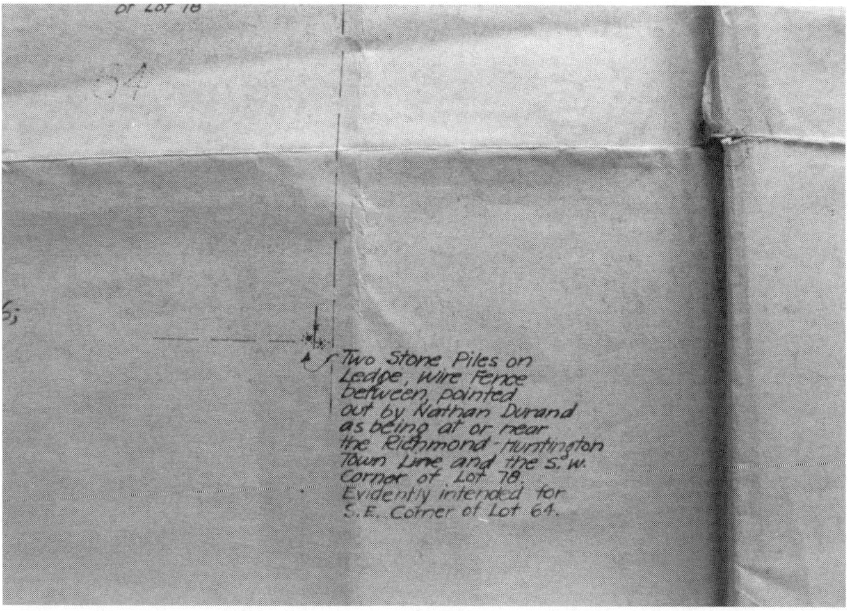

Figure 4.5. Corners in a metes and bounds survey map are usually referenced to easily located reference points, such as large trees, boulders, ridge lines, or other prominent landmarks.

Figure 4.6. Trees are blazed at about chest height with a blazing axe in a way that shows the marks were clearly caused by tools. After blazing, the marks are usually painted (almost always red) to improve visibility.

obvious as possible—ten or twenty years in the future—that the mark was intentionally caused by human effort. A blaze on a young stem will eventually close as the tree grows, but a trained eye looking for a boundary can usually pick out even the most overgrown and indistinct blaze (figure 4.7).

A boundary blaze faces the actual boundary line except when the tree is on the line (figure 4.8). A ring of blazes marks a corner, and when those trees are noted in the survey, they are referred to as *witness trees* (figure 4.9).

To improve visibility, blazes are often painted, though this is usually the work of the landowner or someone other than the surveyor. In most states, only a licensed surveyor can blaze a boundary or refresh an existing blaze, but a landowner or her agent can periodically paint blazes to improve visibility. Repainting blazes needs to be done at least every ten years, more frequently in younger stands. Use a good-quality, oil-based paint in red or some

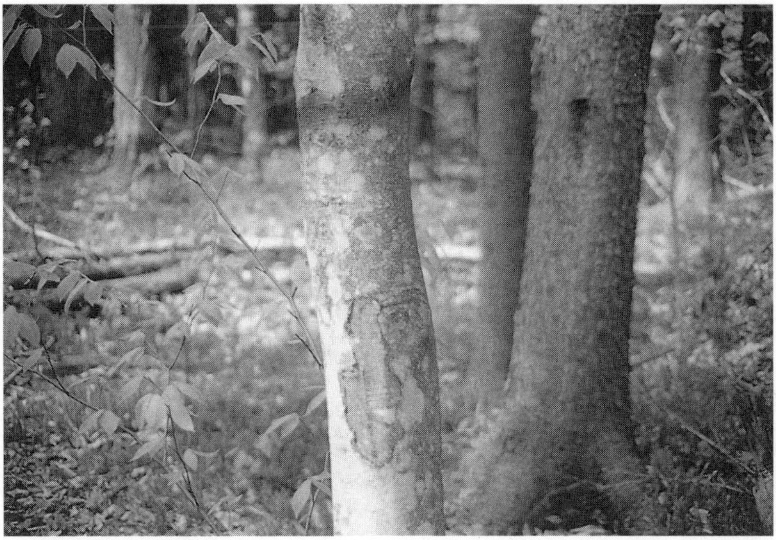

Figure 4.7. To a trained eye, even an overgrown blaze is fairly easy to discern.

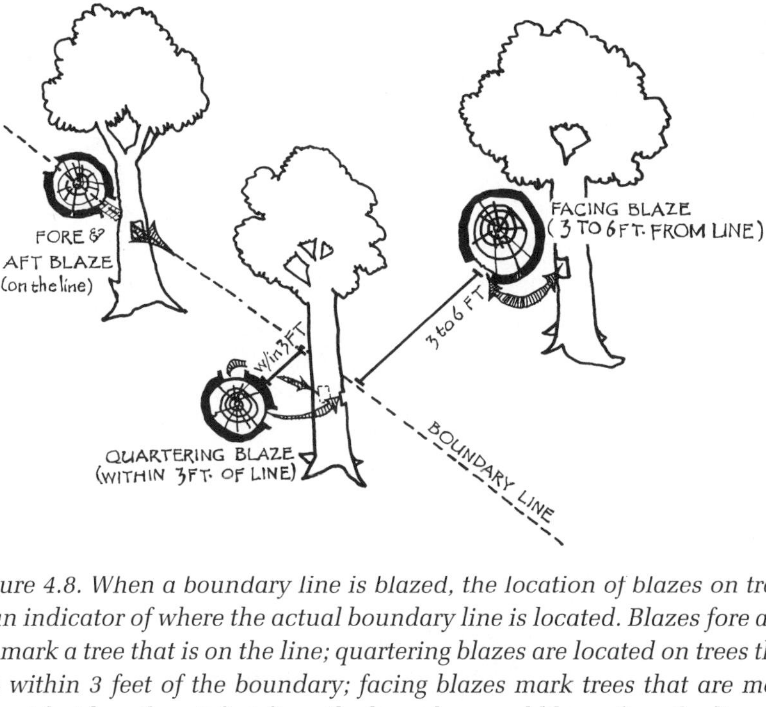

Figure 4.8. When a boundary line is blazed, the location of blazes on trees is an indicator of where the actual boundary line is located. Blazes fore and aft mark a tree that is on the line; quartering blazes are located on trees that are within 3 feet of the boundary; facing blazes mark trees that are more than 3 but less than 6 feet from the boundary, and blazes face the line.

Figure 4.9. In modern metes and bounds surveys, corners are usually marked with iron pins (often abbreviated as "IP" on the survey map). The corner pin is referenced by multiple facing blazes on at least three trees. If the pin is disturbed, the corner can be easily relocated by triangulating from the witness trees.

other bright color. Apply paint liberally and work it into bark fissures around the blaze. Plan to use a gallon of paint per mile of boundary and to dispose of the clothes you are wearing, and the brush, when done. The purpose of painting blazes is to make them obvious and easy to spot, thus doing so is a messy job.

Boundary trees are sacrosanct. Once a tree has been blazed, it is a boundary tree for as long as the tree stands or until the line is remonumented by a surveyor. In metes and bounds states, a blazed tree is a property monument. It can be altered only by the actions of a licensed surveyor. Boundary trees should never be damaged or harvested during a timber sale. Always check with your state forester or municipal official before refreshing blazes on boundaries if you are not sure about the laws in your state.

When a survey is completed, be sure it is appropriately certified by the surveyor and that a copy is properly recorded in the town records. The survey is an essential part of the parcel's title. The same law regarding precedence of claims that applies to deeds also applies to surveys: the earliest recorded claim that is legally valid and accurate will take precedence over all subsequent surveys of abutting parcels that share boundary lines.

A couple of excellent sources of legal and technical information on surveys and boundaries are *Evidence and Procedures for Boundary Location* and *Brown's Boundary Control and Legal Principles* (Robillard and Wilson 2001; Brown, Robillard, and Wilson 2003). Not only do these books touch on the practical aspects of locating and verifying boundaries in the field, they also describe the legal precedents for accepting boundary markers as historically valid and true. If you anticipate entering a boundary dispute, a review of the relevant principles presented in these books will yield valuable information about the strength or weakness of your claim.

Using a Survey to Locate Boundaries

It is always a good idea to know where your boundaries are, especially if you intend to work with the land. Some owners make "walking the boundary" an annual event. It is easy to do. All you need is a copy of the survey or a map with bearings and distances, a compass, and your feet to pace distances. An aerial photograph, available through your county USDA Natural Resource Conservation Office (formerly the Soil Conservation Service), is useful. These maps are also available at outfitting stores.

A common distance measure of surveyors—both in the rectangular system and in metes and bounds—is the *chain*, equal to sixty-six feet. The chain is a useful unit, since eighty chains, or 5,280 feet, is equal to one mile. Also, ten square chains equal one acre, or 43,560 square feet. To estimate your pace, lay out a course of sixty-six feet and walk it four or five times, counting the number of times you plant your right or left foot (i.e., a single pace is two steps, not one). Use a comfortable but deliberate gait, remembering that you will be walking in the woods when counting paces. Average your number of paces in a chain, and you are ready to go. If you have a fairly recent survey, you may need to convert feet into chains before going into the woods.

It is important to keep in mind that a survey is always done as though the land were perfectly flat. To cover the distance of a chain on an incline requires an extra pace or two to account for changes in elevation. Steeper slopes require larger corrections. A surveyor uses special instruments to account for uneven terrain, but for following your boundaries it is necessary to know only that the steeper the incline, the more paces you will need to account for a single chain on the horizontal. After locating a corner the first time, it is useful to make notes about the surrounding terrain so it is easier to locate the next time.

A conventional survey, as discussed in chapter 3, is supposed to be based on true North (directly under the Polar Star). But many early metes and bounds surveys were based on magnetic North (an area near the North Pole that is magnetized by large subterranean deposits of iron ore). Compasses are based on magnetic North, and although the declination of magnetic North from true North can be accounted for, many early surveyors ignored it, causing a legacy of inaccurate boundaries.

New technologies for orienteering, such as handheld receivers that use the Global Positioning System (GPS), are fun to use for walking boundaries and are now quite accurate (figure 4.10). The GPS unit is a signal receiver and computer that reads information transmitted from a constellation of U.S. Defense Department satellites and calculates coordinates—latitude, longitude, and elevation—with an error of less than ten yards; not quite good enough to locate iron pins, but certainly within the range of witness trees.

If you see flagging tape, painted stakes, or other markers along the boundary during your walk, it is a sure bet neighbors are planning work on their side of the line or are having the boundary resurveyed. Survey stakes usually mark the position of the surveyor's equipment when taking measurements, not the actual property boundary. Although a wooden stake may serve as temporary monumentation, the surveyor will eventually establish a more permanent marker. Check with neighbors when you see evidence of a survey along a common boundary, and do not assume stakes found on your side of the line (as you know it) is an attempt to claim a piece of your land.

Figure 4.10. A portable Global Positioning System (GPS) is an inexpensive and easy method of orienteering around your property. (Photo provided by Magellan, Inc.)

Boundary Disputes

Regardless of the system of survey, when people share boundaries, disagreements are inevitable. Such disputes are common where metes and bounds are used, and acceptable resolutions are more difficult to achieve. For example, it is not uncommon for a buyer to believe he was acquiring "130 acres, plus or minus" only to discover after an abutting neighbor's survey that the land is only 95 acres. Almost more troubling than the instant loss of assets is the owner's realization that he or she has been paying taxes on someone else's land. Usually the only thing an owner in these circumstances can do is to hire a surveyor (and possibly a lawyer) to refute or validate the abutter's claim. Taxing authorities will not refund taxes paid in error, on the grounds that it is the responsibility of the owner to ensure a parcel's title is perfect and valid. Neither will the new owner refund the taxes, on the grounds that the previous owner enjoyed the benefits of the land. Such a dispute is an easy way to lose many years of carefully planned and executed work in a stand of timber nearly ready for its first harvest.

The best way to resolve a dispute is with a second opinion. If two surveyors agree, there is nothing to dispute, and you are better off forgetting it. If you have a substantial investment in the timber, the new owner may be willing to work out a deal whereby you can retain timber rights for a specified period of time. The new owner, though, is under no obligation to do so and concessions are agreed to out of a sense of fairness. Threats and demands borne from your outrage at the unfairness of a boundary dispute that goes against you may only sour the new owner, making him or her unwilling to work with you. Bear in mind that even a small portion of something is worth more than all of nothing. Also see chapter 10 for a larger discussion of disputes regarding forest land.

Posting Land, Trespass, and Personal Liability

When you post land, it is the legal equivalent of giving public notice that the property is off-limits except for those to whom you have authorized access. Land can be posted to disallow access for specific purposes (i.e., hunting, fishing, and trapping) or to disallow access altogether (no trespassing). Many owners assume that placing signs along the border of a property is sufficient notice. Most states, however, have strict laws that govern the proper posting of land—laws that may prescribe size and color of the sign, distance between signs, and even the size of letters on the signs. Some states require the name and address and/or phone number of the owner. Also—and this is where many owners fail to effect a proper and legal posting—your state probably requires formal notification with the town or county clerk. Failure to notify the municipality of your posting may subvert your efforts to keep people off your land or limit your ability to prosecute trespassers. Always check with the municipality to learn the rules of posting before setting out markers. In some jurisdictions a proper posting must be renewed each year, and sometimes fees are due.

If you are new to an area, bear in mind that local residents may resent the posting of your lands. Even though it is your right to control access, people in the community may have hunted on your lands, hiked there, or gathered berries for generations. A new owner is under no obligation to continue to provide access to those people, but barring them from the property may cause resentments, which could lead to such problems as vandalism. Before posting, find out who uses your lands and decide if those uses are something you can live with. Get to know people who come onto your land, encourage them to do so, and they will become even more protective of your property than you are. Usually, so long as you do not charge for access, your liability to guests is no greater than your liability to uninvited visitors.

Some owners who post their lands assume it is the best way to avoid personal liability for injuries sustained by uninvited visitors. Although that is a point worthy of clarifying by calling the office of the attorney general in your state, the facts are that posting probably will not provide any special protection from personal liability. This is especially true if you know of hazards on your property, or if you have created hazards to deter access. For example, if you know the location of an old well hole and a trespasser falls into it, you may be liable unless you have made a reasonable attempt to mark the hazard or eliminate it. A deliberate hazard might be an unclearly marked soil berm or ditch across a road you do not want four-wheel-drive vehicles to access. An injury sustained by an uninvited driver of a four-wheeler—even one acting carelessly—may be judged at least partially your fault even though the person was trespassing.

There is also something known as an attractive nuisance. This is a feature on your property, such as a tree house, a pond, a cave, or some other feature that is attractive, especially to children or minors. Generally, you must provide extra protection where there are attractive nuisances. Also, some states have laws dealing specifically with this type of trespass. If anything on your property might qualify as an attractive nuisance, check it out with local authorities, and be sure your postings are proper and legal to protect against liability claims from this type of situation.

The concept of liability is based on society's assumption that there is almost never any such thing as an accident. Someone is ultimately responsible, and the degree to which an individual or company is found to be responsible for losses is a measure of liability.

Liability is always an issue in the acquisition of real estate. It is impossible to obtain a mortgage from a bank without first producing evidence of insurance that includes protection against personal liability claims. Many homeowner policies extend coverage to woodlands routinely or in a special clause known as a rider. Check with your insurer and seek written clarification on the extent of coverage as it applies to forest lands. Some state woodland owner associations offer special liability insurance tailored to the types of claims a forest owner is apt to encounter.

It is impossible to obtain total immunity from potential liability, short of avoiding all interactions with other humans. However, besides insurance, you can defend against claims in other ways. Always disclose known risks clearly and in writing, and have people who use your woodlands accept those risks in writing and indemnify you from losses they may sustain (indemnification is discussed further in chapter 6). Another way to avoid liability is to be sure contractors and others who work on your land have insurance, including personal injury insurance for themselves and their employees. This type of insurance is known as workmen's compensation insurance, and it is required of logging contractors with employees. Request written proof of this insurance, and if you have questions about the coverage, ask your insurer for an opinion.

Access Rights by Tenure

One right among the currently accepted bundle of rights on private land is the right to close land to others. Although being able to exclude people from enjoying the benefits of land seems fundamental to protecting all other rights in the bundle, in many states open access to land is a constitutionally protected dispensation unless specifically disallowed by posting. This open-access condition is intended to allow hunters and gatherers of nontimber forest products (NTFPs) permission to roam in areas far from settlements. Many long-time hunters and gathers believe they have rights to use remote lands so long as it does not detract from the owner's rights to use and enjoy land. These *rights by tenure*, although not documented or recorded, are very real to those who claim them. And many hunters and gatherers believe their rights supercede the claims of those who come later, even a new titleholder.

Realistically, there are no rights to the benefits of land vested in others that are independent of the bundle of rights, so no one can legally claim an access right unless it has been so noted in public records. Absent such written notification, whatever rights someone attempts to claim are really no more than those allowed by the good graces of a current owner. Or, more likely, the owner has no idea who is actually using her land and for what purposes. In most states, a license to hunt or fish is not also a license to use private land. Such access is a privilege to the license holder granted by those private landowners who do not post their lands. Legal access to posted lands usually requires a current letter of permission from the owner.

Access rights by tenure are most analogous to maritime salvage rights that extend to the person who finds an abandoned ship or wreck. Salvage rights can establish a finder's claim superior to that of the owner. The difference between use rights with forest land and maritime salvage rights is that a hunter/gatherer is not capable of establishing claims to the hunting or gathering values that are superior to the owner of record. Property law does not require titleholders to recognize the claims of others unless those claims are noted in the deed or in a contract. Another huge difference between forest access and maritime salvage rights is that a forest owner can legally exclude all others regardless of any historic uses. Even someone who has hunted on a tract of land his entire life can be excluded if the land is properly posted and the owner has not granted a written exception.

There is no question that private forests provide an enormous amount of public benefit, not the least of which is access to those who hunt and gather. Local forest owners are very much aware of these uses and they either condone them or look the other way. New owners, especially people who are not familiar with rural traditions, are likely to look upon these fairly benign uses as trespass. But unless the land has been legally posted, those who wander the woods in search of game or plants are customarily able to do so without written permission. In some states, this open-access dispensation is more narrowly defined, essentially disallowing or limiting a hunter's ability to cross over a fence line or other well-established boundary. Check first with the town or county clerk regarding access to private lands, but any unresolved questions should be addressed to your state's attorney general.

For those new owners who do decide to post their lands, it may pay to first discover who is using the land, then negotiate access rights and put them in writing. Generally, access rights are temporary and thus are not recorded with a property title. When access rights are leased, it is a different matter entirely. Forest management leases are discussed in chapter 6.

Chapter 5

Managing and Using Forest Land

Most people acquire forest land for reasons that have little to do with resource management. Periodic timber sales, roads, creating or maintaining wildlife habitats, and other forest management–related activities are not often factors new woodland owners take into account. They are more concerned with the practicalities of siting a new home, locating water and septic systems, and landscaping. Prospects for utilizing forest resources only become apparent after a few years of getting to know the land. This is when many owners begin to investigate their entire property and, for some, a plan begins to unfold.

Many things in life do not require a great deal of planning; forestry is not one of them. Woodland owners who launch into timber sales or other activities without advance planning are apt to regret it. Thus, the purpose of this chapter is to describe a process for planning the use and management of forest resources.

Establishing Forest-Management Objectives

Sooner or later, a woodland owner learns that owning a forest property is not an entirely passive proposition. Although it is true that an aggressive manager with maximization of resource values in mind has more to do than a passive manager who wants nothing more than to enjoy the natural beauty of forests, both have responsibilities and must put effort into ensuring their respective goals are met. A major difference between active forest managers and passive managers is the degree to which they manipulate forest resources. The motivations of both types of managers may seem worlds apart, but they must have something in common to realize their separate goals—easily articulated objectives.

The most common question forest managers ask of new clients is, "What are your objectives?" This usually precedes a walk through the woodlands, with the manager describing various opportunities. Too often, however, the question remains unanswered. Very few woodland owners can easily say what it is about forest land that makes owning it so appealing. But lacking a well-thought-out answer, opportunities become objectives and the owner relinquishes a degree of control to the manager. In other words, it is left up to the manager to decide what is important, and the owner accepts those judgments. Because managers by training and experience know what is good for the forest, what's wrong with following their advice? Nothing, as long as it reflects your concerns and beliefs about the forest and it meets your long-term goals for the land.

Most woodland owners lack clear objectives, even though forest managers agree that objectives are a necessary prerequisite to owning and managing forest land because objectives control actions (figure 5.1). A woodland owner without them is like a ship without a rudder. Forest-management objectives help identify possibilities and provide a means of realizing them. They also help to assess success or failure, and to channel resources and effort to the areas needing most attention.

Well-stated objectives also describe the purpose of forest ownership by framing the owner's interests within the context of the forest's resource capabilities. It makes no difference if an owner is utilization oriented or otherwise; clear, easily articulated management objectives are essential to all forest owners. Such a simple question, "What are your objectives?" yet most owners do not have an adequate answer. This is not surprising, because even a greatly simplified approach to defining objectives results in hundreds of different combinations.

Consider the case of a woodland-owning couple who are asked to state their top three forest-management objectives. To make it

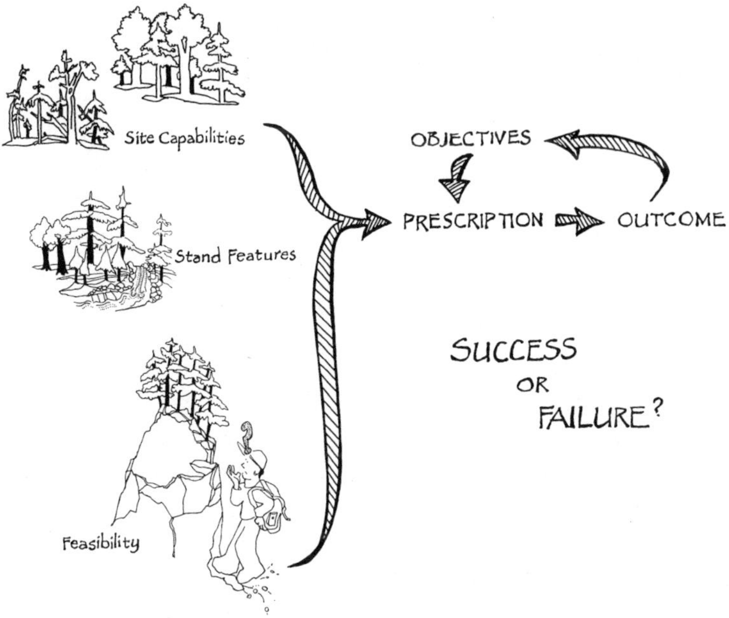

Figure 5.1. Forest-management opportunities and the owner's objectives control actions in the forest. Success or failure of a particular action is a function of well-stated objectives.

easier for the couple, objectives are defined two ways: first, on the basis of forest resource components, such as timber, wildlife, recreation, and aesthetics; second, on the basis of the human benefits they want to maximize, namely, income production, long-term investment, and personal satisfaction. Furthermore, assume that each forest resource component must be related to a human benefit, which is often the case anyway. For example, the couple might agree that one of their objectives is to manage timber resources for long-term investment.

The scenario described above results in a matrix with forest resource components down the side and human benefits across the top (figure 5.2). Because most resource/benefit combinations are not mutually exclusive—in fact, the couple could strive to satisfy all possible combinations—the couple needs to evaluate the extent to which certain combinations are more important than others: they must assign priorities to their objectives. (Remember, this scenario is intended to demonstrate the difficulty of establishing

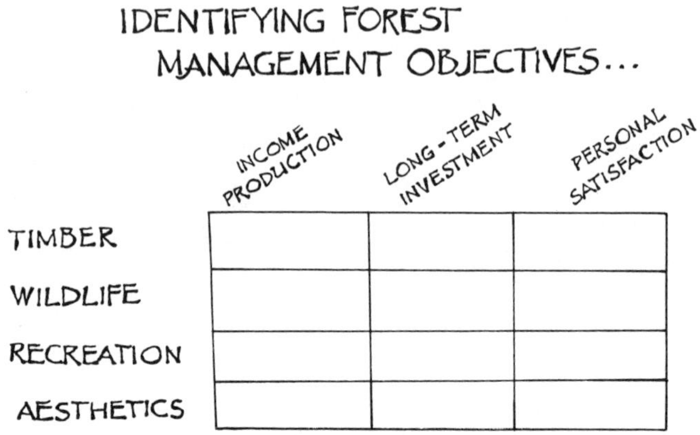

IDENTIFYING FOREST
MANAGEMENT OBJECTIVES...
INCOME PRODUCTION
LONG-TERM INVESTMENT
PERSONAL SATISFACTION
TIMBER
WILDLIFE
RECREATION
AESTHETICS

Figure 5.2. Articulating forest-management objectives is often difficult. If an owner chooses the first three objectives as combinations of human benefits across the top and resource benefits down the left side, so that the cell representing a combination that is of primary importance gets a 1, the combination of secondary importance gets a 2, and the combination of third importance gets a 3—and all other cells are zero—1,319 other choices are excluded.

objectives. For most owners, the difficulty arises when one priority obviates the possibility of another priority. The example used here is intended to illustrate this phenomenon, not to suggest that forest-management priorities are always mutually exclusive. In fact, creative managers find the opposite to be true.)

Asked to identify the three most important combinations, such as "timber for long-term investment," "wildlife for personal satisfaction," and "aesthetics for personal satisfaction," the owners number the corresponding cells in the chart 1, 2, or 3. These are their top three objectives to the exclusion of everything else, so all other cells have a zero. How many other sets of objectives have they excluded? Astoundingly, there are 1,319 combinations other than the one they have selected. (The problem is solved using matrix algebra. The owners have selected one combination out of 1,320 possibilities—12 x 11 x 10 x 1). No wonder forest owners have a difficult time stating objectives.

By putting a 1 in the "timber/long-term investment" cell, a 2 in the "wildlife/personal satisfaction" cell, and a 3 in the "aesthetics/personal satisfaction" cell (and 0 in all the others), the owners in this example have identified themselves as semi-aggressive forest managers, willing to invest time and effort to fulfill a fairly active management strategy. Conversely, a matrix with combinations concentrated in the bottom, right side identify a more passive approach to management (figure 5.3 and figure 5.4).

The real advantage to viewing forest-management objectives as a matrix of resources and benefits is the ease with which one can state objectives once the difficulty of making selections is resolved. For instance, the primary objective for the couple in our example

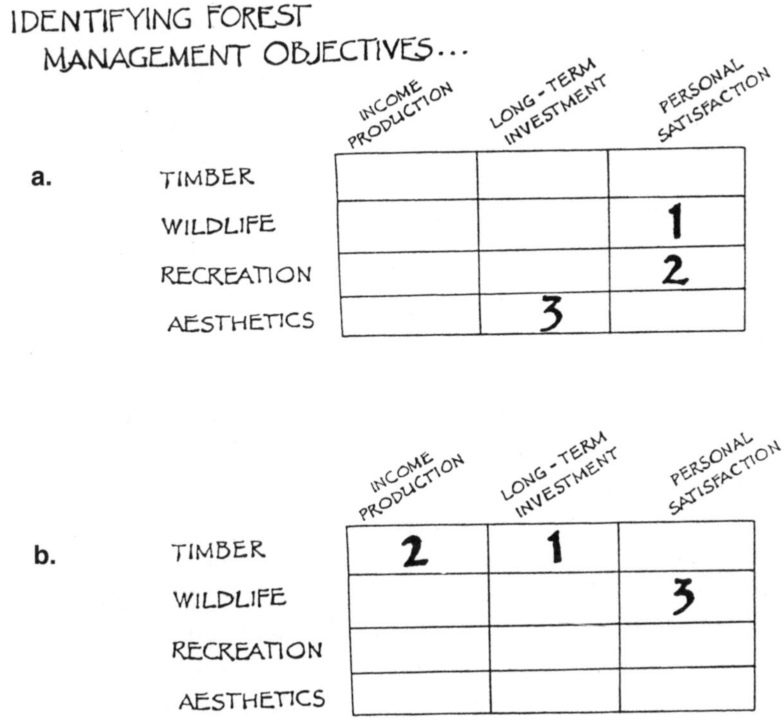

Figure 5.3. In a, the owners choose wildlife for personal satisfaction as their primary objective, recreation for personal satisfaction as second, and aesthetics for long-term investment as third. In b, the owners have established an emphasis on managing timber, which will take priority over other values but not exclude them.

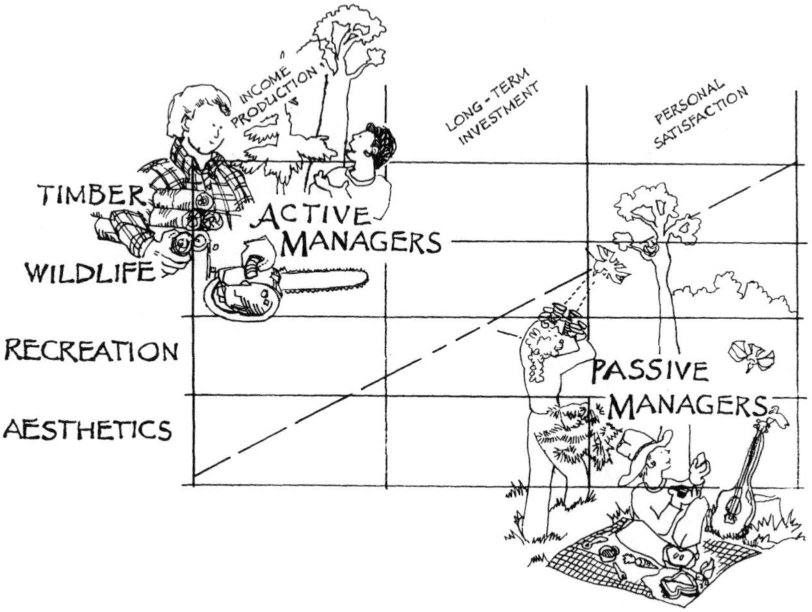

Figure 5.4. Owners who choose combinations in the upper left side of the matrix are committing to more active management than owners who choose combinations in the lower right. Nevertheless, even passive forest owners need clear objectives.

might be stated as follows: manage timber resources on long rotations to maximize long-term investment. The secondary objective is to create and maintain a diversity of habitats for wildlife, especially songbirds. The third priority is to preserve forest aesthetics. Once the priorities are established, a hierarchy dictates that the secondary and tertiary objectives are subordinate to the primary objective. First and foremost is managing the timber resource for long-term investment. Wildlife habitat and aesthetics are subordinate. How does this affect management decisions? In an area designated for long-term timber investment, the manager will make accommodations for wildlife but only to the extent they do not interfere with the primary objective. The manager always has three things in mind: timber investment, wildlife, and aesthetics. There are many circumstances where all three are easily accommodated, but when conflicts arise the hierarchy prevails. Fulfilling a primary objective does not preclude wildlife and aesthetics, such as in this case. Rather, the primary objective defines the context or bounds within which other activities are allowed.

Forestry professionals are usually happy to render an opinion on management strategies and their role is crucial when it comes to recognizing resource opportunities. But the decisions and ultimate responsibility for management activities lie with the owner. Clearly stated objectives greatly facilitate decision-making and help to ensure that forest-management activities, like timber harvests, meet expectations and provide satisfaction.

In some instances the objectives matrix described above does not apply. For instance, if you recently acquired woodland that has been cutover, your options are limited and the best course is probably no action. Even if the matrix does not fit your circumstances, it is still a good idea to have objectives.

Forest-Management Planning

When owners have forest-management objectives in hand, the next step is to develop a plan. The forest-management plan is a document that describes the natural resources on a tract of land. It also includes recommendations detailing how resources can be used to provide a sustained mix of benefits in keeping with the objectives and interests of the owner. Implicit in all forest-management plans, for passive and active managers alike, are the following three elements:

1. A clear statement of objectives.
2. A description of resources, which may be either brief, verbal descriptions for passive managers, or detailed, quantified resource inventories for more active managers.
3. A chronology of major management activities, prioritized according to the owner's objectives and the capabilities of the resources to meet those objectives. The plan documents resource management opportunities and constraints to achieve the mix of benefits required by the owner. It is not solely a timber management plan.

While an owner with more passive interests in forests may get by with a broadly generalized plan, an active manager needs more information to make good decisions. It is usually only active managers who plan, though, most often in anticipation of timber sales. Regardless of their goals, all forest owners should have a long-term (ten to thirty years) written plan for the land.

There are as many different types of forest-management plans as there are professionals who prepare them. It is impossible to say exactly what is needed in each instance, and there is no one plan that fits all. To a lesser or greater degree, however, a plan should include the following ten elements:

1. The owner's management objectives
2. Maps of the property and important resource areas
3. Boundary descriptions
4. Forest inventory data
5. Site and stand descriptions
6. Timber management recommendations
7. Local forest product markets
8. Potential for nontimber benefits
9. Other management recommendations
10. Chronology of major management activities

For the owner whose primary objective is "aesthetics for personal satisfaction," all ten elements are not necessary. However, even if the owner has no intention of managing timber resources, the plan should at least document the fact that there are timber resources on the property. Such an owner would need elements 1, 2, 3, 5, 8, 9, and 10. To demonstrate the importance of the plan elements, regardless of an owner's objectives, consider the importance of each to the total plan.

Owner's Objectives

Besides consideration for resources and benefits, as discussed earlier in this chapter, you need to think about how long you intend to own the land, and how and to whom it will be disposed when ownership is relinquished. For instance, if you believe land will appreciate during your tenure, and one of your goals is long-term investment (i.e., speculation), think about what a new owner will look for; such elements as good roads, large healthy trees surrounding good potential building sites, and other features that will be attractive to a buyer. In contrast to this scenario, your goal may be to pass on a forest-management legacy to children and grandchildren. The objectives you establish today may one day be fulfilled by your heirs. Regardless of your long-range goals for the land, it will be more valuable with clear objectives and a good management plan than without.

Maps

Many different types of maps (or mapped information) can be included in the plan. The purpose of maps is to show the location of the property and to give readers a picture of where various resources are located. The level of detail varies according to the owner's objectives. Useful map information includes topographic data showing the elevation and relief of the land, soils data, habitats, timber stands, roads and trails, human-made features (such as wells and stone walls), and springs and water courses. A well-designed and clearly drawn map is an excellent way to get the big picture of the forest. Gathering map data, however, and drawing and reproducing maps are expensive.

Some foresters use sophisticated computer-aided mapping techniques known as Geographic Information Systems (GIS). When map data are read by a computerized scanner, or digitized, the user can generate maps that include as many different layers as necessary (figure 5.5). The real advantage of GIS is the ability to ask "What if?" questions. For instance, a computer-generated map composed of geologic features, topography, drainage, and soil types would help with road placement and design. The user inputs the ideal conditions for a road then looks at the various alternatives. Once an acceptable alternative is achieved, the road is laid out in the woods. Another advantage of GIS is that once the base map is scanned and digitized, it is a relatively simple matter to print maps. Data layers can be added as necessary.

Geographic Information Systems are still relatively new and

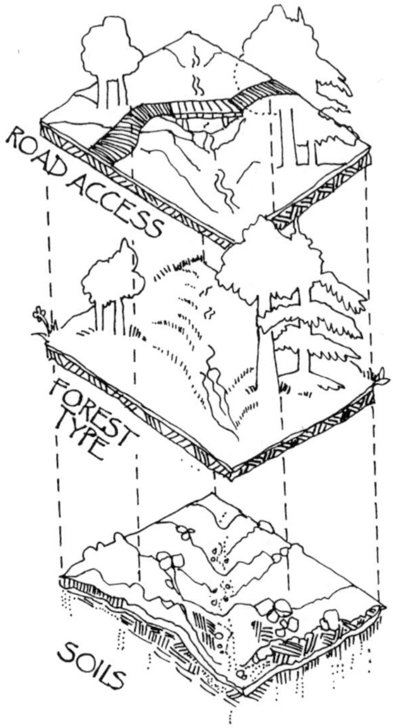

Figure 5.5. Resource data scanned into a computer using a Geographic Information System (GIS), can layer data in different ways to help the manager make decisions.

many foresters do not use them (especially middle-age and older foresters who tend to be less computer oriented, but not always). Instead, they overlay a simple base map with Mylar, using as many layers as they have data or features to show. Most base maps start with a topographic map, then a data layer on soils, followed by forest vegetation and other layers.

Boundary Description

The forest-management plan should serve as a repository for copies of all legal documents pertinent to the forest. This includes a copy of the most recent plat, survey, and/or deed (or at least the boundary description from the deed). Having this information on hand, in one place, makes it easy to locate if it becomes necessary. It is especially important for timber buyers or others doing work on the property to know where the boundaries are (see chapter 6). It also a good idea to note the volume and page of public records that pertain to the property and the property of abutters.

Forest Inventory Data

The need for detailed forest inventory data is proportionate to the amount of timber management the owner expects to do and the current and potential timber values. An active manager with valuable timber needs fairly detailed inventory information, while an owner with more passive objectives does not. The plan should document timber potential even if the current owner is not interested.

A detailed forest inventory requires the technical expertise of a forester. The forest is divided into areas of similar structure and/or species composition. Each area, or stand, is *cruised*, using sampling methods to measure some, but not all, trees. Because a forester measures only a fraction of the trees, statistics are used to verify reliability of data. The timber inventory is only an estimate of volumes, which may be greater or less than actual volume. A good inventory will always show the error of the estimate. In other words, an inventory summary might state: "There are 5,500 board feet per acre, plus or minus 1,500 board feet." Inventory data are of little value without an estimate of error.

Generally, the more valuable the timber, the more detailed the inventory and the lower the error of estimate. Stands of low-value timber do not warrant the expense of an excessively precise inventory. It is not unreasonable, though, to expect errors of 10 percent or less in valuable stands, and of up to 30 percent in less valuable stands.

A good inventory also includes information on the age of trees and on growth rates. Knowing growth rate is useful for planning silvicultural treatments and for "growing" the stand at tax time to figure how your cost basis in timber changes after some has been harvested (chapter 8).

Inventory data are commonly summarized on a stand-by-stand basis in the form of stand and stock tables. A stand and stock table

Stand Number: **1**
Forest Type: Northern hardwoods
Acreage: **20**

Stand Description

Composition by basal area (ft²/ac): Total (Portion ≥ 6" Dbh):

sugar maple 90 (75); yellow birch 20 (5); other 10 (5)

Total basal area: 120 ft²/ac **For trees ≥ 6" Dbh:** 85 ft²/ac

Site index (based on age 50): 70 ft. for sugar maple

Number of stems per acre: 255 **For trees ≥ 6" Dbh:** 160 stems

Mean stand Dbh: 9" **Stand age:** 70

Average annual growth rate: 2.2 percent (+/- 0.2) on volumes

Stand Condition: Excellent; no evidence of any recent defoliation.

Understory: Maple regeneration is thick but small because of dense canopy; shrub layer is absent; buckthorn is present and represents a risk when stand is disturbed.

Merchantable Volume and Value Summary – per acre*
(International 1/4 inch rule)

	Sawtimber		Fuelwood	
Species	**Bd. Ft.**	**Value**	**Cords**	**Value**
sugar maple	2,650	$225	8	$56
yellow birch	325	$38	3	$21
other hardwoods	250	$25	6	$42
Totals	3,225	$288	17	$119

Merchantable Volume and Value Summary – TOTAL STAND

	Sawtimber		Fuelwood	
Species	**Bd. Ft.**	**Value**	**Cords**	**Value**
sugar maple	53,000	$4,500	160	$1,120
yellow birch	6,400	$760	60	$420
other hardwoods	5,000	$500	120	$840
Totals	64,400	$5,760	340	$2,380

**These values are estimates with a range of plus or minus about 8 percent*

gives a detailed picture of what the stand looks like (figure 5.6). If one of your top three objectives involves timber management, statistically valid inventory data are invaluable.

Site and Stand Descriptions

A *stand* is defined as "a collection of trees that is sufficiently uniform in species composition, structure, condition, or age to be distinguishable from surrounding areas" (Smith et al. 1997). A wildlife habitat biologist may refer to a stand as a *cover type*. The collective management of all stands, or cover types, on the property in question is forest management. The stand description may include stand and stock tables, information about the site such as slope and aspect, soils, management limitations, and a measure of productivity. The predominant species of trees and plants are identified, and the structure of the stand is described. The forester also notes any disease or insect problems, or other risks from such factors as fire or wind. Knowing the condition of a stand allows the manager to estimate risk of losses from natural causes during the plan's life. The emphasis in this part of the plan is on potential.

Timber Management Recommendations

If timber is an important resource for the owner, the plan will include recommendations for all stands that have been identified. Each stand has an objective in keeping with the overall management objectives of the owner. For instance, an owner may have wildlife as a primary objective for the forest, but a particular stand may be well suited for long-term timber management. The stand objective describes the desired structure, age of trees, or other conditions that control when the harvesting is to commence. It is based on two things: (1) the

Figure 5.6 (opposite page). Inventory data are presented in stand and stock tables—for which there are no standard forms—that portray the structure, composition, growth rate, quality, and monetary value of stands. With data such as these, a forester familiar with the forest type can develop a fairly detailed mental image of stands.

owner's overall goals and objectives, and (2) the stand's capability to provide benefits in proportion to the owner's objectives.

A timber management recommendation usually includes a prescription, which is a statement describing actions to achieve the objectives for the stand. The prescription should also describe the expected outcome of a treatment. The ability to predict outcomes is the basis on which a prescription is founded. For instance, if a prescription is intended to secure new regeneration of a particular species, there needs to be a guideline to use after the treatment to assess success or failure. In the event of failure, the prescription should identify a plan B, so the original objective is fulfilled. One of the principal faults of timber management prescriptions is not allowing for failure, with procedures to correct the situation.

The timber management recommendations also describe constraints that may affect treatments, such as erosive soils, steep access roads, or other similar conditions. Furthermore, since implementing timber management prescriptions is often the most disruptive of forest-management practices, the forester should describe the risks and trade-offs of a particular treatment. The potential benefits should always exceed risks. In timber management it is better to do nothing than the wrong thing.

Local Forest Product Markets

A good forest-management plan will include information about local product markets for timber and other resources. Some consultants are reluctant to include this in the plan because they feel the information is proprietary. Nevertheless, if you are paying someone to develop a forest management plan, you are paying for information, and information about local markets is usually critical to implementing the plan. All aspects of the plan should stand alone and not necessarily require the services of the person who prepared the plan once it has been delivered. Although it may cause a breach of trust to take a plan developed by a consulting forester and use the information either by yourself or with the services of others, the facts are that you own the plan and can do as you please. An itemization of local markets is not a standard element of most plans, so you may need to request it.

Potential for Nontimber Benefits

The plan should describe recreational opportunities, sites of archaeological significance, scenic vistas, special habitats, unusual or valuable geological deposits, areas for hunting and fishing, and any other nontimber resources on the property. Many forest owners anticipate passing land to children, so it is also a good idea to identify areas where they may want to build. Anyone who has built a house in the forest knows a good site is a very valuable resource. Your children and grandchildren will celebrate your good foresight.

The plan should also identify critical landscapes, such as ridge lines, that require special treatment to preserve the aesthetic appeal of the forest. It should also disclose special considerations for protecting threatened and endangered plant and animal species that might use, or reside on, your land. The manager should attempt to identify local people who use the forest for hunting, fishing and gathering of nontimber forest products (NTFPs). In some parts of the country forest lands are leased to others for hunting and fishing, in particular, but for other uses as well. A good manager will note the potential for securing leases of this nature, which can often raise enough money each year to pay property taxes and other management expenses. Forest management leases are discussed in chapter 6.

Other Management Recommendations

Unique management opportunities, such as small-scale hydroelectric generation, a rare species of wildflower, or an opportunity to improve or maintain habitat for wildlife should be described in the plan. Also included are recommendations on roads and trails, boundary maintenance, stream crossings, or any other activities that need to be undertaken to effect the plan.

This section should also reference any local ordinances, state regulations, or other laws that might affect forest-management activities. For instance, all states have rules to protect water quality during harvesting. Generally, it is the responsibility of the forest owner to ensure those rules are followed. The exact nature of local best-management practices to protect water quality should be spelled out in the plan or clearly referenced so a copy of the rules is easy to locate.

Chronology of Major Management Activities

One of the most useful aspects of the forest-management plan is a chronology of activities that need to take place. With this in hand, the owner knows where to start and can concentrate on tasks that yield the greatest benefits. Some foresters are reluctant to give too much detail for fear the owner will no longer request services. Nevertheless, the plan is like a road map: you should be able to read it and use it without someone else's help. When you pay for forest-management planning services, be sure the document is clear on what needs to be done. Also, planning is not a one-time event. A plan usually has a life of ten to fifteen years. After that, it is time to reassess your objectives, analyze what worked and what did not, and consider the future. If timber management is a high priority, then it is also time to complete a new inventory.

Working with Forestry Professionals

Generally, anyone who makes a career of providing services to forest owners can be characterized as a forestry professional. There are major differences, though, in credentials, motives, and abilities. Most states have no laws that govern credentials, and anyone, regardless of education or experience, can choose any title he or she feels appropriate. The purpose of this section is to provide a clear distinction among the many different types of people who offer services to woodland owners. In a few states, the titles people use and their corresponding credentials are controlled by law. Check with your local state extension forester or state forester (see appendix A) to see if any laws apply.

The Society of American Foresters (SAF) is a professional organization that represents approximately eighteen thousand individuals connected with forest land management. Regular membership is extended to people who have completed a four-year bachelor of science or graduate degree in forestry from an SAF-accredited college or university. The society has minimum educational requirements in a wide range of subject areas that an institution must fulfill to maintain its accreditation. A *forester* in the eyes of SAF is someone who is eligible to be a member, not necessarily a member in good standing. On the other hand, there are many individuals who meet SAF membership criteria who are not members.

It is generally accepted in the profession that a forester is someone who has completed a baccalaureate, master's, or higher degree in forestry. An individual claiming to be a forester should be able to produce a diploma that has the word forest or forestry in it. In other words, a bachelor of science degree in biology would not meet SAF guidelines (unless the person is also a full member of SAF). Where credentials and titles are not controlled by law, the issue of who uses the title "forester" (or makes references to services that only a forester can provide) is the subject of much debate when forestry professionals come together. If you are looking for forestry services in connection with planning or implementing elements of an existing plan, be sure the person you are working with has the necessary credentials: a university degree in forestry from a recognized school and at least some experience in the areas in which you need help.

Public versus Private Foresters

There is an important distinction between foresters in the public sector and those who are private. Public foresters include most research and teaching foresters, and state and federal land managers. They also include extension foresters—mentioned frequently in this book—whose job is to provide education programs for owners, managers, and users of forests. And, finally, there are service foresters employed by the state natural resource agency whose job is to provide one-on-one technical support to woodland owners. Of the public foresters, a woodland owner is most apt to use the services of extension foresters and service foresters. Generally, the mission of these public agencies is not to provide free services but to help woodland owners make good decisions about their woodlands. For instance, a local service forester will visit with a woodland owner, offer an assessment of opportunities, and provide guidance on local services. The service forester is also a valuable source for second opinions. However—and this is a key point—a public employee cannot in any way represent your interests. He or she cannot act as your agent or offer any advice or guidance that favors one source of private services over another. A public forester's job would be in jeopardy if the forester were promoting the services of one provider to the exclusion of others.

In the private sector there are two types of foresters: those who work for the forest product industry and those who sell services to (or act as agents of) private woodland owners and others. The first type is known as an industrial or procurement forester. Also known in the forest industry as a Landowner Assistance Program (LAP) forester, the important thing to remember when working with these foresters is that their first responsibility is to their employer—the mill that is interested in your timber. The individual may be personable, competent, and concerned about your objectives and your woodlands, but there is no ethical way he or she can act as your agent or hold your best interests above those of the employer. When you understand this (and the forester has explained the relationship to your satisfaction), an industrial forester and the implied relationship with a local forest products industry can be an appropriate and rewarding relationship. But don't forget: they are protecting their company's interests, not yours. Also, their services are usually provided in anticipation of a timber sale, for which the company will at least have the right of first refusal, although this is not always a requirement. The industrial forester should not request or accept any direct payments from the forest owner for services. The exceptions to this are instances where the company allows the employee to moonlight as a consulting forester, in which case the forester is presumably in a position to act as your agent and hold your interests above all others. Where there are industry ties, however, know who you are working with and request full disclosure of all potentially conflicting relationships.

The second type of private forester is known as a *consulting forester*. The consulting forester, either as an individual or as an employee of a company that provides consulting services, is in business to represent only the interests of the woodland owner. Either as a private contractor or as an agent (see chapter 6), a consultant's first responsibility is to his or her client. Occasionally, a consulting forester will have a logger or a mill as a client. If such a relationship poses even the remote possibility of a conflict with your interests, the consultant should disclose the relationship and allow you to decide how to proceed.

Consulting foresters offer a wide range of services, but they are usually experts in forest inventory, management planning, and timber sale administration. If you require special expertise in such areas as wildlife habitat, forest finance, and taxation or estate planning, you may need to seek a consultant competent in these areas. Also, all consultants are not equal. Do not assume that a university diploma automatically makes someone a good source of forestry expertise. Always ask for and check references before hiring any professional services.

Another difference between an industrial forester and a consultant is that the woodland owner pays the consultant for services. Payment can take many different forms, but a percentage of gross income from timber sales is common. This method of payment assumes a timber sale will take place, and for this reason it is often an inappropriate way to pay for services. Most consultants are open to other methods of payments, methods that do not rely on immediate timber sales. (The business nature of an owner's relationship with consulting foresters is discussed in more detail in chapter 6.)

Aside from technical competence, some of the most important qualities you should look for in a consulting forester are an ability to listen and to communicate. Sometimes professionals are reluctant to explain their actions to clients on the grounds that the client does not have a technical background sufficient to make explanations short and simple. If there is something you want to know, you deserve an explanation. Many consultants offer an initial visit for little or no charge. This is a great opportunity to get to know each other and discover any communication barriers. Choosing the right forester can be difficult. There are many excellent, highly competent consultants who are poor communicators. Most areas of the country have enough local consultants to give you a choice. Even though working with a consultant is usually a long-term relationship, you should always consider working with someone else if the relationship deteriorates. And remember, the consultant may be the expert, but you are the boss.

Tips on Working with Professionals

The following are a few points to keep in mind when working with forestry professionals:

- Separate the sales pitch from the expertise. Know when information is being used to inform and when it is being used to sway.
- Do not trivialize the forestry professional's expertise. Caring for forests is not rocket science, but there is more to it than meets the eye.
- Be cautious but not necessarily dismissive of contractors sporting new, highly sophisticated equipment. Chances are the debt on the equipment is enough to make you catch your breath, and good practices can readily fall victim to the bill collector.
- "If an offer appears too good to be true, it probably is."
- Be clear about who is paying the expenses of a professional working on your land. Forestry consulting fees usually include ordinary and reasonable expenses (phone, travel, supplies, etc.). An industrial forester's expenses are paid by his company, and a logger is usually responsible for his own expenses. If you have questions about unusual or costly expenses, clarify the matter up front.
- Reserve the right to terminate your relationship at any time for any reason, understanding that you must pay for services already provided. Forest management contracts are the subject of chapter 6.
- If you have no intention of working with a local forest products company that is willing to provide you with forestry services, you should locate a private consulting forester instead. In other words, don't accept free services if you have no intention of granting—at least—a right of first refusal.

- Never proceed with something you do not fully understand. Ask the professional for an explanation or seek answers from the local service forester or extension forester.
- Ask for credentials and do not hesitate to seek documentation. Also, remember that credentials do not guarantee performance.
- If a personal relationship begins to evolve, try to keep it separate from the business relationship. Being close friends with a local logger's family is one thing, but making business decisions on the basis of your friendship is another.
- Discover any agency relationships that may not be clear. For instance, a logger who appears to be an independent contractor is actually an employee of a local mill.
- Do not agree to work with someone just because you know the family, or because the person is related—an uncle, cousin, or brother. This type of arrangement fails more often than it succeeds, and you are probably better off locating someone else. Any ill will from such a decision is quickly forgotten, while memories of a bad experience with a family member can last a lifetime.
- If you have a bad experience with an individual, it is best to sever the relationship and keep the details to yourself. If you must complain, or if someone asks, be careful about what you say and to whom, and how you say it. The reasons for this caution have to do with threats of lawsuits, forcing you to substantiate your claims. Forestry-related disputes are discussed in chapter 10.
- When you have an extremely positive, rewarding relationship with a forestry professional, take the time to write a letter of appreciation. Everyone enjoys congratulations for a job well done, and the letter will go into the portfolio of testimonials from satisfied clients.

Logging Contractors

Most logging contractors are also forestry professionals, defined here as people who make a living providing services to woodland owners. The difference between most logging contractors and most foresters is education. As noted earlier, the SAF recognizes a baccalaureate in forestry or a closely related field as minimum credentials for regular membership. There are a number of foresters—even SAF members—who also provide logging services, but the vast majority of loggers learn their trade on the job. There are vocational agriculture programs, mostly in rural states, that teach young men and women about the logging business. But there is not a single program in the United States that offers a degree in logging. And, despite the fact that many states in recent years have initiated education programs for loggers, there are no third-party accredited training programs for logging contractors.

For most loggers, their credentials are the sum of their experiences, although this is changing and is discussed in greater detail below. The majority of logging contractors are competent, honest, and easy to work with. The public's negative image of loggers is the result of the incompetence, greed, and dishonesty of a very few individuals. One need only ask around to discover the renegades in a logging community. If you learn something about a logger that would compel you to shun his services, it is best to keep your reasons to yourself rather than to confront the logger with what you know. You are under no obligation to explain your decisions to anyone. Unless you know exactly what you are doing and trust the logging contractor implicitly, you should first seek the advice of a consulting forester or the local service forester, although the service forester's ability to render an opinion in this matter is limited.

Recent changes in forest-management practices are causing changes in logging communities. Today, there are fewer fly-by-night operations and fewer loggers. Where loggers used to have jobs lined up for a few months at a time, now they experience a backlog of a year or more. Good loggers are always in high demand.

How to Choose the Right Logger

First, make sure you understand who is actually buying the timber. Sometimes loggers will solicit timber on behalf of a local mill. You might assume it is the logger who is buying the timber, only to discover when the contract is signed that the logger you made the deal with is actually a contractor for a local mill. Always ascertain the identity of the buyer up front. It may not change your plans, but at least you know who's who. Also, be wary of a buyer who is in a hurry to seal a deal for whatever reason. If the buyer is too anxious, that is a signal to reconsider the offer and to seek a second opinion.

Ask for credentials. In logging, experience counts for a lot, but not everything. Usually, the older the woodland owner and the more his or her knowledge is experience based—whatever the field—the more willing that person is to accept the experiences of someone else as adequate credentials. It is very hard to argue with a guy who says he has been working in the woods for thirty years. He may know everything there is to know about felling trees, skidding logs, and trucking to market, but chances are he is only guessing when it comes to understanding the impacts of logging on forest ecosystems. Promising to harvest only trees above a certain diameter is a very common prescription from prospective buyers, but this a prescription for disaster in most even-age forests. Many loggers know better than this as almost all states now have logger education programs that teach principles of forest ecology and silviculture. It is not unreasonable to ask if the logger has participated in continuing education programs, and to wonder why he has not if that is the case.

Another great source of information on local loggers is town or county clerks. They usually know all the stories, even the ones that don't get told. If the name of your logger is unfamiliar to the clerk, this is reason for concern since conscientious loggers spend a fair amount of time in municipal offices, searching land titles and verifying boundaries. The local road commissioner is another good source. At some point, log trucks use public roads and most loggers know it is a good idea to stay on friendly terms with the road commissioner. Your local conservation commission may also have opinions to share on loggers who work in the area. Once a logger's reputation is tarnished it stays with him, and it is usually not too hard to find out why.

Always request references from a prospective timber buyer, follow up on them, and make sure you understand the reasons for endorsements. For instance, an older gentleman gives glowing references for a logger on the phone because, "He always took time to talk with me, and checks came in when I expected them." A visit to this gentleman's property may show that every stick of marketable wood is gone, and what is left of the canopy looks as though a cyclone has gone through it. And, if you learn about the financial aspects of the sale, the seller might have been paid less than half the fair market value for timber. Yet, he is a satisfied client. Why? Because he does not know any better and the logger was nice and conscientious about payments. When you check references, make sure endorsements are well informed and for the right reasons. And, be very suspicious of glowing endorsements.

Ask for a current certificate of insurance for comprehensive liability with specific worker's compensation coverage. Any worker who is injured during a timber sale can file a claim against a forest owner unless there is a worker's compensation policy in place. In addition, woodland owners should also have general liability coverage through a homeowner's policy, or a rider on such a policy. Always check with your insurer before selling timber from your lands.

Good communication with a prospective logger is fundamental. How easy is it to communicate with him or her? Do you understand what she is saying? Do you believe she understands your concerns? Never accept anything on blind faith. If there are communication barriers then it is reason enough to look for someone else. Remember, when the job is done, the logger moves on. You, however, must live with the consequences of the sale for many years. As you get to know the logger, find out what he knows about pertinent laws and regulations. Is he willing to accept liability for violations? If he scoffs at regulations, this is another signal that it may be in your best interest to look for another logger. Why? Because most regulations that govern logging practices hold the woodland owner liable for the actions of others. A logger who gripes about regulations may not be the best person to invite onto your land.

If you are selling a large sum of timber and contemplate a relationship with the buyer that will last for more than a few months, it is good idea to find out if there are any pending judgments against the buyer. Is he up-to-date on child support and/or spousal maintenance? Are there any active court proceedings that may result in a judgment? Knowing this information may seem unnecessarily personal, but the fact is that if someone tries to collect on a judgment, your assets may get confused with those of the buyer.

Always request a sum equal to at least two-weeks worth of harvested timber to be held by the seller, or the seller's agent, as a deposit against just such an event. Buyers resist such performance deposits, but hang tough on this point. While checking into the logger's liabilities, you will also want to make sure he is financially solvent. Any business person who expects you to accept checks as periodic payments should also be willing to give you information about the account: bank name, account number, and a letter to the bank authorizing disclosure of activity, balances, and any information on checks returned within the past twelve months for insufficient funds. A pattern of bounced checks is reason enough to locate another logger. Also, be very suspicious of an unwillingness to share this information even if the logger has never been asked to supply this information in the past. Business is business.

Finally, never under any circumstances sell timber from your land without a written contract. Loggers have been known to bristle at the suggestion of a contract, saying they have always done business with a handshake—implying they believe you don't trust them. Your response is: "I only do business with people I trust. The fact that I want to sign a contract means I trust you." If that does not sit well with the buyer, it is definitely time to look for another logger. Forest management contracts are the subject of chapter 6.

Credentialing of Loggers

Higher timber prices, decreasing supplies of good timber, conversion of woodlands into other uses, a growing controversy about the way we use state and national forests, and a public that is sensitive to environmental issues have all contributed to significant changes in the logging industry. Since the early 1990s there has been a noticeable increase in the number of workshops and short courses offered to loggers. Programs are intended to provide knowledge and skills that can help loggers become more competitive. But they are also intended to provide participants with a credential they can use to help secure clients. Most of these state-level programs are more of a palliative for woodland owners than an honest attempt to improve the knowledge and skills of logging contractors. Detecting the true nature of a logger credentialing lies in knowing how to recognize the difference between a credential as a marketing tool and one that describes an educational background that is likely to have changed the way loggers do business. A logger who flaunts a certificate that acknowledges completion of a set of workshops is not necessarily more or less qualified than someone without these credentials. The only way to verify the value of a certificate is to investigate the organization that awarded it.

Remember, too, there is no education program in the world that can take larceny out of a person's soul. Yes, ask loggers to see their credentials, this will signify they are serious professionals that want to stay up to date. But also ask for the names and contact information of recent clients. Call these references and make sure they are reporting positive experiences on matters that are important to you. Never accept a logger's credentials—or anyone for that matter—without taking a few minutes to verify that the credentials are meaningful and the person is otherwise qualified to work in your forest.

Chapter 6

Forest-Management Contracts

Forest management is all about controlling forest assets. Whether it is for sustained cash flow from periodic timber sales, recreation, wilderness, long-term investment, improved wildlife habitat, or a combination of these and other objectives, management implies control. For most forest owners it is impossible to effect forest management without entering into contracts. Ironically, it is usually the prospect of entering into agreements with others that frightens uninitiated woodland owners away from forest-management opportunities. They reason it is easier to do nothing and avoid conflict. But even the most passively involved forest owner will need to enter into contracts from time to time.

When entering into forest-related contracts, always remember the three essentials of good management:

1. Have a clear idea of what is important—your objectives and an ability to share that vision with others.
2. Locate competent local foresters, wildlife biologists, loggers, and others whom you trust.
3. Always use good written contracts to ensure your concerns and interests are understood and protected in dealings with others.

In all states, with the exception of Louisiana, laws governing contractual relationships are enumerated in the Uniform Commercial Code (UCC). Developed in the early 1950s, and adopted in most states by the mid-1960s, the code is composed of ten articles whose purpose is to unify rules of conduct in business relationships and thereby facilitate interstate commerce. Covered here is only a small portion of the UCC that relates specifically to the types of transactions forest owners are apt to encounter during their tenure with the land. Most of the technicalities of contracts as outlined in the UCC fall outside the scope of this book and the code varies slightly among states. Some excellent, introductory-level textbooks on business law are available that present most details of the UCC, primarily through case studies (Frascona et al. 1984).

For most people, the subject of legal contracts conjures a negative image of human interaction: we have been led to believe contracts are a necessary evil to keep others honest and to avoid being cheated. We see contracts as a means of forcing behavior, to compel people we do business with to act according to our conditions with the threat of being sued if they do otherwise. Contracts are a buffer to the outside world; they are immutable, sacrosanct, and a good way to pin somebody down, or be pinned. Contracts, many of us believe, are the only way to make deals with people we do not trust. They are the moral equivalent of using the carrot as a stick. And, perhaps the greatest misunderstanding of all--only lawyers can develop contracts. None of this is true, and the person who sees legal contracts as a means of effecting any of the above conditions is a victim waiting for a catastrophe.

Contracts are simply a means of formalizing communication between people, and whether we know it or not, most of us enter into contracts more than a few times every week. From implied contracts at the self-service gas station to oral agreements, such as with the kid who mows the lawn, almost all circumstances that involve an exchange of promises—either expressed or implied—will form a contract.

Virtually all contracts related to forest management should be in writing. A good rule of thumb is this: anytime you make an agreement with someone to do something that will take more than a day to complete, get the details in writing.

Finally, view contractual relationships in a positive context. Some people in the forestry community take offense when offered a contract to sign, saying, "A handshake has always been good enough for me." If you trust the person and intend to do business, follow up the handshake with a letter or memo outlining the points on which you have agreed. If problems arise down the road, you will be glad to have something in writing, and if certain conditions are met, the letter itself may be viewed as a written contract.

Introduction to Contracts

By definition, a contract is a promise, or set of promises, exchanged between two or more parties that create a legal obligation to perform. It is important to understand the distinction between an agreement and a contract. An agreement may be a manifestation of mutual assent between parties, but it does not necessarily constitute a legal obligation to perform. The difference between an agreement and a contract is that the exchange of promises represents value to the parties, value they would not otherwise be required to share if not for the terms of the contract.

All contracts, written or verbal, have the following four basic elements:

1. Evidence of agreement, or a manifestation of mutual assent, is essential to the formation of a contract. All parties must clearly understand the terms effecting a "meeting of the minds." A good contract also clearly demonstrates the definite intentions of the parties to perform the contract and that promises and commitments have been exchanged. The condition of mutual assent implies that willingness and understanding are basic to a contractual relationship.

2. Consideration is value exchanged for the commitments of others. Usually thought of as money, consideration is anything of value given to secure the promises of others, including another promise.

3. Legal capacity of the parties to a contract implies the court will acknowledge a participant's ability to create a contract with others. For instance, a person judged mentally incompetent does not legally have a capacity to contract, presumably because there is no way the first condition—a meeting of the minds—can be met. In most states, minors (under the age of twenty-one in all but a few states) have only a limited capacity to contract. If you enter into a contract with an individual who has only a limited

capacity to do so, you may be forced to uphold your end of the bargain while the person of limited capacity is let off the hook. This is important to keep in mind for owners who commonly hire young people to help around the tree farm.

4. Legality. The contract must encompass only actions, terms, and conditions that are not illegal. Any form of consideration that is apt to be viewed by a court as an agreement to perform an illegal activity may result in a void or voidable contract. For instance, a promise to steal a piece of equipment and deliver it to another party in exchange for promises from others (whether those promises are legal activities or not) is an illegal contract.

If any one or more of these four elements is missing, a contract may be judged void, voidable, or illegal. The first and third elements are more conceptual and obscure than the elements having to do with consideration and legality. It is usually easy to ascertain consideration in a contract but not always as easy to determine if there was a meeting of the minds. A contract delivered by a timber buyer to an elderly and infirm woodland owner, who may be incapable of understanding all the terms, could be voided simply on the grounds that there was no meeting of the minds.

Contracts can be implied or express, and express contracts can be written or oral (figure 6.1). An express contract means the terms agreed to were certain and stated by the parties, while an implied contract, as suggested by the words, means that by their actions (or inaction) a contract is assumed to exist between the parties. For example, an owner watching someone paint his or her equipment shed cannot refuse to pay by arguing that no contract exists. The owner's inaction—failure to stop the other party from working—may be viewed as an implied promise to pay. Although each type of contract varies in the degree to which terms are specified (or assumed), an implied contract has all the force of law that an express contract does.

The UCC requires that some contracts be express and written to prove their existence. For instance, contracts for the sale of land or for the sale of an interest in land (such as timber and other resources) need to be in writing. Contracts between parties for the performance of services generally do not need to be in writing. (The

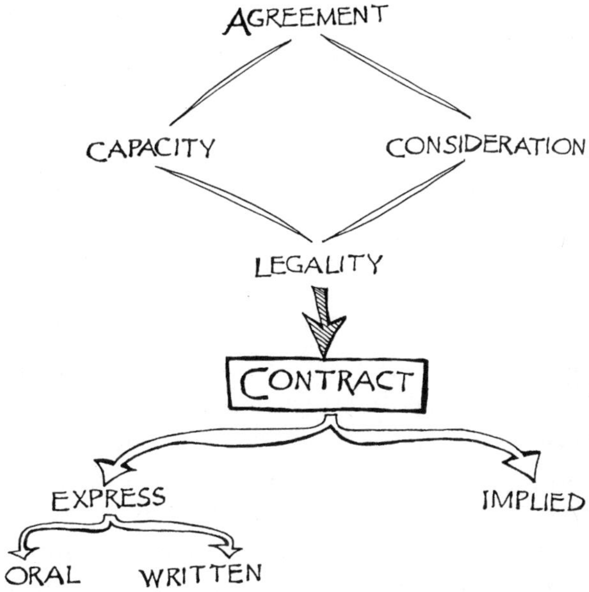

Figure 6.1. The four essential elements of a contract can be stated in specific (express) terms—oral or written—or implied based on the actions or inactions of the parties. Generally, forest-management contracts should be express and in writing.

UCC, as it applies to the sale of timber and other assets from land, is discussed later in this section.)

In its simplest form, a contract can represent a single promise between two parties. For example, you promise to pay a forester five hundred dollars for an undefined inventory of woodlands. This is called a *unilateral contract* because it involves one promise—to pay five hundred dollars—dependent on completion of an activity. When the inventory is delivered, the forester can expect payment regardless of the fact that there were no performance expectations to judge the acceptability of the inventory data. It is called a unilateral contract because the forester has not made any promises. This is a perfect example of a bad contract, because there are many different types of inventory, from a cursory walk-through to a detailed, statistically validated survey of timber volumes. Also, if time of performance is not stated, reasonable time is implied, which may be considerably longer than you think is reasonable. Contracts for services should always take the form of a bilateral, written contract—with an expiration date—unless you know the service provider extremely well.

There is no such thing as a standard contract in forestry practice. If the four conditions are met, a legally binding contract can be developed on the back of a napkin. The term *standard* usually means a form commonly used by the party offering the contract for signature. In forestry transactions, it is often the timber buyer or the provider of services who will offer a contract to the woodland owner. Among merchants, however, it is commonly the seller who first offers the terms of a contract. The buyer then either accepts the terms, rejects the offer, or submits a counteroffer. A forest owner offered a contract can extract elements to which he or she agrees and draft a new contract for signature by the other party. This is regarded as a counteroffer, and depending on the complexity of the terms, consideration and reconsideration of counteroffers are forms of negotiation.

Nothing should prevent you from developing your own contracts. Should a discrepancy arise, a decision as to who is at fault will be based solely on the terms of the contract and all the events that have occurred since the contract was formed. For these reasons it is important that the text of the contract cover all aspects of the relationship between the parties. It is not necessary to have an attorney draw up a contract for it to be binding on the other party. But it is usually well worth the cost to seek an attorney's opinion on a contract, particularly if it is someone else's. The cost of this service can usually be recovered at tax time.

The following are a few other points to keep in mind before signing forest-management contracts:

- Include an *indemnification clause* to limit your liability for the actions of others. When the other party accepts an indemnification clause, he or she agrees to "save and hold [you] harmless" for damages or injuries that might arise as a result of the contract. There are limits, of course, to which this type of clause will apply. In other words, it probably will not provide full protection if you are actually liable for an injury or loss.

- Specify an expiration date but include a clause that allows extensions for good cause, at your discretion.
- Eliminate any wording or reference that appears to be outside the scope of the contract.
- Get the other parties to agree to settle disputes using arbitration (see chapter 10). A common practice is for each party to select an individual to help arbitrate and then the parties (or the arbitrators) agree on a third arbitrator. Decisions of the arbitration panel are final. This can be an excellent alternative to going to court.
- Request a cash performance bond if any of your assets are at stake (which is always the case for timber sales).
- Include a paragraph that clearly states the outcome or products you expect from the contract. Do not hesitate to do this; the other parties will tell you if your demands are unreasonable.

Always have someone witness the contract—an individual who can be easily located even after a few years, preferably a notary.

- If you decide to sign a contract developed by someone else, have your lawyer look at it and explain your concerns so the lawyer knows what to look for.
- Finally, include a paragraph stating that you will write a letter to the other parties upon full performance indicating the contract is complete and you are satisfied with the outcome. The letter formally states that in spite of any other documents, statements, implied circumstances, or facts to the contrary, your contractual relationship is complete. In other words, the contract has been successfully executed.

Purchase of Services

A service provider is someone you contract with to perform a task. The key element to understanding your relationship with the provider is this: you are purchasing the result of services rendered and not the right to control how the services are provided, except as specified in the contract. Also known as a work order, the contract for services can be express or implied, oral or written. It can be unilateral (I'll pay you a thousand dollars to survey my land), or bilateral (you promise to complete the survey within thirty days). Most written work orders are bilateral, with the timeframe and other performance conditions clearly spelled out. If it is your intent to control how services are provided, you either need a detailed work order or you may want to consider developing an agency authorization, which is discussed later in this chapter.

There are many different types of forest management-related service providers you can expect to encounter—from realtors to heavy equipment operators, surveyors, accountants, and others. The most common forestry service provider woodland owners are apt to encounter is a consulting forester. Private consulting foresters can provide a wide range of services, from locating boundaries to mapping and inventory. They can also administer timber sales and help with some of the business aspects of management. Best of all, by having no conflicting ties with the wood-using industries, a private consulting forester can represent your interests and yours alone. In other words, under certain circumstance described below, a forester can act as a fiduciary.

When entering into service contracts, a clear understanding of the product is essential. For example, a contract to develop a forest-management plan could result in a few pages of general statements about the land coupled with a hastily sketched map, or it could result in a comprehensive and detailed document with inventory data, management options and consequences, and a series of carefully drawn maps. In a contract that does not define product expectations, both documents are apt to be viewed equivalently. If there were a discrepancy that ended up in court, testimony on what is fair and reasonable given the facts would weigh heavily in the court's judgment.

Another point to bear in mind about work orders or service contracts is to know what you are not purchasing. An agreement to develop a forest-management plan is not necessarily an agreement to begin implementing the plan. One of the most common errors of this nature involves boundary surveys. The owner's concept of a survey is a carefully drawn map with distances and directions, and a survey area with marked boundaries. Unless requested in the contract, most surveyors will not mark the boundaries as part of the survey.

Contracts for services are a useful method of purchasing services as needed. Because they must be carefully negotiated each time a new contract is developed, however, and may not provide you with an adequate degree of control, they often fall short when working with a professional over a period of years. If you have located a forest manager you trust, someone who is easy to speak with and who understands your concerns, a far more useful and satisfying contractual relationship may be one that authorizes the manager to act in your behalf. Clear communication, flawless rapport, and a high degree of trust are essential prerequisites.

When working with independent contractors focus on the following:

- Once the contract is signed, you do not have a right to control the actions of the service provider except as outlined in the contract. Be clear at the outset about any conditions you want met.
- Payment for services can be arranged many different ways, but a portion of the payment (up to one-third of the total) should be held until the contract is fully executed.
- Expenses to complete services are commonly paid by the provider, except as outlined in the agreement. For instance, a client may be charged for phone calls and travel expenses, but not for secretarial time or copying expenses. Include a clause in the contract that spells out agreed upon expenses and require a current certificate of insurance from the contractor or his agent.
- Be sure the contractor has workmen's compensation insurance for his or her workers and that any subcontrators are also covered. This is a form of liability insurance that protects the employer and the clients from claims of workers injured on the job. Also, check to see if the contractor carries general liability insurance and that it is adequate to cover damages or injuries to others that might occur during execution of your contract. Some owners will request that the contractor's insurer list the owner as coinsured during the life of the contract. Check with your insurer.
- Clearly state that the contractor is not an employee, and that nothing in the contract should be construed as an employer-employee relationship.

- Pass liability for compliance with applicable laws and regulations to the contractor, who should be willing to attest to the fact that all laws and regulations will be followed. Bear in mind, though, that most laws of this nature are written so that the landowner is ultimately liable for compliance.
- If the service provider will be handling money for your account, be sure the money is held in an escrow account and that you will be provided a complete accounting when the contract is finished.
- Generally, a service provider is not necessarily your agent, so be sure the wording reflects the exact nature of your relationship. Some work orders or agreements will refer to the service provider as your agent. Unless that is your intent, change the wording.

Although forestry service contracts are most common between woodland owners and forestry professionals, there is no reason they can't exist between professionals, such as between loggers and consulting foresters. The relationship may sound anomalous, but it needn't be. When a logger hires a consulting forester for services, there are risks associated with divulging client identity until the consultant has agreed to the terms of a contract. Aside from the fact that it is egregiously unethical for a consultant to abscond with a logger's client, the contract should carefully spell out appropriate channels of communication, making it clear that the forester is providing services for, and reporting to, the logger who is paying for those services. Under no circumstances does a consulting forester have the right (or duty) to compel a woodland owner to break a prospective agreement between logger and landowner. Until such time as a relationship of trust develops, the contract should specify a punitive monetary remedy in the event a logger's client decides to work with the logger's forester, rather than with the logger. Also, all parties to service contracts between loggers and consulting foresters should be reminded that it is illegal (in all states) to compel someone to breach a contract with another person, especially for the sake of personal gain.

Agency Authorizations

Common law, which varies from state to state, describes an *agent* as a person with a fiduciary responsibility to someone he or she represents. A fiduciary has a legal duty and authority to act for the sole benefit of another. The relationship can be implied or express, oral, or written; as long as the agent is doing things solely for the benefit of the parties he or she represents, it is an agency relationship. For the sake of discussion, the entity the agent represents is known as the *principal.* The parties with whom the agent enters into contracts for the benefit of the principal are known as *third parties.* In forest-management situations, the woodland owner is the principal, the agent may be a consulting forester (or anyone the principal authorizes), and the third party is anyone with whom the agent enters into contracts for the principal (figure 6.2).

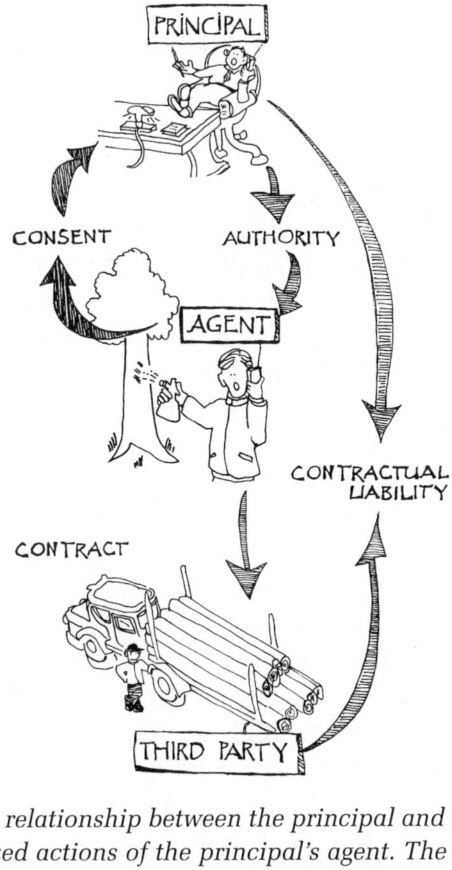

Figure 6.2. The relationship between the principal and third party created by the authorized actions of the principal's agent. The agent must be acting with the authority of the principal, and the third party must know this to be true.

How does an independent contractor differ from an agent? You buy only the results of a contract with an independent contractor. But if a person is acting as your agent, you have a right to control his or her actions. An agent can also enter into contracts that are binding on the principal while avoiding personal liability for the contract (assuming it is perfectly clear to the third party that the agent is acting in the principal's behalf and the principal's identity has been fully disclosed).

A written agency authorization is also known as a *power of attorney*. When the scope of an agent's activities is strictly defined, it is called a *limited* power of attorney. If the limited power of attorney is also a contract between the agent and the principal, the law of contracts applies. Setting up an agency relationship is an extremely powerful way to work with professionals, but it is not without risk. The scope of authority vested in the agent by the principal must be clearly spelled out, and an agency authorization should usually have an expiration date of twelve months or less with a provision to extend if the principal so desires.

Because you have the right as principal to control the activities of your agent, each of you has expectations regarding the other's behavior. It is generally accepted that the agent's duties to the principal include performance, loyalty, obedience, care, accounting, and information. The principal's duties to the agent include compensation, compliance with the terms of the agency, reimbursement for expenses sustained by the agent, and indemnification—to "save and hold harmless" the agent in his or her dealings with third parties in behalf of the principal.

A contract for an agency relationship, besides outlining the scope of the agent's authority, should identify a form of consideration (i.e., money) to make the contract binding. In this case, consideration takes the form of a retainer, a fee paid to the agent that can be credited against compensation due the agent when acting in your behalf. The retainer is like an advance and most likely will not include the total compensation the agent can expect.

The contract for agency has two parts: (1) the limited power of attorney granted to the agent by the principal, or the exact scope of the agent's authority; and (2) the contract, which besides satisfying the four elements of a legal contract, lists the procedures by which the agent is expected to fulfill his or her duty to the principal.

It is not unreasonable for the contract to require regular written communication from the agent, or for the agent to seek prior written approval before entering into certain types of contracts—such as timber sales. The contract should also clearly describe the special nature of what is otherwise viewed as an employer-employee relationship. Unless it is your intent to hire the person as an employee, you need to state clearly that the agent is not an employee but a person you have entrusted to act on your behalf according to the limited power of attorney. This is tricky and may require some legal advice from local attorneys who have experience in this area. If something goes wrong, it is usually the agent (or the agent's survivor) who claims he or she was acting as an employee and burden is placed on the principal to prove otherwise.

Here are some other points to consider:

- List the powers of the agent as exclusionary; that is, if not specifically listed, the agent does not have authority to act without your written consent.
- If the agent is empowered to make purchases for you, notify merchants to that effect.
- If the agent is empowered to sell timber for you, notify local log buyers.
- Reserve the right to terminate the agency contract at any time for any reason, but be willing to pay what is due the agent for services rendered prior to termination but not yet accounted for.
- If you are concerned about legal incapacitation during the agency, you may want to have your lawyer create what is known as a *durable power of attorney*, which is not affected by the subsequent disability or incapacity of the principal.
- An agent cannot be used to act in behalf of someone who is already legally incapacitated. For instance, if the principal has only a limited capacity to contract, the agent must operate under the same limitations.
- Anyone can act as an agent for another, even a minor. But remember, the law of contracts applies: you may not be able to enforce performance by a minor.

- If the agent exceeds the scope of his authority, it is the agent, not the principal, who is responsible for any contracts or claims, unless the principal ratifies, or accepts, the agent's actions.

The agency authorization is especially useful to absentee woodland owners, or to any woodland owner who wants to take full advantage of the expertise and services of local professionals. A good agency agreement obtains a commitment from a professional to act only in the best interest of the client whenever actions are required. Since the owner is empowering another person with the ability to make decisions (as spelled out in the contract), the owner must trust the agent to always make good decisions. Generally, the owner is attempting to obtain the commitment of an employee but without taking on all the responsibilities of an employer. For this reason the agency authorization must clearly spell out that an employer-employee relationship does not exist. In an agency authorization, the full relationship between principal and agent is described in the contract. But when an agent is viewed as an employee, state law will prevail over any terms set forth in a contract.

Forest-Management Leases

A lease is a type of contract that grants property rights to a person (the lessee), usually for a specified period of time. The property can be personal property (goods) or real property (land). The difference between the two is that personal property is tangible, something the lessee can possess and use, while real property deals with more intangible rights the lessor is willing to grant the lessee, such as the right of access. In northern New England, owners of mature northern hardwood forests will often lease the right to gather sap in the spring for maple syrup production. A lease is a way for an owner to allow others to use property while enjoying the benefits of income—the rent a lessee is willing to pay for those uses. While the owner (lessor) still holds title to the property and is responsible for property taxes, leasing is a great way to help defray the costs of owning forest land. The laws governing contracts apply to leases.

Forest management leases usually require the lessee to install improvements, so it is not uncommon for the lease to extend five to ten years or more. For example, a sugar maker lessee bears the cost of tailoring sap-gathering tubing to an area that is to be tapped. It would be impractical to sustain the expense of tubing if the lease were good for only one year. Generally, if the lessee's activities do not require an expenditure of capital, lease life can be shorter. The longer the lease, the more the lessee should be willing to pay.

In some parts of the country, mineral exploration companies will approach forest owners to lease the right to explore for oil and gas and other valuable minerals. Those leases are usually long-term, and the rent is paid up front as an inducement to sign. There is also a *royalty* provision if the company locates exploitable minerals on the property. At face value, a mineral exploration lease looks like a good deal. The problems arise when a lease is exercised and access roads are poorly designed and other site disturbances are not corrected before the crew moves on to the next site. Be wary of mineral exploration leases. Always seek a legal opinion before signing one, and don't sign if you are not completely comfortable with the deal. If there are valuable minerals in your valley, one or more of your neighbors probably will sign, and eventually you will hear about it.

Observe the following points when signing leases:

- Be sure you first own the rights you are leasing. For instance, some forest owners do not own mineral rights on their lands. You cannot sign a mineral exploration lease if you do not own mineral rights.
- The lease will create an imperfection on the title. An astute lessee will record a long-term lease with the town or county to protect his or her interests if the property goes up for sale.
- Always reserve the right to cancel the lease for cause with adequate and reasonable notice to the lessee. Spell out the circumstances that would cause you to cancel the lease.
- The lessee should be willing to post a bond or provide a deposit to cover the cost of damages or to compensate the owner for failures on the part of the lessee.
- A lease to use your woodlands should be nonassignable in the absence of your prior written approval. In other words, the lessee cannot pass rights to another person without your permission.

Fee-Based Recreation on Private Woodlands

Considering all the costs of owning and managing forest lands—in addition to ad valorum property taxes and the time-value of money—many forests in the United States are not sustainable—economically or ecologically. This is especially true in areas where larger tracts are being parcelized into smaller properties, and where lands traditionally dedicated to forest values are converted into second homes. Nevertheless, the cost of owning land eventually becomes an issue, even among those owners who acquired woodlands for reasons other than forest benefits. When owners discover that even highly sustainable forestry practices are incapable of footing the bill, the prospects of raising revenue by other means becomes appealing. There are lots of ways to use forest land to raise revenue, and many don't require compromising other objectives, or even the use of extractive practices. In fact, leasing forest rights is becoming an attractive alternative source of revenue, and forest recreation leases in particular are an emerging area of interest among owners and managers.

Although the concept of obtaining income from forest recreation is still emerging in most of the United States in other areas it has become tradition. For example, in the pine forests of the Southeast many owners of tracts larger than fifty acres—and virtually all owners of large holdings (five hundred acres and up)—lease their lands for hunting and fishing. Sportsmen will gladly pay for the experience of hunting on well-managed lands, and woodland owners are pleased to have them.

Fees are determined by the woodland owner and cover all lease costs; including legal fees, liability insurance, posting expenses (if necessary) and—best of all—property taxes. Total lease cost divided among an agreed upon number of hunters (so as to not overhunt game populations) is usually a minor expense to the lessee(s) compared to all other incidental expenses hunters will bear.

Some forest owners who recognize the potential to tap into local outdoor recreation markets will offer other services including blinds, guides, ATVs, and lodging that can vary from primitive cabins to a fully-appointed, luxury lodge. In fact, some forest owners who initially leased woodlands to help pay property taxes on a timber investment have developed lucrative, full-time businesses with a regular clientele. In other words, timber is now subordinate to recreation and for the first time woodlands are a sustainable investment.

Leasing of forest use is not limited to hunting and fishing. Some owners have discovered that people will gladly pay for recreational activities like cross-country skiing, off-road biking, rights to gather nontimber products from forests, and for other uses. But selling recreation, especially when it excludes local people who have always had free access to forests, is not without risk in some areas. Local people who claim rights to land by tenure for gathering, hiking, hunting, and other fairly benign uses, resent owners who exclude them, especially when those rights are then sold to an outsider who can afford to pay. In regions where recreation leasing is a new concept, restricting access can be a difficult decision. Nevertheless, the titleholder to land—and taxpayer—has the right to control how their lands are used, and if a recreational enterprise is necessary to make forests sustainable, it is the owner's prerogative.

For many forest owners, the opportunity to develop an alternative source of income from forests is the only way to keep lands intact. But most ventures are not passive; they require the cooperation and assistance of family members. Developing a recreational enterprise on one's forests is not a decision to be taken lightly.

In some regions, good camping spaces in state parks are sold out months before seasons open, most of the popular woodland trails have far exceeded reasonable carrying capacities, and it does appear as though public investment in outdoor recreation is poised to increase by legislative mandate in most states. The only way to meet growing demand is through private investment: fee-based outdoor recreation on private forest lands. Demographic trends indicate that not only will Americans have more leisure time in the future, but they will be looking for experiences that help families reconnect with land; and they will pay for those experiences rather than wait in line at public facilities.

Timber Sale Contracts

According to the American Forest and Paper Association, 2 to 3 million private, nonindustrial forest owners will enter into contracts each year for the sale of forest products. Less than a third of those transactions involve any type of professional forester, and a majority of sales do not involve written contracts between buyer and seller. Yet the law requires a written contract if the sale involves more than five hundred dollars worth of timber to be cut by the seller, or—a more likely scenario—timber is to be cut by the buyer. In the first instance, timber is treated as "goods" under the Uniform Commercial Code (UCC 2-107); in the second instance (the buyer does the cutting), it is viewed as a sale of an interest in land. Both conditions require a written contract to prove the existence of an agreement between the buyer and seller. Aside from the fact that it is plain good business to "get it in writing," when you are selling timber a written contract is required in every state except Louisiana.

One of the only practical ways to change or improve forest conditions for wildlife, recreation, or timber production is through periodic timber sales. The sale provides income to help cover the costs of owning land and, by manipulating the vegetation, an owner can influence forest conditions for many different uses. The trick is to generate income while improving forest conditions. In most parts of the country, harvesting timber solely for the sake of income production is not a valid strategy. Most successful managers see timber as a by-product of forest management that aims to improve investment, create wildlife habitat, and sustain other less tangible but no less important forest values, such as ecosystem health.

Always look for four parts in a timber sale contract (figure 6.3). Usually, the first paragraph identifies the buyer, the seller, and any agents. This may seem obvious, but it isn't always. For instance, you may sign a contract with a timber buyer, and then a week later a logger you have never met shows up and immediately violates the spirit of the contract. The logger may be the buyer's agent, but he is more apt to be an independent contractor. He is responsible only to the mill who bought your timber, and the mill has purchased the result of his activities, not the right to control his behavior. How do you resolve that situation? The buyer should divulge the names of people retained to harvest timber and should also be willing to show you a copy of any agreements with a third-party logger (the work order). The work order should convey exactly the same conditions you have placed on the buyer, with it being the buyer's responsibility to supervise the activities of the contractor. Anyone who will be involved in the sale should be identified.

The what, where, and when of the contract identifies the species to be harvested, the products (i.e., sawtimber versus pulpwood or other products, such as poles for pilings), the precise location of the sale (preferably with a map showing the boundaries of the sale area and surrounding property boundaries), the duration of the contract, and a listing of circumstances that may dictate when harvesting should be suspended, such as during wet ground conditions. A timber sale contract should always have an expiration date, with provisions to extend it for cause.

Often a timber sale contract will identify only the principal products, such as sawtimber (the main trunk of the tree), but not the by-products, such as cordwood in the tops of trees. If it is the intent of the buyer (or the timber harvester) to remove wood from the tops for sale, it should be listed as a product in the contract and the seller should be credited for its value. From an income tax perspective, sellers are better off to sell the tops in standing timber rather than sell wood from tops after trees have been felled (a standing tree is an interest in land, the sale of which is considered to be a sale of capital; income from tops lying on the ground is considered to be ordinary income, taxed at higher rates).

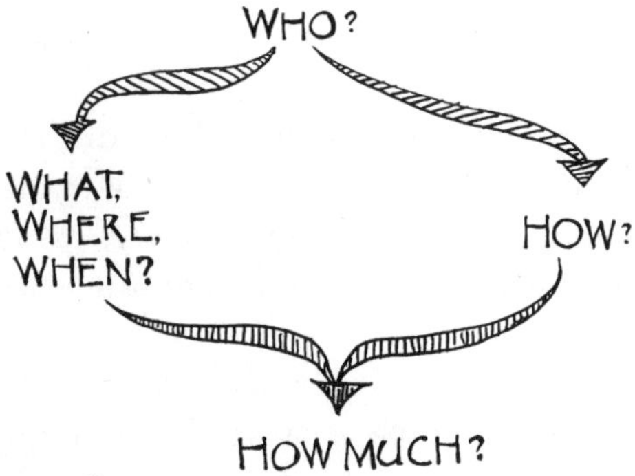

Figure 6.3. Look for these critical elements in a timber sale contract.

The seller is also responsible for ensuring the buyer knows where timber is located. And it is usually the seller who proposes access routes to harvest areas. To ensure compliance with the terms of the contract, it is a good idea to confirm that the buyer is well oriented to the sale area. If, after the sale is completed, there are claims of trespass from an abutting neighbor, the seller's efforts to ensure that the buyer was well informed will help protect against liability.

The how of a timber sale contract details all of the conditions a seller requires of the buyer. It addresses such conditions as treatment of slash after harvest, reseeding roads and landings, access routes, and specifications for skid trails and haul roads. It might also specify the type of equipment the buyer will use on the site, and any other special conditions the seller requires, such as protection of wildlife den trees and preservation of stone walls and cellar holes. If the landing is near the seller's house, be aware of the fact that loggers often start work before first light, and they work on weekends, too. Sellers who like to sleep in on weekends should specify limitations on work hours.

Always retain the right to suspend the operation for any cause, but especially during ground conditions that could be injurious to tree roots. In the North, every spring has two to four weeks when frost is leaving the ground. During this period, all but extremely sandy soils are susceptible to damage from heavy equipment. Known as mud season, it is a time when logs are scarce and loggers go without work. Notwithstanding, a seller should reserve the right to suspend harvesting during those conditions, or run the risk of damaged timber, washed-out roads, polluted streams, and angry neighbors.

A seller should place as many special conditions on the sale as needed to feel comfortable. Remember, however, that each condition requires special attention from the buyer, which means more time and less money. Thus the seller should also be willing to accept less money.

The contract should identify timber volumes and the means by which those volumes are to be measured. There are at least three major methods used to estimate the volume of boards in logs, known as log rules, and they all differ (as described below). Each region has its own traditional log rule. In the Northeast, the International 1/4-inch rule prevails; in the Midwest, the Doyle rule is common, and on the West Coast, they use the Scribner Decimal C rule. Local variations exist for each of these rules, so it important to know how the timber is being measured. Sometimes the final harvest volume is not known when the contract is negotiated. Even so, the contract should provide some hint as to how much timber is to be cut and removed from the land during the course of the contract.

Log Rules in the United States

The challenge for a log buyer is to estimate volume and value of rectangular products that a skillful and consistent sawyer can obtain from cylindrical raw materials. It sounds so straightforward and easy, but the facts are precision (the ability to obtain the same results consistently; repeatability) is elusive and accuracy is often more a function of experience than instrumentation. Of the two—precision and accuracy—log sellers are more concerned with the former, while log buyers are far more concerned with the later. One is looking for consistency and repeatability, the other is more concerned with how close any particular estimate is to actual yields, especially after factoring in losses from squaring logs off, kerfs, edgings, and shrinkage. In an attempt to reconcile precision and accuracy, and to account for losses during processing, manufacturers have over the years developed three different models to estimate lumber yields from logs: diagrammatic methods, mathematical formulas, and tally studies; three different approaches to arrive at the same solution.

A diagrammatic method, as the name implies, is based on an optimized sawing pattern diagrammed on the end of each log. Diagrams and sawing patterns vary with log diameter and the sawyer knows exactly how to handle each log; from the first pass through the head saw until the final board or cant.

Mathematically based log rules employ a formula that optimizes lumber yields from a tapering cylinder, which is a better approximation of log shape than cylindrical. Calculations also assume the sawyer's goal is to optimize lumber recovery, and the formulas account for the usual volume losses in saw kerfs, slabs, and edging. An advantage of the math-based rules over diagrams is they are far more sensitive in accounting for losses in misshapen logs, such as in those with sway or crook. Also, the guidelines for handing defects from seams, old wounds, branch stubs, and so forth are easier to apply.

A mill-tally log rule is one that evolves from actual lumber yields from logs that arrive at a mill over a period of time. Accurate rules require volumes of data and consistency on the part of the sawyer. Presumably, mill tally rules integrate all the factors that affect volume and value recovery, including consistent inaccuracies of the sawyer. These were the first log rules to disappear because of their highly subjective nature. It is ridiculous and unreasonable for a log seller to be penalized by a sawyer's errors, so why build these errors into the systems used to tally wood arriving at the mill? None of the recognized log rules in use today are based on data from mill tallies, although local mills will adjust their volume and value estimations based on knowledge of local factors that consistently affect yield recovery. For example, a local mill knows exactly how much volume and value it can expect to lose on local logs that come in with butt injuries, or from the effects of stem-boring insects.

Over the course of two centuries these volume-estimation models—diagrammatic, mathematical, and mill-tally—have spawned more than 95 "recognized" log rules known by at least 185 different names (Freese 1974). Diversity was due to a lack of standardization in procedures not variation in trees or markets, and log sellers were at the mercy of log buyers who used log rules that were most favorable to the mill. Variety notwithstanding, all rules were variations on the themes mentioned above. Names like Dimick's Standard, Fifth-girth Method, Thurber, Dusenberry, Partridge, Favorite, Los Angeles, and Goble Rules—even the "Logger's Favorite Rule," were all based on the same two parameters: log length and diameter. Eventually statutes that mostly came into existence after World War II required standardization, paring nearly one hundred log rules down to three common rules used today: Scribner rule, Doyle rule, and the International 1/4-inch rule.

Scribner is probably the oldest of the "method" rules based on diagramming. It is far more common in western states where they use a variation called "Scribner Decimal C" that rounds estimated log yields to the nearest ten feet. Scribner is also very similar to one of the oldest formula rules, the International 1/4-inch rule, which is probably the most common log rule used in North America. Doyle is also a formula rule used in the mid-Atlantic and central regions, usually for transactions involving high-value hardwoods. It is a buyer's rule because it tends to disfavor log sellers, especially when calculating useable volumes in smaller diameter logs (table 6.1). The Doyle rule consistently underestimates volumes in logs of diameters less than thirty inches. For this reason, most landowners and loggers avoid Doyle if at all possible.

In pulpwood markets or in markets that use wood for fuel, products are measured by weight (commonly *green tons*, especially when the product form is *chips*), or cubic volume (either in total cubic feet, or in *cords*, a common and traditional unit of measure in forestry). A cord is 128 cubic feet of wood, bark, and air, when the product form is *sticks* (pulpwood cut to four-foot or eight-foot lengths), or firewood in various lengths that can be easily stacked into a pile that is four-by-four-by-eight feet.

Minimum log length varies with markets, but a standard log length in the United States is sixteen feet, plus a *trim allowance* of four to six inches, measured along the shortest side of the log (which is the top side of a felling-notch in a butt log; an important point to remember when calculating trim allowance). In the East, a very common product length is eight feet plus a four-inch trim allowance. In some markets it is called a *log*, but in others it is correctly called a *half-log*. Log rules will vary in allowable log lengths, but two-foot intervals beginning at eight feet (eight, ten, twelve, fourteen, etc.)—usually to a maximum defined by the market—are called *standard* lengths.

Required minimum log diameters vary by species and buyer. Most softwood mills in the East will accept a minimum *tip* diameter of six inches, but the minimum for hardwoods is ten inches, although some mills will accept smaller diameters for *clean* logs. Minimum log diameters are much larger in the West.

Local mills regularly publish and distribute among its suppliers a page that describes log specifications. The *spec sheet*

Table 6.1. Comparison of log rules for 16-foot logs (with a 4-inch trim allowance).

Log Diameter* (inches)	Board Feet: International 1/4-Inch	Board Feet: Scribner Decimal C	Board Feet: Doyle
6	20	20	4
7	30	30	9
8	40	30	16
9	50	40	25
10	65	60	36
11	80	70	49
12	95	80	64
13	115	100	81
14	135	110	100
15	160	140	121
16	180	160	144
17	205	180	169
18	230	210	196
19	260	240	225
20	290	280	256
21	320	300	289
22	355	330	324
23	390	380	361
24	425	400	400
25	460	460	441
26	500	500	484
27	540	550	529
28	585	580	576
29	630	610	625
30	675	660	676
32	770	740	784
36	980	920	1024
40	1220	1200	1296

* Diameter measured from inside bark at the small end of the log.

lists minimum log lengths and diameters, trim allowances, and the rules for volume deductions from logs that have defects. Also included are grading rules and prices. And, it is not uncommon for mills to offer premiums for selected species, and/or for logs that are exceptionally valuable. Log buyers have also been known to offer mileage allowances to offset the expense of hauling high-value logs.

The two factors that determine log values are volume and grade. Of the two, grade has the biggest effect on value. As noted earlier, the process by which a tree is manufactured into logs has a major effect on value. The only way for a woodland owner to win in the marketplace is to locate a buyer who has the skill and motivation to process standing trees so as to maximize value over volume. For example, a tree with a merchantable height of twenty-four feet can be processed into three half-logs to maximize volume yield, or it could be processed into two, twelve-foot logs with less volume, but worth 20 percent more due to higher grades. Unless the logging crew is regularly informed of grade-premiums, in this case for twelve-foot logs, the company stands to lose 20 percent every time the option to create twelve-footers is converted to half-logs. For this reason, everyone on a logging crew needs to know the effects of prevailing log rules on volumes and values, and each week the crew boss should notify log makers of spec sheet changes that can have an enormous effect on the timber seller's bottom line.

Timber Sale Methods

The method of payment is an important issue for the seller and buyer to resolve. Traditions vary from region to region, but the timber seller's strategy is to ensure that payments are prompt and in the correct amount. Prepayments are not uncommon, and if the amounts are more than a few thousand dollars, the seller should require a cashier's check or a bank-certified check. The method of payment often depends on the type of sale, of which there are three: *lump-sum sale*, *mill-tally sale* (also known by the IRS as a "pay-as-cut" sale), and *sale on the basis of shares.*

The lump-sum sale is the most risk-free method for the seller. The buyer agrees to pay the seller a lump sum for the right to harvest designated timber, regardless of the actual volume the buyer recovers. It is the buyer's responsibility to ensure the sale volume is accurate, and he or she bids accordingly. The owner, who cannot possibly be held responsible for poor utilization standards of a logging crew or for internal defects revealed at the mill, is paid based on the estimate of volume in standing trees. The contract can specify a payment schedule for large sales or a single payment when the contract is signed and before harvesting begins.

In a mill-tally sale, the buyer agrees to pay the seller so much per unit of wood, the units to be determined when the wood is measured or tallied at the mill or at some other location such as a weigh station or scaling yard. The risks for the seller are these:

- Who will ensure the logging crew is maximizing log values in the woods?
- How will the owner know which mills are taking delivery of his logs?
- Who actually owns the logs once they leave the property?
- Who is liable if a logging truck carrying logs to market gets into an accident?

Following are the answers to those questions (assuming the conditions of a mill-tally sale):

- There is no way to control utilization standards of logging crews short of constant supervision or some sort of incentive that gives loggers an interest in maximizing log values.
- One can keep track of log loads, but it is tedious and consulting foresters rarely do it. Log scale and grades are usually determined at the mill.
- As far as ownership of the logs is concerned, the title is shared between the buyer and the seller until the logs are first measured at the mill (unless the seller passes title in the contract).
- The seller may be liable if a log truck carrying her logs gets into an accident. For this reason, the contract should pass title to logs (or at least pass liability) when they leave the seller's landing. An attorney can help craft a specific clause in the contract to pass title—and responsibility—for logs to the buyer the moment the buyer's truck leaves the property.

A sale on the basis of shares is really a consignment sale. The buyer (usually also the logger) agrees to pay the seller a percentage of the mill-delivered price for the logs. The percentage varies between 30 and 40 percent share to the seller (depending on timber values; sellers receive a higher percentage of more valuable logs). Of the timber sale methods, this is the most risky for the seller. Why? Because it is the equivalent of the seller going into business with the logger, and in doing so placing complete trust in that person's technical capabilities as a logger and on his or her own business practices as a partner. The same risks as for the mill-tally method apply as well.

Regardless of the method of sale, most woodland owners should seek the advice and guidance of a private consulting forester before selling timber. It is the consultant's job to represent the interests of the owner and to see that all the conditions of the contract are met and that payments are made on time. When a consultant is involved, his fees for administering the sale are often paid as a commission from the gross proceeds of the sale. This is accepted practice throughout the country. However, the owner should be aware of a potential conflict of interest when a consultant is paid on commission: The more timber sold, the higher the forester's commission, whether it is good forestry or not. Most consultants will disclose this situation before the sale; some consultants do not. It is perfectly acceptable to pay a consultant on the basis of commissions, as long as you understand the implication of doing so. Also, because of the potential for conflict of interest, it is probably impossible for a consultant to hold a limited power of attorney (or even act as a fiduciary) in connection with timber sales. The best situation is to tie payments to services rendered, not to commissions on sales.

Before signing a contract to sell timber, follow these ten steps:

1. Clearly establish your ownership goals and objectives, and the specific management objectives to be met by the sale.

2. Have the harvest area cruised to establish current timber volumes, both growing stock and potential harvest volumes. Also, estimate the growth rate of your trees.

3. Develop a prescription—exactly how will forest vegetation be changed and what is the expected outcome?

4. Develop marking guidelines to help implement the prescription.

5. Mark the stand and tally harvest volumes.

6. Identify contract conditions (restrictions) and draw up a sample contract.
7. Solicit bids and show the sale area.
8. Review bids and select a buyer. (Do not reject other bidders yet.)
9. Check the references of the successful bidder.
10. Review the contract conditions with the buyer, amend if necessary, and sign the contract in front of witnesses.

If there is a discrepancy during the sale, the written conditions of the contract are the only source a court (or arbitration panel) will use to identify a breach of contract. Therefore, it is essential that all conditions are clearly spelled out in writing and that the contract anticipates as many foreseeable circumstances as possible. Once the contract is signed, oral promises mean nothing in court. If you forgot to spell something out and cannot live without it, put it in writing, have all affected parties sign it, and append it to the contract.

The following are some other ideas to keep in mind when developing a timber sale contract:

- Review the elements of a good contract, described earlier in this chapter.
- An indemnification clause to "save and hold harmless the seller" is essential. Require workmen's compensation and personal liability insurance of the buyer.
- Require the buyer to post a bond (10 to 15 percent of the estimated sale value) or provide a sum of money to be held in escrow to ensure performance of the contract.
- Include a paragraph that requires parties to arbitrate disputes before going to court (arbitration is discussed in chapter 10).
- Payments either go directly to the seller or to the seller's representative (the consulting forester, assuming the forester is acting as a fiduciary). If payments go to a consultant, be sure you understand how and when payments are to be dispersed to you. Also, be aware of the fact that any payment of more than six hundred

dollars must be reported to the IRS on the appropriate Form 1099 (discussed in greater detail in chapter 8).

- Do not allow the contract to be assigned to other parties without your prior written permission.
- Require full disclosure of all other parties (subcontractors) who may be involved in the contract. For instance, include the name of the heavy equipment operator hired to put in roads.
- Clearly spell out the terms under which the contract will be considered fully executed, and the timing and method for refunding deposits.
- Specify practices that will result in improvements to the land after harvest. For example, have timber extraction trails designed so they can easily be converted to hiking and cross-country ski trails.
- Always reserve the right to terminate the contract for good cause with adequate notice to the buyer.
- When in doubt, seek a second opinion.

Finally, if you are not absolutely comfortable with the arrangements, do not sign the contract. The advantage of dealing with timber is that it is a crop that will not spoil (even after severe damage from ice, hurricanes, and other natural causes there is usually plenty of time to effect a sale, which is contrary to what most buyers will claim). You can delay your decisions indefinitely, or at least until you are sure the contract does what you want it to do. If you do not understand any elements of the contract, have your consulting forester or your lawyer explain them before signing.

Chapter 7

Ethics in Forestry Practice

Someone once said ethics are all the things we learn by the age of six, usually on the lap of a parent. It is a matter, we are told, of recognizing right from wrong. We are encouraged to choose a path of right behavior that is standard, not special, and we learn responsibility. In time, we come to recognize the obligation we have to other people and to the world we live in. Our ethics form the basis of a social contract that exists among humans. If not for this contract, human behavior would be unpredictable, chaotic, and violent.

The formation of ethics is a cultural phenomenon. What is acceptable in one culture may be taboo in another. It is almost impossible to predict correct behavior in a foreign culture without hints about what is acceptable and what is unacceptable. The purpose of this discussion is to view forestry and forest management as a culture unto itself and to describe acceptable and unacceptable practices forest owners are apt to encounter.

Most of the ideas presented here were inspired by, or extracted from Lloyd Irland's book *Ethics in Forestry* (1994), a collection of essays on various interpretations of situations where questions of ethics arise.

Excessively One-Sided Transactions

A free-market system operates on the premise that both the buyer and the seller are equally knowledgeable about the product and the price. For most woodland owners who periodically sell timber, this is not the case. They know woefully little about the products they sell and even less about fair prices for those products. A forest owner will sell board feet by the thousands without the slightest idea of what a single board foot is. And it is common for a seller to accept the estimates of a buyer without any possible means of checking the accuracy or veracity of those estimates. When a woodland owner relies exclusively on information from a buyer, it may be an excessively one-sided transaction. A one-sided transaction is not necessarily unethical, but it has the potential to be unless the buyer explains to the seller the one-sidedness of the deal. It is unethical for a buyer to take advantage of the ignorance of a seller even if the seller is acting out of greed. And it is illegal to mislead a seller to compel him or her to enter a transaction. Though these statements may seem obvious and irrefutable, in real life they are not. In a capitalist society, we are taught that business is business, and there is no requirement to suffer a fool's folly. Businesses make money with information, and a woodland owner selling timber is entering the wood products business, if only briefly. One can easily argue that it is not the responsibility of the buyer to educate the seller, especially if it means less profit for the buyer. From a strictly business perspective, an uninformed woodland owner is fair game. But if the buyer's advantage is excessive, it is not a fair transaction.

What is the buyer's obligation in this circumstance? It is to tell the woodland owner that, as the buyer, he cannot protect the owner's interests and that the owner should seek guidance from someone who can. The act of informing someone of a one-sided transaction is sufficient to remove the specter of unfairness. The buyer is under no other obligation to educate the seller, and the seller is under no obligation to act on the advice of the buyer.

The best way for a woodland owner to avoid an excessively one-sided timber transaction is to employ the services of a consulting forester. The cost of those services is usually more than offset by the financial advantage of the forester's knowledge.

Conflict of Interest

When a person has an interest in a transaction substantial enough that it does or might reasonably affect his or her independent judgment in acts he or she performs for another, it is a conflict of interest (Barry 1994). For example, in an excessively one-sided transaction, the buyer has a conflict of interest in his relationship with the seller. The conflict arises from the buyer's first responsibility to his or her own interests or those of his or her employer. Another example of conflict of interest is when a person shows favoritism for direct or indirect personal gain. An employee choosing a material supplier because of personal promises the supplier makes to the employee is an example of favoritism and is a conflict of interest. Any use of one's position for personal gain is potentially a conflict of interest.

Offering or accepting undisclosed payments, bribes, or kickbacks as the basis for a business transaction is often illegal, fraudulent, and a conflict of interest. In forestry, finder's fees are common. It is a payment, usually from a timber buyer to a third party, for information that leads to a timber purchase. Although a finder's fee does not always constitute a conflict of interest, there are circumstances when the payment or acceptance of those fees is unethical. For instance, if a finder's fee is paid by someone who then represents the interests of the person the information applies to, the payer of the fee is obligated to tell that person about the fee. Otherwise, it could be a conflict of interest. A consulting forester who pays a finder's fee to obtain a new client is obligated to tell that client about the fee. Failure to disclose the fee will violate the new client's trust and may create a conflict of interest for the consultant.

Another example of a conflict of interest involves related payments from more than one source. An example of a related payment is when an agent of the woodland owner accepts a premium (a reward or a kickback) from a mill for delivery of highly valuable logs while also accepting payments from the owner for services. In this case, the agent has an obligation to tell the owner about the other payments. If the owner is realizing the best possible market for her timber, the consultant might argue the extra payments are irrelevant. Be that as it may, at the heart of the transaction is a client's timber, thus the client has a right to know all aspects of any side deals—even if those deals are solely for the benefit of the client.

The best way to avoid conflicts of interest is to fully disclose all the facts of a situation to all the parties involved in a transaction. For example, a consulting forester who provides services in exchange for a commission paid from the gross proceeds of a timber sale has an obligation to explain the potential for conflict of interest to his client. The conflict arises from the fact that the forester has a financial interest in the transaction (the commission), which might reasonably affect his independent judgment. That is, the more timber he marks, the more he gets paid. The consultant's obligation to his client is to explain the potential for a conflict of interest, even if the consultant never intended to take advantage of the situation. There is nothing inherently wrong with proceeding in a situation where there is potentially a conflict of interest, as long as there is full disclosure to the parties who might suffer unfavorable consequences.

In many forestry communities, consulting foresters will provide services to woodland owners in exchange for a portion of gross income from timber sales. Although this method is steeped in tradition (going back to a time when the principal service offered by a consultant was administering timber sales, and gross receipts were well correlated with a consultant's efforts), the potential for conflict of interest using commissions is too great to warrant its use today. Nevertheless, consultants who prefer using timber sale commissions as the basis for payment can continue to do so provided they disclose the potential for conflict of interest with their clients. Many will accept the risks, but it is the client's right to do so after the facts have been disclosed.

Code of Ethics

Although ethical behavior is largely voluntary, grossly unethical behavior may be judged illegal. Yet it is not illegal to be unethical, but only to the extent that it does not cross into the realm of illegal activities. The continuum between ethical and illegal behavior is unbalanced (figure 7.1), with a broad range of interpretation between ethical and questionable practices. What one person may view as ethical, another sees as questionable. Depending on the facts and circumstances, it may be difficult to judge. As one moves along the continuum from questionable to unethical, it is easier for objective observers to agree on when someone has crossed the line. The distinction between a questionable practice and an unethical one is more obvious; there are fewer shades of gray. The distance between unethical and illegal behavior is very narrow, but the definition is even more obvious. In other words, it is easier for people to agree, because the boundary between unethical and illegal is usually well defined and easy to interpret. A person who behaves in a grossly unethical fashion is probably also acting illegally.

Recognizing the need to interpret situations in forestry practice that may be questionable or even unethical, such professional societies as the Society of American Foresters and the Association of Consulting Foresters have developed codes of ethics. The codes consist of a list of canons or statements to which all members agree. The statements are necessarily broad and subject to interpretation, and only rarely is a member formally charged with a violation. An official finding of a violation almost never happens. Most members of these national societies and other similar local professional organizations are aware of their society's code of ethics. But only a few members know the code well enough to paraphrase even one or two of the canons. This is not to suggest that members who cannot recite the canons are inherently unethical. Ironically, the opposite is usually true: the member who knows the canons by rote is the person you want to watch!

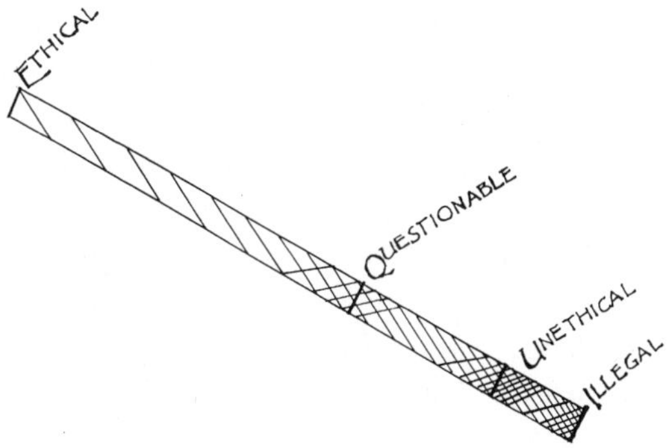

Figure 7.1. The continuum between ethical, questionable, unethical, and illegal behavior is unbalanced. In forestry, there are many shades of gray between ethical and questionable behavior, but there is almost no distinction between unethical and illegal behavior. Grossly unethical behavior is also illegal behavior.

Most members of professional societies do not need a code of ethics to determine right from wrong. The codes are more for putting the public's mind at rest than for governing the behavior of the society's members. But the canons also define a boundary of acceptable behavior for those few professionals who operate on the fringe of ethical and questionable practices.

Mollie Beattie, a good friend and now deceased colleague, once said (jokingly), "'Your society [referring to SAF], upon request, will send you a copy of the Code of Ethics, suitable for framing.' The collateral question is, suitable for framing whom?"

The codes are often misused by dishonest individuals who hide behind them or by righteous people pointing fingers. The codes developed by professional societies are necessary, however, and occasionally useful. But steer clear of people who talk about their society's code of ethics rather than behaving in an ethical fashion.

When you work with forestry professionals, as a client you can expect—at a minimum—three things. First, that the nature of your business dealings will be held strictly confidential. It is unethical for someone you do business with to discuss the nature of your relationship, or anything related to a transaction, with third parties. Second, anything other than total honesty and complete loyalty as it relates to your business dealings is unacceptable. It is unethical for a professional to switch loyalties as may be convenient for him or her, and dishonesty is always unethical, whether you are the victim or someone is being dishonest with another person but in your favor. Tolerating unethical behavior is in itself unethical. Finally, you have a right to expect technically sound and acceptable management practices of the professionals with whom you work. It is unethical for professionals to profess technical proficiency in areas where they are unskilled. And it is wrong for a professional to implement practices without knowing if the practices are regulated locally or if other special conditions apply.

Licensing, Registration, and Certification of Professionals

There is a recent trend for states to control forestry activities and the actions of people who provide services to woodland owners. The purpose of these efforts is to limit the severity of cutting, to ensure forest ecosystems are protected, and to protect the public from people who claim professional competency but have none.

Cutting restrictions and forest protection mechanisms take the form mainly of notification statutes, which require the owner to file a plan when harvesting more than a certain threshold amount of timber. To see if your state or local area requires a permit to harvest timber, contact your state extension forester (appendix A). In some locales, permitting is based on access to public roads, on protecting water quality, or even on some obscure (and possibly illegal) local ordinance aimed at controlling timber harvesting. If there are such ordinances in your area, you must comply with them. Generally, the requirements are fairly easy to satisfy. As the landowner, it is your responsibility to be sure your forest-management operations comply with local laws. Yes, a competent consulting forester should know the law and can advise accordingly. But, regardless of a consultant's advice—good or bad, right or wrong—it is the landowner's duty to uphold the law.

Some states are requiring foresters, loggers, and other woods workers to document and maintain credentials to provide the types of services they offer. The statutes take on many different forms, but they are largely intended to help the public understand the extent of a person's competence, and/or to require full disclosure of the professional's relationships with the wood-using industry or others whose interest may be in conflict with those of the forest owner.

A certification program is the least restrictive method of controlling the credentials of people who offer services. Certification usually is voluntary and often sponsored by a professional organization. It commonly requires members to have attained a certain level of professional competence and to make a commitment to maintain that competency. When certification is required by statute, it takes the form of a registration. For foresters or loggers to provide services, they must comply with the certification requirements. To maintain the certification, they must usually complete continuing education programs and adhere to a standard of conduct or a code of ethics. If an individual fails to complete the requisite education or violates the standard of conduct, certification is suspended.

Licensing is the most restrictive form of controlling credentials. It is only rarely used, because forestry is somewhat obscure and poses minimal threats to human health, safety, or welfare. Most states reject licensing because of the expense associated with maintaining a board of licensure and on the grounds that only a small portion of the population benefits. The difference between licensing and registration is in the degree to which the controlling authority takes responsibility for licensees. A licensing authority assures the public that people with licenses to practice have achieved a minimum level of competency and that the licensee will perform in an acceptable and professional manner, in accordance with all laws and regulations. Registration does not usually provide the public any guarantees other than of credentials. Regardless of the method—certification, registration, or licensing—each has a standard of conduct by which professionals are expected (or required) to abide.

The American Forest and Paper Association, under its Sustainable Forestry Initiative, has recently asked member companies to require education programs for its loggers. To comply, a logger must complete a state-by-state defined curriculum within a certain time. Significantly, this is the first time the forest industry has required any conditions on the procurement policies and practices of its members. It is not a certification program, however, and currently no standards of conduct are required of loggers who complete these programs. The SFI education requirement is not a certification program, but it looks like one.

The element that licensing, registration, and certification programs have in common is a standard of conduct or code of ethics that people are expected to abide by to maintain their status. Consumers of professional services must remember that the behavioral standards of certification or licensing are not necessarily a performance guarantee. It is very difficult, almost impossible, to resolve a complaint with a licensing board. Therefore, it is up to the woodland owner to judge a professional's character and to know when and how to enter and break off a professional relationship.

Environmental Ethics

Many people have come to realize that, besides the social contract we have among ourselves, we also have a responsibility to the earth and to all the other organisms with which we share the planet. Having a sense of environmental ethics implies that consideration is always given to the effects of our activities on plants and animals, and on future generations. Forests are complex, though, and it is not easy to predict the results of our actions. Often, what is good for one species may spell doom for another, or seemingly dire and irreversible outcomes may turn out to be temporary. How then does one know when a practice is right or wrong? The answer is: it depends—on the motivations of the forest owner, on the long- and near-term forest management objectives, and on the degree to which practices preserve the integrity of an ecosystem. For example, a forest owner who harvests timber solely for production of income without regard to the health and condition of the forest after the harvest is acting unethically; a forest owner who harvests timber for income, but only to the extent that long-term productivity is protected and adequate consideration is given to wildlife species that use the forest, is acting ethically. The irony in these examples is that there may be little difference in the financial outcome for both owners, but one of them is doing the right thing by exercising a little extra care in the interest of other species and of future generations.

Making the right decision is not always easy. Some forest owners believe it is highly unethical to disturb the forest in any way. Yet we need the products of forests and have demonstrated we can harvest timber without sacrificing other values. Human use does not need to be destructive or to obviate use by other organisms. Careful planning with an eye to the future and empathy for other organisms will almost always lead to the right decision. We are fortunate to live in a time when our knowledge of forest ecosystems is expanding rapidly. As our understanding increases, so does our ability to make the right management decisions.

Certification of Forest Practices

The forest certification movement emerged in the late 1980s in response to careless logging in tropical forests. First played out by large companies felling huge swaths of rainforest for wood production and land clearing, even recently enacted laws have not stemmed the flow in some third-world countries. The developed world's taste for exotic woods feeds a growing market for tropical hardwoods that rivals, in some circumstances, markets for illegal drugs. Of course, most American and European consumers have no idea that the picture frames, moldings, fine furniture, and other such products they buy are supporting devastating practices far from home. Felling and extracting a single, three-hundred-year-old tree can take a small crew a couple of weeks to accomplish, leaving behind many hectares of damage from vines that rake the forest floor like anchor chains as the crop tree falls.

When conservation groups started getting the word out about these practices, there was so much market inertia that it seemed as if cutting would stop only after all the valuable trees had been harvested. Change was slow, too slow for those who witnessed the effects of crude timber extraction practices in tropical forests. Governments of third-world countries were fairly quick to react, but powerless to control the steady stream of now illegal exports. It is impossible to stem the flow of wood without stanching demand and this is where the concept of forest certification was born. Educate consumers about the perils of buying tropical woods, they stop buying them, eventually demand dries up, and local people are encouraged to use more sustainable practices.

Forest product certification got started as a way to eliminate lucrative markets for sensitive tropical hardwoods. In theory, the eventual groundswell of demand for certified wood will mostly displace demand for uncertified wood, and everybody wins. So far, this has not proven to be the case, but changing the habits of consumers takes time and there is a lot of money betting that green products, harvested from certified forests, will catch hold in a big way.

Fortunately, we don't have the same forest utilization problems in the United States as in tropical regions, but there is still room for improvement in the way we harvest and use forests. Our forest use problems are different but the principles behind good practices that define sustainable forests are exactly the same: use the best methods to harvest and extract timber while protecting forest soils and habitats. A certified forest is one that—above all else—maintains the integrity of forest ecosystems; human use is secondary. A certified forest product is akin to organically grown produce, which has established a substantial niche market in the grocery industry in less than twenty years.

American forest industry has had a love-hate relationship with forest certification since it arrived here in the early 1990s. There is no middle ground, no fence-sitting. Those who embrace it see new marketing opportunities and an emerging consumer that wants more from products than just service. Those who hate it decry another layer that spreads profits thinner, or unnecessarily increases production costs. But, as with most things, truth lies somewhere between the extremes: yes, it costs more to produce products from certified forests, but manufacturers who produce green products believe consumers will increasingly demand these products and profitability will follow. This in spite of the fact that recent trends have proved otherwise: American consumers tend to be more cost conscious, choosing the lower-priced item over the more earth-friendly one, at least for now.

Large lumber retailers are attempting to expand their green-certified product offerings, but the jury is still out as to whether consumers will create enough demand to make it worthwhile. And there is a healthy debate between environmentalists who fashioned the certification movement with formation of the Forest Stewardship Council (FSC), a Germany-based worldwide organization that pioneered forest certification in 1993, and the American Forest and Paper Association (AFPA), which represents forest industry in the United States. The issue is: Whose imprimatur is more meaningful, and who is eligible to inspect whom?

FSC is presently the only worldwide forest and forest product certification organization. It espouses ten principles to which a woodland owner or wood manufacturer must adhere to receive and maintain certification. The principles require an ecosystem-approach to management and a commitment to sustain wood production while protecting plant and animal diversity, wildlife habitats and other forest values. Third-party "auditors," usually foresters but manufacturing control experts as well, visit candidate woodlands and wood product businesses to determine whether or not the practices meet FSC standards. To qualify, the components of products must be auditable as to chain-of-custody from forest to consumer, and every step of the process must meet FSC guidelines. Producers that adhere can market products with the FSC logo. Retailers advertise the earth-friendliness of their products. Woodland owners who supply green-certified timber are assured their practices protect forest ecosystems, and consumers can feel good about saving the planet.

To date FSC has certified about 20 million acres in the United States, and more than 100 million acres in sixty countries. The key to its program is third-party certification and verification of the chain-of-custody. Periodic audits of certified forests and producers ensure that standards for practices and products are continuously maintained. The costs for initial certification and subsequent audits are high, and this has been an issue with small primary wood processors and woodland owners who don't yet feel that those costs can be easily recouped by selling FSC-certified products. So far, most are right; but some producers have obtained niche markets for their products and are doing quite well. Others see certification as an investment in the future.

AFPA, which sponsors the popular Tree Farm program (through its American Forest Foundation) in addition to representing wood-using industries in the United States, developed the Sustainable Forestry Initiative (SFI) in 1995, a few years after it appeared that FSC was making progress. Coincidental or not, critics say AFPA's purpose was to thwart third-party certification, to squelch a movement created and controlled primarily by environmental interests. Its forest certification efforts are closely tied to the Tree Farm program and requires third-party audits same as FSC. The difference is that the audit process is controlled by forest industry, creating the appearance of a "fox in the hen house" and throwing consumer credibility out the window. Without credibility it is not long before consumers and woodland owners begin to feel like they are paying for the equivalent of air in the cereal box.

AFPA also requires its members who want to use the SFI concept to accept and adhere to a broad set of principals, same as FSC. But the organizations differ on things like the allowable maximum size of clearcuts (AFPA says 120 acres, FSC supports smaller treatment areas), and on the use of chemicals (AFPA says they are essential, especially herbicides in plantations, FSC advocates practices that don't use chemicals). The "them-versus-us" posture of the debate risks losing faith of consumers and woodland owners altogether, but it is doubtful even a feud will stop what amounts to a brand-recognition dispute.

The forest certification process under either FSC or AFPA is fairly simple. A review is initiated by the woodland owner. Depending on the size of the owner's holdings and complexity of the landscape, a small team is assembled to review the owner's forest management plan and to judge the effects of practices on the ground. The team is composed of a forester or two, a wildlife biologist and others, depending on the owner's resources. For example, if the owner's land encompasses areas that are of archeological significance, the team may include an archeologist. After reviewing the owner's plans and practices, the team writes a report that describes their findings, including recommendations for changes that will protect ecosystems or improve resource sustainability. Based on the final report the certifying agency will either accept the land, the owner and his practices, deeming the land *certified*, or it will outline changes the owner must put in place before certification is issued. Only after the owner has satisfied all conditions is the land fully certified, and products from the land can be sold as such. The forest is certified until the next review, usually scheduled at five years or whenever the certifying agency has reason to believe the forest is no longer certifiable. The woodland owner pays the cost for all reviews.

Recognizing the need to streamline the review process so as to attract more private woodland owners, FSC now certifies forest managers. Whether or not a forest is certified is still the owner's choice, but if the owner is a client of an FSC-certified manager, the process is simpler and the expense far less than an owner dealing directly with FSC. AFPA is attempting to tie forest certification into its Tree Farm program, but so far the two have not been an easy match to work with.

In recent years a third certification program has emerged, touting itself as a middle ground between FSC and AFPA. Sponsored by the National Woodland Owner's Association and the National Forestry Association (very closely related organizations), *green tag forestry* is portrayed as a moderate-cost alternative to owners of smaller woodlands in the United States and Canada who want their lands and practices certified. For more information on green tag forestry, visit: www.greentag.org.

The rivalry between FSC and AFPA aside, critics of forest certification say it is a fad. With no discernable difference in products other than label and price, consumers who don't feel wealthy and magnanimous will always pick the best buy, conscience be damned. Tough times have an effect on consumer preferences, but most experts still agree that forest certification will become more prevalent, not less.

Tolerating Unethical Behavior

When we tolerate unethical behavior in others, either by looking the other way or by taking advantage of someone else's inappropriate behavior, it is unethical. It is wrong for us to espouse a standard that we live by while accepting lower standards of others; this is especially true if we stand to gain from another's transgressions. For example, it is unethical for a mill that purports to be environmentally sensitive to accept timber from a logger who is notorious for unethical practices. The act of buying logs from people like that is supporting and reinforcing bad behavior, and the mill is just as guilty as the perpetrator.

People associated with forestry are often judged by the bad behavior of a few who act in disregard for any appropriate or reasonable standards. It is not necessarily our responsibility to confront renegades, but it is important to speak out when confronted by people who associate the bad behavior of a few with the entire community. Unless you have facts to support the allegations you could make, however, it is best to criticize practices rather than people. Making oral statements of facts that are injurious to the reputation of others is called *slander*. There are many ways to criticize bad behavior without taking things to a personal level. Making injurious written statements of facts is called *libel*. Both are punishable as *torts*, noncontractual, civil wrongs that results in injury to another person. The validity of purported facts in slander or libel is a defense, and the injured party must prove there was intent to cause injury and that a loss has been sustained.

Although not nearly so egregious as openly tolerating unethical behavior in others, failure to accept responsibility for one's actions is a distressingly common form of unethical behavior. It is easy to point a finger, to plead ignorance, or to otherwise avoid responsibility. Often a subordinate—the last person hired—takes the brunt of criticism for someone else's failing. Recognize failures to accept responsibility and know that they are symptomatic of behavior that could easily lead to much more serious transgressions. "Acting ethically is acting courageously" (Irland 1994). Taking responsibility for one's actions—especially when it is easy to blame someone else—is acting courageously.

A Case Study in Forestry Ethics

In Vermont we have a forty-eight hour curriculum for logging contractors known as LEAP, an acronym for Logger Education to Advance Professionalism. The program is voluntary and covers a diverse curriculum that includes a daylong workshop on professionalism and ethics. Our approach to teaching ethics includes the use of case studies, where loggers in small groups are asked to review the facts of a scenario and to answer questions about the ethics of various decisions made by the characters.

The exercise is initially intimidating, because the characters and situations are true to life. Eventually, a lively discussion ensues, and the exercises become a favorite part of the workshop for participants. They learn that, although it is not always easy to state why a particular action is right or wrong, instincts can help. They also learn that it is easy to change the thinking of their peers just by speaking up.

Following is one of three case studies we use during the workshop. Read the scenario, give careful consideration to the facts, and think of ways that potentially unethical actions could have been avoided. Then try to answer the questions that follow. An interpretation of the scenario and some answers to the questions follow the case study.

Final Thoughts

In most parts of the country, the people who make up the local forestry community are well known. Their reputations precede

A Case Study in Ethics

A logger gets a call from a friend who recently heard that his wife's uncle is thinking about selling his timber. The 140-acre woodlot is fairly well known locally, not much harvesting has been done over the years. Aside from a little fuelwood, there have been no commercial timber harvests on the property for more than sixty years. There may be as much as a million feet of mostly hardwood sawtimber of much-better-than-average quality. The friend suggests to the logger that he give Uncle John a call, gives him the phone number and even offers some ideas on how to sway Uncle John to sell. But, if Uncle John does decide to sell, the friend wants a cut for making the referral without Uncle John knowing his involvement in the transaction.

Next day the logger parks his pickup and hikes up into Uncle John's woodlot to have a look see. The area is a beautiful stand of one-hundred-year-old-plus sugar maple and yellow birch. Even a light cut will yield easily accessible, mostly high-quality sawlogs.

The logger calls Uncle John and discovers that he is interested in selling some timber, but not all of it. With virtually no understory over most of the woodlot, Uncle John expresses concern about getting a new forest started underneath. The logger suggests a *selective harvest* and Uncle John agrees.

When the logger and Uncle John meet a few days later, the logger agrees to pay so many dollars per thousand for maple and birch, and he also agrees to document log volumes with mill-tally slips. After much discussion, they agree that only trees larger than fourteen inches will be harvested, the logger assuring him that what is left after the harvest will provide perfect conditions for regeneration.

During harvesting, the logger sorts logs on the landing and brokers them to various mills, receiving a premium that amounts to 15 percent to 20 percent more than he agreed to pay Uncle John.

1. How should the logger have handled the "tip" from his friend?
2. Does Uncle John have a right to know about the conditions of the referral?
3. How could the logger handle the referral to avoid questionable ethics?
4. Was it acceptable for the logger to visit the woodlot without Uncle John's consent?

5. Given Uncle John's concerns about silviculture (over strictly income production), is it ethical for the logger to act as he did—giving what amounts to silvicultural assurances without the credentials to do so? Is there another way?
6. Is it ethical, in this instance, to buy the timber based on fixed stumpage rates and mill-tallys when the logs were actually brokered from the landing?
7. Are there any conflicts of interest? If so, describe them.

Questions 1, 2, and 3. There is nothing wrong with paying a finder's fee for information. If the logger anticipates a business relationship with Uncle John, however, he is obligated to disclose his source, especially if Uncle John asks. The logger might have suggested to the friend that the two of them approach Uncle John together. If the friend is unwilling, the logger should wonder why and consider walking away. Or the logger could approach Uncle John, tell him the source of his information, pay the finder's fee, and risk his friendship with the source. Either way, Uncle John has a right to know that someone gave the logger a tip about his timber. Also—as a friend—the logger may want to advise the tipster to first speak with his wife, since Uncle John is on her side of the family.

Question 4. It is common practice in most parts of the country for buyers to "road-cruise" timber and to walk onto lots that are not posted. In this case, the logger was doing so based on a tip, and contemplating a future business relationship with Uncle John, he should have first asked permission to walk his land. If the logger had no prior knowledge of Uncle John and his woodlands, and the land was not posted, it is probably OK for the logger to walk on the property. If, however, the logger anticipates a future business relationship with the woodland owner, he may want to obtain permission to visit the land.

Question 5. Unless the logger has credentials to do so, it is unethical for him to advise Uncle John on silviculture. Proper credentials to give that type of advice would include a B.S. in forestry and sufficient experience with similar prescriptions in the timber type. The logger may have many years of valuable experience as a timber harvester, but that does not qualify him as silviculturalist or as a forester. Also, there is no such thing as a "selective harvest," which presumably means only that someone has selected trees for harvest. Diameter-limit cutting in this circumstance—to regenerate northern hardwoods—is probably the worst possible practice to use. The logger should have sought (with Uncle John's permission) the advice and guidance of a local consulting forester, with the understanding that the consultant would be working for the logger, not for Uncle John. It would be totally unethical for the consultant to approach Uncle John independent of the logger or try in any way to steal the logger's client, even if the consultant believed Uncle John and his forest would be better off not dealing with the logger. (If the consultant is troubled by the Uncle John/logger relationship, after informing the logger of his concerns, he could make his case to Uncle John, but then he must walk away from the situation.) The logger runs the risk of Uncle John hiring a consultant of his own, but there is no other way. The logger can only hope that his honesty and forthrightness will eventually be rewarded. If Uncle John is overcome by greed, though, the best thing may be for the logger to walk away.

Questions 6 and 7. If it is understood and agreed to by Uncle John that he is to be paid a fixed rate for stumpage by the logger, who is also the buyer (and this is a key point), then there is nothing wrong with the logger brokering logs to the higher-paying markets, assuming Uncle John is paid according to the agreed-upon terms. It looks like a "related payment from more than one source," and it would be if the logger's agreement is to pay a percentage of the payments he receives from log buyers to Uncle John. However, assuming the logger is the buyer (which is another reason he cannot honestly advise the client on silviculture without a conflict of interest), there is no problem brokering logs to other markets. But, because the brokering is taking place on the landing—that is, on Uncle John's land—the logger has a duty to tell him of this activity and to seek the landowner's approval to do so. By inviting buyers onto Uncle John's land, the logger has exposed him to liability and he has a right to know this.

them. One need only listen to hear stories of the thieves and incompetents. The stories of good deeds are not nearly as well known. Nothing will sully a professional's reputation more quickly than dishonesty, and it is almost impossible to reverse a tarnished reputation. But a bad reputation is irrelevant to someone who cares little about honesty and protecting forest ecosystem values.

To avoid becoming one more victim, always ask for credentials and references of the people with whom you work. What sounds like a good deal offered from a person of questionable ethics may turn out to be the worst deal of your life. And if you willingly tolerate the questionable practices of others for your gain, you are just as responsible as the person acting in your behalf. Also, expect to be victimized by others if your standards are low.

Chapter 8

Forest Taxation

"The only certainties in life," according to Benjamin Franklin, "are death and taxes." It is human nature to avoid the inevitability of both, but only one is a matter of degree. It stands to reason then that the objective of a taxpayer is to pay as little as possible, but no less than what is owed. The facts are, however, that most people pay too much, and this is especially true of forest owners. The purpose of this chapter is to describe the three primary forms of taxation that affect woodland owners—property tax, income tax, and estate tax—and to suggest ways forest owners can avoid paying more than is due.

In society, taxes are a necessary hardship, a burden we all share because taxation is one of the only means of raising revenue to expend for the public good. Most people oppose taxation not because of an unwillingness to pay their share but on the definition of *public good*. We resent paying taxes because we are unsure how those tax dollars will be used and who will benefit.

From society's perspective, a tax must meet certain criteria to be successful. It must be perceived as reasonably fair and equitable. If it is not, compliance is low and the cost of collection is high. People must also accept the authority or purpose for which taxes are levied, and they must feel that they have a say in how revenue is spent. In the United States, most people believe that taxation should be progressive: those who have more are taxed at a higher rate than people who have less. Of the three types of taxes discussed in this chapter, income taxes and estate taxes are progressive, while the property tax is not. Property tax is an example of a flat tax because it is the same rate for all taxpayers regardless of their ability to pay. Sales tax is another example of a flat tax on consumption. Flat taxes are often mistakenly referred to as regressive taxes (i.e., tax impact goes down as income goes up), because the proportion of tax to income is higher for a person of low income than for a person of high income.

Tax liability should be simple to calculate, definite, and efficient to administer. People need to know a tax is a regular and periodic obligation, not a whim of the taxing authority. Also, the cost of collecting the tax must be substantially less than the revenue raised; in other words, the tax must be efficient. Finally, from society's perspective, a tax must be economically neutral. A tax burden should not cause wild, destabilizing swings in economic activity that would tend to destabilize local economies (Gregory 1972).

Tax equity is an elusive concept. Theoretically, it is the point where one's ability to pay is roughly equal to the taxpayer's perception of benefits received. When ability to pay far exceeds the perception of benefits, the taxpayer is apt to feel as though the burden is excessive. Even if a person has an infinite ability to pay taxes, he is restrained by feelings that his tax burden is out of proportion to the benefits he can expect to receive.

Equity is almost always an issue among forest owners, because land values on which taxes are levied are not necessarily a reflection of ability to pay, and forest lands require few or no services of the community. Because forests do not cost the community very much (nor do they put more kids in local schools), why then, a forest owner argues, are my taxes so high?

A taxing authority, whether a local town or county, or the federal government, is guided by two principles: (1) It must raise sufficient revenue to cover its obligations, and (2) its policies must promote (or at least not disturb) economic stability while fostering growth at a sustained and acceptable level (Gregory 1972). Local communities traditionally raise revenue through property taxes, while state and federal governments have relied on more progressive taxes, such as the income tax.

Property Tax

Property tax, also known as an *ad valorem* tax (Latin for "at value"), is levied on the fair market value of real estate and, in some parts of the country, personal property—both tangible property, such as cars and boats, and intangible property, such as stocks and bonds. It is the primary source of revenue for local municipalities, and for that reason it is jealously guarded as one of the few means of local control left to residents.

Local tax rates are determined by allocating the total cost of running the municipality (including the cost of public schools in most areas, which is 70 to 80 percent of the total) over the assessed value of property in the town, also known as the *grand list.* Periodic assessments, usually based on arbitrary rules and often notoriously inexact, are used to compile the grand list. When the municipality approves a budget, often by popular vote, the tax rate is determined by dividing the budget by the grand list. For example, a town with a $385 million grand list and a budget of $7.5 million will have a tax rate of $1.95 per $100 of assessed value ($7.5 million / $385 million). In some areas of the country, the tax rate is expressed as dollars per thousand dollars assessed value, also known as the *millage rate* or *mil rate.* In the example above, the mil rate would be $19.50. A taxpayer can quickly figure property tax liability as $19.50 for every thousand dollars of assessed value. If an owner's forest land is assessed at $250,000, the property tax—at a mil rate of $19.50—is $4,875.

In many areas of the United States, property taxes are the principal source of funding for schools, and the majority of revenue raised goes to the public school system. Wealthy communities have the best schools, but because recent state supreme court decisions (Vermont, New Hampshire, and elsewhere) have found that adequate funding of public education is a state responsibility, the structure of local property taxes—and school funding—is changing. Wealthy communities are enraged about sharing their ability to raise revenue with poorer communities for what they see is a responsibility of state government. Exactly how sharing occurs is still the subject of much debate, but the overall effect is that of a statewide property tax.

Collecting property tax is a relatively simple matter of multiplying the tax rate times the assessed value of each taxpayer's property and sending out bills. In many communities, taxes are spread over two to four payments in a year. Some communities will offer an incentive rebate to people who pay their taxes in one payment. If a taxpayer disagrees with an assessment, he or she can launch an appeal first with a local board of civil authority, then through the court system. Local appeals are fairly common, but court battles over property taxes are not.

It is pointless to appeal an assessment unless you have documented an error or oversight in the assessor's figures. Unfortunately, this almost always involves neighbors, since their assessments are the basis for comparison. Winning a small concession on your property taxes may not be worth alienating neighbors and friends. Also, launching an appeal on the grounds that all forest land is overtaxed will not work. The review board is charged with reviewing each case independent of another. Its job is to resolve disputes, not to change public policy. Most taxpayers use moral outrage as the impetus for an appeal. They soon learn how quickly moral outrage turns to frustration in front of a citizen's board that must make decisions on the basis of facts, not feelings.

It is common practice, where state law allows, for a community to manipulate assessments so that tax rates appear to be lower than they really are. In this way, a community can attract businesses and development and then shift the tax burden onto the new properties. Some states require municipalities to assess property at 100 percent of fair market value. This is almost always the case in states where there is an attempt to equalize revenue for schools in property-poor versus property-rich towns. Forest owners with land in communities that assess property at less than fair market value have little grounds for appealing their assessments. In states where full fair market value assessments are required by law, forest owners quickly learn that careful forest-management practices and a commitment to long-term forest use have virtually nothing to do with assessment of fair market value.

Property assessment is purportedly based on fair market value of an asset at its potential highest and best use—in an economic sense. The problem with this concept as it relates to forest land is that it requires land be assessed as though it were being held in inventory for development, since development (from the perspective of the keepers of the grand list) is the highest and best economic use of the land. Many tragic stories are told of tree farmers with developable land being taxed out of business and forced to sell. The irony of this situation is that most people in the community would prefer to see forest land remain intact. Studies have also shown that the increased tax revenue from developed forest land usually falls far short of the extra costs to the community for services demanded by people moving into the town, including the cost of new schools for their children. Developed land costs a community more than undeveloped land, and the community that encourages development gets sucked into a revenue spiral that is nearly impossible to escape.

Most states have programs that allow forest land to be taxed at its current-use value rather than fair market value. Requirements vary, but generally the owner must agree not to develop the land. If the land is sold, the new owner usually has the option of continuing the former owner's uses or changing the use and paying a penalty. In some states, a forest owner must grant a lien or an easement—in favor of the state—which stays with the title forever or until the land is developed or the lien is reacquired by the current owner. The purpose of these programs is to allow individuals to practice long-term forest management without the annual burden of property taxes based on nonforest uses.

Many forest owners do not participate in these use-tax assessment programs because they feel as though the state is dictating how land is to be managed, or they are concerned about clouding the title with liens and easements. Those are valid concerns, but until all property is assessed based on its current—not potential—use, forest land in developing areas will continue to be overtaxed. An owner who intends to keep land intact and to pass on a forest management legacy has more to gain from current-use taxation programs than he or she—or future owners—stands to lose. For more information on these programs, contact your state extension forester (Appendix A) or call the county or town clerk. Every state now offers an alternative to ad valorem taxation of forest lands.

Finally, property taxes are considered an annual expense by the Internal Revenue Service and can be deducted each year on Schedule A for people whom the IRS calls timber investors or on Schedule C or F for people in the business of managing forest land. The difference between "investors" and people who the IRS say are "in the business" is discussed later in the section on reporting income and expenses from forest management. For those investors who do not file Schedule A, annual property tax payments can be added to the cost basis of the property and recovered when property is sold. Adding periodic costs to the current cost basis of property is known as capitalization.

Yield Tax

Some states tax income from timber sales, either in addition to a property tax based on less than fair market value or as a stand-alone tax. When assessed in addition to a property tax, the *yield tax* is sometimes called a *severance tax*. The good thing about a yield tax is that it is assessed when land is generating income. By itself, a yield tax eliminates the annual economic burden of property taxes (or lessens the burden) in years when there is no income from timber sales. With a yield tax, the owner is given an incentive to grow higher-value products over longer rotations.

Although the yield tax appears to be the perfect solution to increasingly burdensome ad valorem property taxes, it has not been widely accepted. In states where it is an alternative to annual property taxes, and taxpayers have a choice, forest owners tend to stick with the property tax. Why? Because they fail to see any clear advantage of one form of taxation over another, and they fear the uncertainty of delaying tax liability to some indefinite time in the future. People would rather pay an annoying but certain amount each year than an unknown sum in the future.

Contact your state extension forester (appendix A) to see if there is a yield or severance tax in your state. Bear in mind that from an economic perspective, a yield tax is much preferable to an annual property tax. Also, in some states it is customary for the timber buyer to pay the tax, or it is a fairly easy matter to set up the sale contract in such a way that the buyer is responsible for it.

Income Tax

IRS rules as they apply to timber are obscure and confusing. To make matters worse, it is almost impossible to obtain a consistent opinion from the IRS on a timber tax question, and tax laws are constantly changing. What references to timber that do exist in IRS literature are, at best, misleading and in some instances wrong. Even people who are very familiar with IRS rules are lost when it comes to reporting income and expenses of a timber sale and the experts on timber taxation do not always agree. Why all the confusion? In part, it is because subsections of the IRS Code deal specifically with timber. Those subsections are intended to apply mostly to timber-using companies that also own and manage forests. The rules (Subsections 631[a] and [b] of the IRS Code) allow those companies to treat the sale or cutting of timber as a long-term capital gain. This is a special rule, because timber can be viewed as a wood-using company's inventory, or "stock in trade." Generally, other types of companies—from manufacturers of computer chips to disposable diapers—cannot treat income from the sale or use of inventory (i.e., microchips or diapers) as a capital gain. However, non–wood using companies can treat the sale of standing timber they might own as a long-term capital gain under the same rules available to wood-using industries. The advantages of the rules to the timber industry (and other business entities) make interpretation of the same rules as they apply to nonindustrial forest owners (nonbusiness entities) confusing and difficult, both for taxpayers and for the IRS.

The purpose of this discussion of income tax rules as they apply to timber transactions is to describe a fairly simple and straightforward way for most woodland owners to report income and expenses. Although the methods presented here meet the information requirements of the IRS under the Paper Work Reduction Act, and have been accepted by at least a few revenue agents in the northeast, they have not been formally approved by the IRS. Because some of my recommendations, especially as they apply to filing Form T (discussed later), are contrary to strict interpretations of current IRS rules, readers are cautioned to seek other opinions, especially if their circumstances differ substantially from those discussed here.

If you live in a state that has an income tax, chances are the tax is pegged to your federal tax liability, with no special steps necessary to report income from timber sales. In some states, however, the income tax is figured separately, and the rules on capital gains may differ from IRS rules. Also, your state may have a special tax on capital gains that is independent of income from other sources. Special rules may also apply if you live and pay taxes in a state that is different from the state where you sold the timber. Contact your state extension forester for information on local rules that may apply to income from timber sales.

Timber Sale Income and Capital Gains

Internal Revenue Service rules on taxation of income from capital gains have changed many times since the Taxpayer Relief Act of 1997, the first major change in more than ten years. Significantly, new laws are more favorable to investors and so are more forest-owner friendly than before. The tax rate on capital gains income used to be tied to holding period, or the amount of time an asset is owned before being sold. Under current law, timber sold after December 31, 1997 must have been held more than twelve months to qualify as a long-term capital gain. Beginning in 2004, the maximum tax rate on capital gains is 15 percent (for timber sold after May 6, 2003). Taxpayers in lower income brackets (either the 15 percent or 10 percent brackets) pay a tax rate of 5 percent on capital gains (again for timber sold after May 6, 2003).

Self-employment taxes (a self-employed person's payment into the Social Security system) are not assessed on profits from the sale of capital, whereas "other" income is subject to the tax. Self-employment tax is an important consideration for anyone who is apt to be viewed by the IRS as a sole proprietor or partner in a timber business, or individuals who are retired and have little or no income from wages or other sources. Long-term capital gains income is not taxed for Social Security purposes, and income from capital gains does not reduce Social Security payments. Unless your strategy is to build up your Social Security trust fund account, timber should always be sold in such a way as to allow treatment of profits as capital gains and not as other income. Many inexperienced forest owners report income from timber sales as "other" income on Form 1040. Amounts reported on this line are taxed at the higher ordinary income tax rates and are also assessed for self-employment tax (the net self-employment tax rate is 15.3 percent on income of four hundred dollars or more).

Another reason to report timber sale income as a capital gain: capital losses can be used to offset up to three thousand dollars of ordinary income in a particular year, and—a big advantage for some taxpayers—capital losses can fully offset capital gains. This means that a person who, say, loses in the stock market can use those losses to offset the capital gain from a timber sale so that no tax is paid on income from timber. A small consolation, but an advantage nevertheless. The law also allows carry-over of capital losses until the loss is fully recovered.

A forest owner should always sell timber in such a way as to allow capital gains treatment (see chapter 6). This means selling standing timber, not logs or the products of trees. It is a fine distinction and one not most IRS revenue agents are apt to question, so even if the method of sale is unclear, a taxpayer should still report income from a timber sale as a capital gain. In most circumstances, capital gains are reported on Schedule D, but to comply with IRS rules, you should attach a page to further explain the transaction. (Attachments to Schedule D are discussed in more detail below.)

Establishing Cost Basis of Forest Assets

One of the major tax advantages of a timber sale is the ability to offset income from the sale with a portion of the original purchase price of land and timber. Known by the unfortunate term depletion, what the woodland owner is doing is subtracting the cost of timber from gross sale income to figure profit. Although used in reference to timber sales, depletion is usually a process whereby a resource owner estimates the extent of a nonrenewable resource, like gravel or coal, then recovers the cost of the resource as it is extracted. The difference between mineral deposits and timber is that timber volumes and values can be readily estimated and verified, whereas one can only guess the extent of a mineral deposit. When forest owners deplete the cost basis they have tied up in timber, all they are doing is subtracting the original cost of the timber to figure net profit. The concept of depletion is to timber what depreciation is to equipment used in a business; the taxpayer recovers cost as the timber or equipment is used up.

The cost basis of any asset is the sum of its costs up to the present. It is composed of the original cost plus allowable amounts that may have been added to the basis over time, less any amounts that may have been recovered through depreciation or depletion. When an asset is sold, the taxpayer subtracts its current cost basis before figuring gain or loss from the sale.

Although the concept of cost basis is simple, it is not always easy to calculate, especially for timber. Why? Because timber is usually purchased with land, buildings, and other improvements all for one price. Before a woodland owner can recover the cost basis of timber sold, he or she must first determine what portion of the total cost basis of all assets is attributable to timber. This process is one of making an allocation to different accounts. In the example that follows, the owner has set up two accounts, land and timber. Only that part of the total cost basis that is *reasonably and fairly* allocated to timber is subject to depletion. Land is never depleted until it is sold outright. To determine if an allocation to timber is correct, the IRS applies the test of reasonable and fair to support its determination.

For many woodland owners, the cost basis of land and timber is attributable mostly to the original purchase price of the property. However, any carrying charges, such as taxes, interest, and insurance, not taken as a deduction in the year they were incurred can be added to the cost basis.

Consider the following example and assume there have been no additions to the basis and no deductions up to the current year:

Ms. K acquires 130 acres of forest land in the spring of 1997. She paid $45,500, or $350 per acre. An inventory of the timber was completed by a forester in the fall of 2005. He estimated the current inventory to be 456.2 mbf (thousand board feet) and 1,593 cords. He also estimated average annual growth rate at 2.2 percent. The forester deducted the equivalent of nine years of forest growth (actually, nine growing seasons) to arrive at an estimate of the volume when the land was acquired: 375.05 mbf of sawtimber and 1,310 cords of fuel-quality wood (figure 8.1).

The value of the timber inventory on the date of purchase: sawtimber = $31,879 ($85/mbf), cordwood = $9,825 ($7.50/cord). The unit values for sawtimber and cordwood were obtained from information on timber sales in the area in 1997. Total timber value on the date of purchase was $41,704 (sawtimber + cordwood).

The 1997 fair market value of timber is estimated to be about 92 percent of the total purchase price of land and timber combined. Although this may seem reasonable to the woodland owner, it will not seem reasonable to a revenue agent during an audit. The IRS stipulates that the cost basis of assets must be allocated according to the separate fair market value of each asset independent of the other, and bare land never has a value of zero or less.

> Ms. K investigates the value of her land as bare, cutover property. After much prodding on her part, she finally obtains a realtor's estimate of what her land would have sold for in 1997 without the timber on it. The realtor believes the property might have brought $90 per acre for the tract as bare, cutover land. The 1997 fair market value of bare land is $11,700 (130 acres times $90/acre). She has a letter to this effect on the realtor's stationery and will use it if necessary to document and defend the fair market value of bare land.

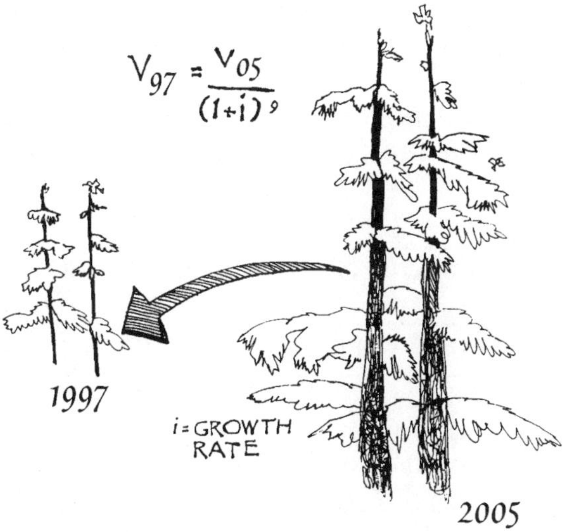

Figure 8.1. Discounting applied to a current forest inventory is used to estimate inventory at some point in the past.

With information on the fair market value of each asset (independent of the other), she can allocate her cost basis to the land and timber accounts as shown in table 8.1. It is important to remember that cost basis is the amount of money that an owner has tied up in the asset, not the current fair market value.

The allocation must be reasonable and fair, not arbitrary. In fact, Ms. K may have been able to argue that because of limited access, steep topography, or other constraints on nonforest uses of the property (such as for development), the fair market value of bare land is an even smaller proportion of the total basis of the property. Despite the claims of some economists that cutover forest land can actually have a negative value (after all, who wants to buy cutover land and pay taxes on it?), the IRS insists that some portion of the total cost basis of land and timber be allocated to a bare-land account.

Once the allocation to separate land and timber accounts has been made, the timber account can be further divided into subaccounts for regeneration, young growth, or other product categories. This is especially important if and when Ms. K decides to sell timber. She can create as many subaccounts as she likes, but in this example she sets up two—sawtimber and cordwood. Again, she allocates timber cost basis according to the separate 1997 fair market value of each asset, but divides the cost basis for the asset by its current (2005) inventory to obtain the "unit basis for depletion," as shown in table 8.2.

When timber is sold, its cost basis can be depleted in proportion to the amount of current inventory that is harvested. If 25 percent of

Table 8.1. Allocation of cost basis to separate land and timber accounts.

Asset	Fair Market Value	% of FMV	Cost Basis
Land	$11,700	22	$10,010
Timber	$41,704	78	$35,490
Totals	$53,404	100	$45,500

Note: The allocation of $35,490 to the timber account is based on Ms. K's calculations that show 78 percent of the total FMV of land and timber combined is fairly attributable to timber—$45,500 x 0.78. The balance of purchase price is attributable to bare land, in this case $45,500 x 0.22. Essentially, Ms. K paid $45,500 for $53,404 worth of assets; she got a deal.

the current inventory is harvested, 25 percent of the current timber cost basis can be recovered. An easy way to do this is to create a unit basis for depletion by dividing the available cost basis by the current inventory. In this example, for every thousand board feet Ms. K sells in 2005, she can deduct $59.12 from gross sale income.

In future timber sales, Ms. K must recalculate the unit basis for depletion by completing an inventory before the sale, or by growing the residual inventory by the average annual growth rate (figure 8.2). Whatever basis is available at that time is divided by inventory to calculate the unit basis for depletion. Because forest stands grow (while the cost basis of assets usually stays the same or shrinks as basis is recovered during timber sales), the unit basis for depletion gets smaller and smaller with each succeeding sale. The only time it ever reaches zero is if the entire inventory is sold, or when land and timber are sold outright.

If you have acquired forest land in the past thirty years, you should investigate the cost basis of your property. Most forest land (especially in the East) acquired before the mid-1970s probably has an original cost basis that is so small compared to the current value of timber as to not warrant the trouble of calculating cost basis. Furthermore, a valuable stand of sawtimber on a good site today may have been a relatively low-valued stand of pole-size timber as little as ten years ago. The allocation of cost basis can be done at any

Table 8.2. Allocation of the 2005 timber cost basis to separate sawtimber and cordwood subaccounts.

Asset	Fair Market Value	% of FMV	Timber basis	Unit basis for Depletion
Sawtimber	$31,879	76	$26,972	$59.12/mbf
Cordwood	$9,825	24	$8,518	$5.35/cord
Totals	$41,704	100	$35,490	

Note: The allocation of timber cost basis to product subaccounts is handled in the same fashion as the original allocation in table 8.1. In this example, it is the separate FMV of sawtimber and cordwood on the date of acquisition that is used to make the allocation to timber and cordwood subaccounts. The unit basis for depletion is the total amount in each subaccount divided by the current inventory. For sawtimber it is $26,972 divided by 456.2 mbf, which is the inventory immediately preceding the sale in the fall of 2005.

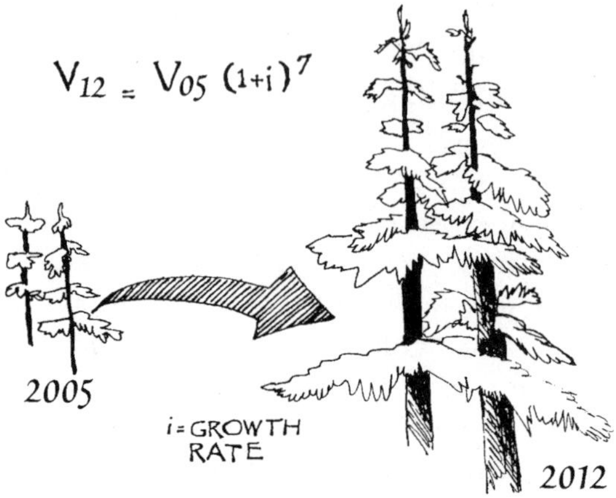

Figure 8.2. Compounding applied to a current forest inventory is used to estimate inventory at some point in the future; in this case, after seven growing seasons.

time. However, it must reflect the actual fair market value of timber on the date the property was acquired.

When land is acquired by gift, the donor also gives whatever basis he or she has in the land. The cost basis for the new owner is the donor's basis plus any gift taxes that might have been paid. For land acquired by inheritance, the cost basis of the property is "stepped up" to the fair market value as of the date the decedent passed away, except as noted below (the stepped up basis rules are slated to change in 2010, as noted later in this chapter). This includes the share attributable to a "joint tenant with rights of survivorship" or by "a tenant by the entirety" who dies. For instance, when a husband and wife own woodlands as joint tenants and the wife dies, half the basis they jointly held in the timber is stepped up. This is an important point to keep in mind when planning your estate. Giving forest land with little or no cost basis may, in the long run, be more expensive to your children than if they were to inherit the forest. Also, if you are faced with having to sell timber to help pay the expenses of an illness preceding the death of a spouse, you are better off waiting until after the spouse dies to take advantage of the stepped-up basis.

Beginning in tax year 2010, the stepped-up basis will no longer apply. The basis of inherited assets will be equal to the decedent's basis or the fair market value of the assets when the decedent died, *whichever is less.* The good news, however, is that the law will allow a stepped-up basis of up to $1.3 million per decedent, which should cover most forest owners. On property passing between spouses there is an additional $3 million step-up in basis. Since spouses are treated as separate taxpayers, the first spouse to die can pass up to $4.3 million in stepped-up basis to a surviving spouse, but when the surviving spouse passes the limit is $1.3 million. On jointly owned assets, these rules apply to half the total value, as noted in the previous paragraph.

Forest-Management Expenses

There are three types of costs borne by forest owners that are not tied to timber sales: annual expenses, carrying charges, and capital expenditures. Keeping track of costs is important because eventually these costs can be used to offset income. This is known as recovering costs, since the effect is to lower taxable income in the year the costs are claimed. The costs associated with timber sales are handled differently. All reasonable and necessary timber sale expenses are deducted from the gross proceeds of the sale to figure capital gain. (Timber sale expenses are discussed in more detail in the next section.)

Annual expenses include such costs as foresters' fees, expenses of maintaining boundaries, road maintenance, equipment depreciation, and other similar expenses that are annually recurring and short-term in nature. Carrying charges include costs such as taxes, interest expenses, insurance, or any recurring costs that maintain or protect the value of assets. Capital expenditures include the cost of purchasing more land, permanent improvements to the land (such as a pond or a house), and the cost of tree planting.

In most circumstances, a taxpayer is better off (financially) to recover expenses in the same year they are incurred, because inflation dictates: "A dollar today is worth more than a dollar next year." Unless a forest owner is materially and actively involved in managing the land, however, annual expenses can be recovered only to the extent of investment income. Carrying charges can be annually expensed or added to the cost basis of assets, at the discretion of the taxpayer, but capital expenditures must be capitalized and recovered only when the capital is sold (there are exceptions to this rule, as described below). For an investor in timber, there are limitations on the extent to which management expenses can be deducted from other (noninvestment) sources of income.

If a forest owner's annual expenses are substantial, it is an advantage to be "materially and actively" (IRS language) involved in management of the forest. This is the IRS's test of who is and who is not "in the business" and is discussed in greater detail below. Also known as the Passive Activity Loss Rules promulgated by the Tax Reform Act of 1986, the purpose is to severely limit the extent to which limited partnerships can create business losses on paper solely for the purpose of sheltering from taxation income from other sources. Fortunately, for forest owners the test to determine who is and who is not in the business is based on the facts and circumstances of each situation. If a woodland owner (and spouse) can demonstrate they have done all that is necessary to the manage the forest for which they are claiming the expenses, they will generally be viewed by the IRS as "in the business." This type of taxpayer would report annual forest-management expenses and carrying charges on Schedule C or Schedule F, although Schedule F is for farming businesses and Schedule C is for any type of business. Forest businesses should probably use a Schedule C. There is some dispute among experts as to which schedule—F or C—is more appropriate for forest owners. Most favor Schedule C, but all agree that consistency—using the same form each year—is of primary importance.

If a woodland owner investor does not itemize deductions on Schedule A, there is no way to report annual forest-management expenses and carrying charges, such as taxes. A strict interpretation of IRS rules is that annual expenses not recovered in the current tax year should not be added to the basis of assets. Many taxpayers, however, do so, using the argument that an annual expense not claimed in the current year becomes a carrying charge. The flaw of this argument is that an item once treated as an annual expense must always be treated as an annual expense.

Of the cost items most owners will want to expense—or deduct from current income—in a given year, property taxes should be at the top of the list. Even timber investors who itemize deductions using Schedule A can report property taxes and are not limited by the Passive Activity Loss Rules. However, if you have never reported property taxes on Schedule A (because you have never itemized deductions), you should be able to sum them up for the years you owned the property and add them to the total cost basis. A portion of those costs can then be recovered each time you sell timber. Woodland owners who are "in the business" can report annual expenses on Schedule C or Schedule F. Those who are not in the business of growing forests should try to associate expenses with timber sales. As long as the expense is "ordinary and necessary" (IRS language) it can be used to offset income from the sale of timber.

Passive Activity Loss Rules and Accelerated Depreciation

In 1986, during the second term of the Reagan administration, Congress passed what experts have touted as one of the most significant tax reforms since the income tax was adopted to raise revenue for the Civil War in 1862. Inauspiciously named the Tax Reform Act of 1986 (TRA), it was intended to be "revenue-neutral" by increasing taxes on businesses to pay for lower taxes on individuals. Since 1986 there have been more changes in the tax code (ten including four changes since 2001) than at any other time in the history of income taxation. But none of the other changes—before or since TRA—have had as much effect on the way people pay taxes.

By far the most stunning effect of TRA was empowering IRS to set boundaries on the long-standing concept of "regular, continuous and substantial" as the acid test of a taxpayer's involvement in a business. And it did so with the addition of two words: "material participation." The idea was to create a clearer distinction between taxpayers who wanted to *appear* to be involved in a business from those who actually *are* in business. Why? Because without requiring material participation it was easy and perfectly legal for wealthy taxpayers to use IRS rules to shelter income from taxation using sophisticated tax avoidance schemes. The result: ordinary taxpayers were paying a disproportionately large share of tax burden in the United States while wealthy, savvy individuals used tax shelters to pay little or no tax.

A pre-TRA tax shelter usually involved heavily financed real estate with grossly inflated "book" values. Accelerated depreciation of business assets and other book expenses charged to the company would create losses, but only on paper. These book losses were passed on to owners of the company who then used the losses to offset high salaries or taxable fees. Not all but some highly paid professionals with large taxable incomes used tax shelters to do just that: shelter their otherwise taxable income from taxation. Before TRA, losses of any kind could be used to offset income from any source. Those who could afford to buy into such ventures might have, say, two hundred thousand dollars of taxable salary offset with two hundred thousand dollars of paper losses in a company that was set up to lose money. And the cost of participating in such a venture was often 10 percent or less of the tax advantage, so in early 1980s tax shelters were very popular among the rich and well paid.

When TRA came along it split the definition of "business" into two realms: (1) an "active" business in which the taxpayer is a material participant on a "regular, continuous and substantial" basis, and (2) a "passive" business in which the taxpayer has no involvement except as a source of cash (i.e., tax shelters). With a stroke of a pen, Congress correctly categorized pre-TRA tax shelters as passive businesses. IRS developed two hundred pages of interpretive rulings to distinguish the two realms, and the taxpayer's guide, which is a condensed version of the interpretive rulings, is known as the "Passive Activity Loss Rules" (PAL), discussed below.

The genius of TRA was that it forced taxpayers to allocate their annual income into three different sources or "baskets": (1) wages, salaries, fees, and other income from active business ventures; (2) investment income including nonbusiness related interest, dividends, annuities, and income from the sale of capital assets held for investment; and (3) income from passive business ventures, defined according to PAL as income from a business in which the taxpayer is not a material participant. The heart of tax reform and the most revolutionary concept of TRA was this: losses can offset income only from the same source. In other words, judging a business venture on its ability to produce loss for the purpose of sheltering income from taxation was no longer attractive.

Before TRA most woodland owners preferred to be viewed as investors in timber because it afforded more flexibility in the way they sold timber, and there were few limitations on recovering the expenses of owning and managing forest land as itemized deductions on Schedule A. Timber businesses, on the other hand, were forced to sell timber using only one or the other of two methods. But they, too, were allowed to recover annual expenses. A timber investor's ability to recover the expenses of owning and managing forests (costs of consultants, hired labor, travel, equipment, interest on borrowed funds, and other expenses related to managing the investment) is limited to the extent of investment income (except property taxes which are still fully deductible for woodland investors who itemize deductions on Schedule A).

A woodland owner who is a material participant in a timber business, on the other hand, can recover forest management expenses against any source of income, provided: (1) it is a valid business with a profit motive, as opposed to an investment or hobby; and (2) the owner can prove that he or she is a "material participant" in the business.

Generally, an activity that shows a profit in any three out of five years is considered a "business" by IRS. But given the irregular nature of income from most forestry ventures, IRS uses other factors to determine if an activity is an investment or a business. These other factors include a combination of observations, such as: Does the owner have any expertise? Does the owner act like a business person or like an investor? How successful is the owner with the activity and are assets generally appreciating? How much time does the owner devote to the business? Does it appear as though the owner has a personal attachment to the activity or the assets? (In other words, have trees been given names?) How does the purported business compare to the owner's other assets?

It is the impression created by these factors and others taken in total that determine if an activity is truly a business or something else. For example, a lack of expertise taken by itself is not determinative. But if it appears as though the owner has strong emotional ties to the forest, or the "work" he or she does is actually recreationally therapeutic, it is apt to be viewed as something other than a business. Remember, most of the tax shelters that were eliminated with TRA involved real estate ventures, so businesses involving land that have regular expenses and only infrequent income are already suspect.

Once an activity is declared a business, the taxpayer must then demonstrate material participation in order to recover expenses against all other sources of income. It is a fairly safe bet that a taxpayer who successfully argues that an activity is a business will also pass one or more of the six passive activity loss rules, but not always. A material participant is a taxpayer (including jointly filing spouses) who:

1. Contributes more than five hundred hours annually (combining the efforts of spouses)—roughly the equivalent of one day per week—to the business with unlimited help from others.

2. Contributes more than one hundred hours annually—roughly the equivalent of one day per month—to the business with the sum of days contributed by others not exceeding twelve.

3. Contributes substantially all of the business activity with virtually no help from others.

4. Contributes less than one hundred hours per year to the activity in question, but the activity is considered "significant participation" in a larger related venture involving five hundred hours or more in total (a woodlands business as part of a farm, for example).

5. Is viewed as a material participant by any of the other tests in any five of the preceding ten tax years.

6. Participates at least one hundred hours annually and the facts and circumstances prove the taxpayer is participating "regularly, continuously and substantially" in the business.

There is a seventh test that involves personal service activities, but IRS has decided these activities do not apply to the business of growing trees.

To prove material participation it is necessary to support the facts of only one of the above tests. Although circumstances vary and this will have a bearing on which tests are most relevant, generally items 3 and 6 above are the conditions most owners of valid timber businesses will pass. According to IRS, "the extent of a taxpayer's activity may be established by any reasonable means. Contemporaneous daily time reports, logs or similar means *are not required* if the extent of such participation can be established by other reasonable means."

The term "other reasonable means" can include things like appointment books, calendars, personal organizers, computer records, or narrative summaries to back up statements of services performed and the amount of time devoted to each. Nevertheless, forest owners who want to establish themselves as material participants of a business must be able to allocate time to activities that fit the "facts and circumstances." Activities such as: communication with managers and others, recordkeeping (but different from what an investor would do), planning, business-related travel, labor, maintenance and repair, supervision, education (reading, workshops, and study), working with neighbors, and advocating for the cause of good practices in forestry.

Other forms of evidence that will support both the claim that an activity is a business, and that the taxpayer is a material participant include: a separate bank account for forest land, a notebook or diary concerning forest activities, an up-to-date forest management plan, agency relationships with service providers (as opposed to contracts for services), a library on forest management, invitations to school groups to your forest, subscriptions to related periodicals, active membership in a local forest association, capital gains reported on Form 4797 (when the buyer cuts timber) and ordinary gains and management expenses on Schedule C or F, and—finally—keep Form T (for "Timber") up to date. All of the above represent the sorts of things a forestry-oriented business would do. Taken together they represent a "reasonable means" of proving the relevant facts and circumstances of the business relationship an owner has with forests.

So what is the significance of the PAL rules? What is the principal advantage of holding and managing forests as a business rather than as an investment? Up until May 2003, the benefits were marginal. One of the biggest expenses of owning land—taxes—is still fully deductible for timber investors as well as for businesses. And most other major management expenses are usually incurred in connection with timber sales and so can be used to offset sale income.

In 2003, the Jobs and Growth Tax Relief and Reconciliation Act (JGTRRA) was passed providing incredibly lucrative savings for businesses that purchase new equipment, from early May 2003 until the end of tax year 2005. A quadrupling of the Section 179 deduction that allows businesses to write-off a portion of new equipment expenses in the first year of service is responsible for most of the savings. Before JGTRRA, only the first twenty-four thousand dollars of business equipment was deductible as a Section 179 deduction. The balance was depreciated over three to thirty-nine years, according to IRS depreciation schedules (most forestry equipment will qualify as three to seven year assets; buildings have longer periods).

In October of 2004, the American Jobs Creation Act (AJCA) extended the Section 179 benefits and other accelerated depreciation methods until the end of tax year 2007.

In 2004, the Section 179 deduction was $102,000 (on new or used equipment, provided it is new to the business), and the rules also allow a "special first-year depreciation allowance" of from 30 to 50 percent of the balance (but for newly manufactured equipment only) even before figuring normal first-year depreciation. In 2005, the amount jumped to $105,000, and in the last two years of the law amounts increased by a cost-of-living factor. So long as the total equipment expense is less than $410,000 (the threshold was half this amount before JGTRRA) the rules apply as stated above. On purchases that exceed this amount, the allowable Section 179 deduction is reduced dollar for dollar. For example, the allowable Section 179 deduction on equipment purchases totaling $450,000 is $65,000 ($105,000 less $40,000, the amount exceeding the $410,000 limit). Here's how it works.

> A forest owner purchases two pieces of equipment in 2005: a mid-size tractor outfitted with an arch and winch for skidding logs and a portable bandsaw mill. The total cost is $68,000. She reports the entire amount as a Section 179 deduction on Form 4562 (for figuring depreciation and amortization) and carries the amount over to Schedule C or F as an "equipment depreciation expense."

If the woodland owner in this example has a marginal tax rate of 20 percent (in other words, she pays twenty cents on every extra dollar of income), she saves $13,600 (20 percent of $68,000); or the equivalent of paying $54,400 for $68,000 worth of equipment. And it makes no difference if the equipment is purchased outright or financed. Despite the fact that a bank or manufacturer "owns" most of the asset, the tax benefit still goes to the buyer. Business interest expenses and sales taxes are also fully deductible.

If the purchase was in 2003 or 2004 she can still take the deduction by filing an amended return. In 2003 the deduction limit was one hundred thousand dollars for purchases up to four hundred thousand dollars. On equipment purchased before May 6, 2003 (the day after JGTRRA was signed into law), the old rules apply, which means the Section 179 deduction tops out at twenty-four thousand dollars.

Under JGTRRA, virtually any equipment that has a business use can qualify including trucks and many sport utility vehicles. In fact, due to an oversight, the accelerated depreciation benefits described above also applied to more than fifty sport utility vehicles and pickup trucks whose gross weight exceed six thousand pounds. Since many businesses were using the deduction to purchase fully appointed, luxury sport utility vehicles—when a more reasonably priced sedan would have worked just as well—Congress determined to close the "luxury SUV loophole."

Under the AJCA, after October 23, 2004 a vehicle must weigh more than fourteen thousand pounds (or have a specific use such as a modified body on a lighter chasse) in order to qualify for the $105,000 Section 179 deduction. Stock vehicles weighing less than seven tons, but more than three tons, are limited to twenty-five thousand dollars. And so the luxury SUV loophole is closed.

A woodland owner who purchases a new vehicle for the tree farm business must still be able to demonstrate that the vehicle is used at least half-time for business purposes. Section 179 deduction amounts are figured in proportion to business use. In other words, if a new truck is used 80 percent for business (and the balance for personal use) then 80 percent of the purchase amount is available for accelerated depreciation benefits.

Reforestation Costs

Costs associated with getting a new crop of trees started are known as reforestation costs. These costs must be capitalized; that is, they are added to the cost basis of property and recovered when the property is sold. There is an exception to this known as the Reforestation Tax Incentives. For reforestation expenses sustained before October 22, 2004, the taxpayer can claim a 10 percent investment tax credit on the first ten thousand dollars of 2004 reforestation expenses. A tax credit is a dollar-for-dollar savings in tax liability. In addition, reforestation expenses up to ten thousand dollars (and minus half the tax credit mentioned earlier) can be amortized and deducted over the next eight years. Reforestation expenses in excess of ten thousand dollars should be capitalized in the timber account.

The rules are now substantially different for reforestation expenses after October 22, 2004. The investment tax credit has been eliminated but the first ten thousand dollars of reforestation expenses can be deducted in 2004 and subsequent years. Furthermore, any amount in excess of ten thousand dollars can be amortized over eight years.

The Reforestation Tax Incentives are a huge advantage in areas of the country where forest stands are replanted after harvest. It allows the taxpayer to recover a major portion of the cost during the first few years of the new stand. Without this program, the taxpayer would need to wait until the first timber sale to recover a portion of reforestation costs borne many years earlier. These incentives are available only for trees that are being planted for fiber production. They are not available to nurserymen and Christmas tree growers. Also, the tax benefits are subject to recapture if the land is sold for, or converted to, other nonforest uses.

Virtually every state that relies heavily on replanting has detailed information on using the tax credit, which is claimed by filing IRS Form 3468 for individuals (Form 3800 for businesses). The amortization is calculated on Form 4562, which is included in the standard Form 1040 package sent to most taxpayers. The costs of tree planting and site preparation for natural and artificial regeneration are practices eligible for the investment credit and amortization. For more information on reforestation and related tax incentives, contact your state extension forester (see appendix A).

Forestry Assistance Programs

Ever since the Clarke-McNary Act of 1924, agricultural committees of Congress have provided technical and financial assistance to private nonindustrial forest owners. The purpose of these programs is to encourage owners to manage their lands for tangible benefits like timber. The U.S. Department of Agriculture coordinates these efforts through the U.S. Forest Service. Technical assistance and cost-share funding is available for a wide variety of forestry activities, including: reforestation, site preparation, tree planting, thinning, pruning, fertilization, prescribed burning, watershed restoration, creating and protecting wildlife habitats, and protecting forests from insects, disease, and wildfire.

Financial assistance to private owners is provided mostly in the form of cost-sharing grants. Depending on the program, cost-share payments are reported as income or excluded from income. For some types of payments there is an optional excludable portion. IRS has approved exclusion of payments from income for the following programs: Forestry Incentives Program (FIP), the Forest Stewardship Incentive Program (SIP), the Forest Land Enhancement Program (FLEP), the Wetlands Reserve Program (WRP), the Environmental Quality Incentives Program (EQIP), and the Wildlife Habitat Incentive Program (WHIP). Payments to farmers under the Conservation Reserve Program (CRP) are generally excludable from income, except for tree planting cost-shares, which must be reported as income. Whether or not cost-share payments are excluded, the payments are still reported on the recipient's tax return.

With the 2002 Farm Bill, the alphabet soup of federal cost-share assistance programs was mostly eliminated or, rather, replaced by a single program: FLEP. The current complement of forestry assistance programs available directly to private owners are listed in table 8.3. Only those listed as "financial" provide money—often in the form of cost-share payments—to woodland owners. Programs listed in table 8.3 as "technical" provide services to owners but no cash payments.

Table 8.3. Forestry assistance programs available to nonindustrial private forest owners.

Program	Type of Aid	Eligible Recipient	Activities
Forest Land Enhancement	Financial	Owners	Forest improvement practices
Forest Legacy	Financial	Owners	Easements to maintain
Emergency Reforestation	Financial	Owners	Site prep and planting forest uses
Forest Health Protection	Technical and financial	Owners	Disease and insect control
Wood Product Marketing	Technical and financial	Owners	Domestic and export marketing
Forest Stewardship	Technical	Owners	Forest planning, education

Source: Gorte 2004.

Financial incentive programs are intended to make forest investments more appealing by sharing the costs of cultural practices before stands are capable of generating income from timber. Generally, these payments may be excluded from income by the taxpayer (except as noted earlier), but that may not be the best strategy. If payments are excluded, the tax benefit is subject to recapture if the owner does not maintain the practice, or if land use changes. In many instances, though, forest owners receive many thousands of dollars each year, and it may be to their advantage to exclude the payments from income, especially if they have every intention of maintaining the practice. Going forward, virtually all of the forest practice cost share programs will fall under FLEP. Recipients of federal cost share payments can expect to receive a Form 1099-G from the agency that issued the payment. Since 1099s are also filed with the IRS, a cost share recipient must account for payments in the year they are received.

The Forest Legacy program is a special type of financial assistance that helps woodland owners who want to protect their forests from development. Since its inception, however, the program has been underfunded, resulting in keen competition for grants. The purpose of grants is to buy well-managed forest lands from owners, or to obtain an easement that prevents conversion of lands to developed uses. Forest Legacy is discussed further in chapter 9.

Reporting Income and Expenses from a Timber Sale

It is a wise forest owner, regardless of status as investor or business, who plans forest-management expenses to coincide with timber sales. Income from the forest helps pay expenses and all "ordinary and necessary" (IRS language) expenses can be subtracted from the gross proceeds of the sale to figure gain. The more expenses, the lower the gain, the less tax paid.

What are "ordinary and necessary" expenses? Just about any expense that is related to ensuring the timber sale is executed according to plan. Travel, phone calls, lawyers, accountants, and consulting foresters, possibly even a portion of the cost of doing a property survey, are apt to be viewed by the IRS as ordinary and necessary. Overnight accommodations in January at a ski resort for a nonresident woodland owner, including lift tickets (for the owner and her forester), probably would not qualify as ordinary expenses of a timber sale. To meet the test of "ordinary and necessary," the expenses must first be "reasonable and fair" (IRS language).

The costs of a forest inventory and management plan—at least for the areas to be harvested—are ordinary and necessary expenses, as are the costs of gaining access. With a little extra planning, a timber access road can make a fine trail for hiking, skiing, or snowmobiling. A log landing can be cleared with a future house site in mind and the expense of wildlife habitat improvement—again, with a little extra planning—can be billed as ordinary and necessary timber sale expenses. Don't get too carried away, though. IRS rules say only the portion of a cost associated with the timber sale can be deducted. If you obtain extra services that are too obvious, such as site clearing or trail building, you must estimate the cost of those services and report them as income from the sale.

The profit, or capital gain, from a timber sale is gross income, less expenses, less depletion. If you are an investor in timber (which the IRS is apt to view many forest owners as), you report the sale on Schedule D and use an attachment to explain sales price and how you arrived at the reported gain (see figure 8.3 and figure 8.4, later in this chapter). If you are in the business of growing forests, the sale is reported on Form 4797 (with the same attachment) and the result is carried over to Schedule D. Use an attachment to show how you arrived at the sale price and how you have figured gain. Any portion of the sale that results in ordinary gain is reported on Schedule C or F.

Form T. It is probably not necessary to file IRS Form T, the Forest Industries Schedule, but this is where my opinion differs from other timber tax experts. The infamous Form-T-for-Timber is an information form only—it does not materially alter the tax you owe. Nor does it contain computations you need to perform to ensure your figures are correct. The purpose of Form T is to help the taxpayer calculate and maintain the unit basis for depletion of timber resources. It is also intended to help the IRS develop a history of the basis of forest assets in the event of an audit. IRS rules say anyone who claims an "allowance for timber depletion" must file Form T. But because the form does not materially alter tax liability, for most forest owners my opinion is that it need not be filed. A taxpayer who can demonstrate acceptable procedures for figuring the cost basis of timber, and can document adjustments to cost basis as assets are acquired or sold, has fulfilled the information requirements of the IRS. However, Form T is an excellent worksheet for figuring unit basis for depletion and keeping track of the basis of assets. For a forest owner who is actively involved in timber sales, or in the acquisition and sale of forest assets, it is good idea to obtain a copy of Form T and keep it up-to-date. But it is probably not necessary to file it every time timber is sold. An attachment to Schedule D or to Form 4797, typewritten on a plain sheet of paper and stapled to the appropriate form, should suffice to explain the particulars of a timber sale with enough detail to allow the IRS to do its business if your return is questioned.

To obtain a copy of the correct Form T, be sure you specify the "Forest Industries Schedule." Another Form T is used to report income and expenses of a trust; if you ask for "Form T," more than likely you will get the trust document. Tax forms are now available online at www.irs.ustreas.gov/.

A strict interpretation of IRS rules states that anyone who claims a deduction for depletion of timber assets must file Form T. Some timber tax experts believe this is especially true for taxpayers who are claiming to be a business. Those same experts believe Form T filed in the year of a timber sale will help prevent an audit, although there are no data to support this claim. Most revenue agents are not familiar with Form T, so seeing it attached to a return that is being examined may imply the taxpayer knows what he is doing. Regardless, there should be no penalty for not filing Form T if you have handled the cost basis of timber assets properly and the correct amount of tax has been paid. A properly prepared attachment to Schedule D should suffice, especially for timber investors—the vast majority of people who sell timber. Bear in mind, however, that using an attachment to Schedule D versus filing Form T is strictly the opinion of the author.

A Timber Sale Scenario. If you have never reported income from a timber sale, chances are good that much of what you have read in the past few sections is vague. The purpose of this section is to summarize procedures for accurately reporting income from a timber sale, and to give an example of how it is done.

You need three pieces of information to report the income and expenses of a timber sale: (1) preharvest forest inventory and average tree growth rates, (2) an accurate estimate of harvest volumes, and (3) a composite summary of timber sale income and expenses. If this is your first sale and you have not yet established the cost basis of forest assets, you will also need historical information on standing timber (also known as stumpage) and bare land prices in your area, as discussed earlier. At a minimum you will need to know how much your timber was worth (fair market value) on the date you acquired the land, and how much the bare land was worth independent of the timber.

It is almost impossible for most forest owners to estimate items 1 and 2 without the assistance of a forester. Item 1 is necessary to determine the unit basis for depletion preceding a sale. And, if you have not yet allocated the cost of land and timber to separate accounts, average growth rate is used to grow the stands in reverse (also known as *discounting*), back to the date you acquired the land. The concept of discounting is exactly the same as compounding the interest and principal in a savings account but in the other direction (see figure 8.1 and figure 8.2). A caveat of discounting is that it assumes average annual growth rate is constant, which is not usually the situation in forest stands. So long as the forests in question have not changed product classes (from cordwood-size trees to sawtimber-size trees) during the discounting period, however, using an average annual growth rate for periods of ten years or less should not be a problem. Reinventory stands after ten years.

The second item—an accurate estimate of harvest volumes—is necessary for bookkeeping purposes. By subtracting actual harvest volumes from presale inventory, you can estimate the postsale inventory or how much is left in the stand after the sale. Using average annual growth, you can grow postsale inventories to estimate available volumes for another sale within a ten-year period. For instance, if you have a sale in the same area three years after the first sale, just grow the inventory left after the first sale by the average annual growth rate (see figure 8.2). This will tell you the current volume immediately preceding the sale, which is used to calculate the unit basis for depletion for that sale.

The third item—a composite summary of timber sale income and expenses—is necessary for obvious reasons, but the information is not always readily available. If you work with a consulting forester, part of his or her services should be to maintain a summary of timber sale income for you and to deliver a copy when the sale is completed. If you work directly with a timber buyer, it is usually your responsibility to keep track of receipts from the mill. Keeping a record of expenses is also your responsibility. Expense claims of more than twenty-five dollars will require a receipt, and only ordinary and necessary expenses are allowable. An expense that is only partially attributable to the timber sale must be apportioned accordingly. For example, if you obtain legal advice on a timber sale contract at the same time you are obtaining legal advice on other matters, only the portion of the cost of services associated with the timber sale can be counted.

Consider the following scenario. It is a continuation of the cost basis scenario described earlier in this chapter. If you are not familiar with the case of Ms. K and her forest land, you may want to first review the facts presented earlier. Ms. K decides to sells timber in 2005. Her forester has completed a presale inventory and discounted the current inventory for nine growing seasons at an average annual growth rate of 2.2 percent. With these data, and with information on timber prices and cutover forest land prices in 1997, he helps Ms. K allocate the original purchase price to separate land and timber accounts. He takes the cost basis attributable to timber and figures the unit basis for depletion available in 2005.

In the fall of 2005, Ms. K and her forester implement a "timber stand improvement" prescription across the entire property that yields 149.5 mbf of low-quality hardwood sawtimber and 455 cords of fuelwood. They used a "lump-sum" timber sale method (discussed in chapter 6), and received eighty-five dollars per thousand board feet of sawtimber and ten dollars per cord of fuelwood. The other facts of the sale are as follows:

Gross Income: $17,257.50

Sale Expenses:
$1,800.00 Forester fees
$80.00 Phone calls
$175.30 Travel expenses
$250.00 Lawyer fees
TOTAL $2,305.30

Depletion Allowance for Timber:

[Harvest Volumes x 2005 Unit Basis for Depletion = Depletion Allowance]
149.5 mbf x $59.12/mbf = $8,838.44
455 cords x $5.35/cd = $2,434.25
TOTAL $11,272.69

Figure Long-Term Capital Gain:
Gross Income – Sale Expenses – [Depletion Allowance = LTCG]
$17,257.50 – $2,305.30 – $11,272.69 = $3,679.51

Before 2004, the IRS had strict rules about the various timber sale methods and who could use which method. Generally, businesses were required to use somewhat riskier sale methods while investors were allowed to use sale methods that afforded the seller more protection. Of the three primary sale methods discussed in chapter 6, the lump-sum sale method is the most risk-free method for the seller. Mill tally sales and sales on the basis of shares, on the other hand, involve a higher degree of risk for the seller. So long as Ms. K sold timber infrequently under the old rules (interpreted by the IRS to mean "no more than a few times" during one's tenure with the land), she could use the lump-sum method. Forest owners who are apt to be viewed as timber businesses by the IRS were disallowed from using the lump-sum method.

Beginning in 2005, however, the rule changed—by an act of Congress. Now anyone—business or investor—can use the lump-sum sale methods with no restrictions on frequency. In other words, it is no longer necessary for the seller to "retain an economic interest" (IRS language) in timber until it is measured. This is a very significant rule change that affords a much greater degree of protection for forest owners.

Returning to the example, Ms. K uses a lump-sum sale method and reports the sale on Schedule D with an attachment that explains how the capital gain is calculated (figure 8.3 and figure 8.4).

If Ms. K was attempting to establish herself as a timber business, she could still use the lump-sum sale method but otherwise she would report income from the sale according to the provisions of IRC Section 631(b). As a business, she may also want to report the sale on Form T.

If she decides to cut the timber herself (or hires a subcontractor to do the work) she must report income from the sale under the provisions of IRC Section 631(a). The primary differences between subsections (a) and (b) have to do with the involvement of the timber owner in the conversion of standing timber into logs. Section 631(b) is for outright timber sales of timber-owning businesses, and section 631(a) is for timber-owning businesses that want to treat the cutting of timber as though it is a sale of capital to itself. (Why such a ridiculous premise? Only standing timber can be treated as a capital asset; once it hits the ground it is an ordinary asset. Section 631(a) allows a timber-owning and log-using business the capital gains advantage on the conversion of

Part II **Long-Term Capital Gains and Losses—Assets Held More Than One Year**

	(a) Description of property (Example: 100 sh. XYZ Co.)	(b) Date acquired (Mo., day, yr.)	(c) Date sold (Mo., day, yr.)	(d) Sales price (see page D-6 of the instructions)	(e) Cost or other basis (see page D-6 of the instructions)	(f) Gain or (loss) Subtract (e) from (d)
8	TIMBER	4-1-97	10-15-05	14952 20	11272 69	3679 51
		—	SEE	ATTACHMENT —		

9	Enter your long-term totals, if any, from Schedule D-1, line 9	9	
10	**Total long-term sales price amounts.** Add lines 8 and 9 in column (d)	10	14952 20
11	Gain from Form 4797, Part I; long-term gain from Forms 2439 and 6252; and long-term gain or (loss) from Forms 4684, 6781, and 8824	11	
12	Net long-term gain or (loss) from partnerships, S corporations, estates, and trusts from Schedule(s) K-1	12	
13	Capital gain distributions. See page D-1 of the instructions	13	
14	Long-term capital loss carryover. Enter the amount, if any, from line 13 of your **Capital Loss Carryover Worksheet** on page D-6 of the instructions	14	( )
15	**Net long-term capital gain or (loss).** Combine lines 8 through 14 in column (f). Then go to Part III on the back	15	3679 51

Figure 8.3. Sample Part II, Schedule D, Form 1040, reporting timber sale income for 2005. Note the reference to an attachment that explains how sale price is calculated.

timber into logs.) Section 631(a) is commonly used by Christmas tree growers who are allowed to treat the conversion of standing trees into Christmas trees as a capital transaction (if the trees are more than six years old at the time of harvest and sold without the roots attached).

For more information on subsections 631(a) and 631(b), see *Forest Owner's Guide to the Federal Income Tax* (2001). Another excellent source is the National Timber Tax website: www.timbertax.org/. Remember, forest owners who are (or appear so to the IRS) in the business must file under the provisions of either IRS Code Section 631(a)—if the taxpayer cuts the timber—or under Section 631(b)—if standing timber is sold to a buyer.

Deductions for Timber Losses. Losses in timber caused by fire, storm, flood, or any other sudden, unpredictable event can generally be deducted against income in the year the loss occurs. The loss must be "sudden, unexpected, and unusual" (IRS language) to qualify as a

Attachment to Schedule D (Form 1040)
2005
for
Mrs. K
123–45–6789

Volume of timber sold:

149.5 mbf of mixed hardwoods and 455 cords of fuelwood in standing culls and tops.

This was a lump-sum sale that took place during October and November of 2005. Timber was paid for at the following rates specified in our contract:

Sawtimber: $85.00 per mbf
Fuelwood: $10.00 per cord

*Recovery of the cost basis in timber through depletion is based upon an allocation of the original purchase price of land and timber to "**Land**" and "**Timber**" accounts according to the separate fair market value of each asset on the date of acquisition (4–1–97). The following unit rates of depletion are based on the total adjusted cost basis in the timber account divided by the standing inventory of timber and fuelwood immediately preceding the sale:*

2005 Depletion Units

Sawtimber: $59.12
Fuelwood: $5.35

Sales price (col. d) is calculated as follows:

Gross Income: $17,257.50

Less the following sale-related expenses:

Consulting forester	**($1,800.00)**
Phone & Travel	**(255.30)**
Lawyer fees	**(250.00)**
Sales price:	**$14,952.20**

Cost or other basis (col e) is calculated as follows:

149.5 mbf times $59.12/mbf plus 455 cords times $5.35/cord = $11,272.69

Gain (col f) is calculated as follows:

Sales price [$14,952.20] - Cost basis [$11,272.69] = $3,679.51]

Figure 8.4. Sample attachment to the Schedule D, Form 1040, in figure 8.3, describing how sale price is determined.

casualty loss. The IRS has taken the position that losses from drought do not meet the test. However, there are instances when—on appeal—losses from drought "of unprecedented and extraordinary severity" were treated as casualty losses. Losses from pollution, insect infestations, or disease depredations usually are not considered "sudden, unexpected, or unusual" enough to be accepted as casualty losses. Also, even though a flood can create a casualty loss, losses from flooding in flood-prone areas do not qualify. Keep in mind, too, that a casualty loss cannot exceed the timber's adjusted basis (which is not the same thing as fair market value). The loss is figured by first estimating gross loss then subtracting income received from salvage and any insurance payments. For more information on casualty losses of timber, see *Forest Owner's Guide to the Federal Income Tax* (2001), mentioned earlier.

Form 1099. Whenever you receive payments of six hundred dollars or more from another nonwage source, the payer is required to file a Form 1099 with the IRS. The purpose is to allow the IRS an easier method of tracking money changing hands. If you worked with a consulting forester during a timber sale, the forester may have acted as the banker for the transaction (assuming you established a fiduciary relationship with the consultant). All stumpage or log payments went into the consultant's escrow account, and from that account he or she drew payments or commissions and then issued payment(s) to you. In a case such as this the consultant is required to file a Form 1099-S reporting the gross income from the timber sale (less commissions or other payments). The figure reported on Form 1099-S is "gross sale income" used to figure "sales price" in Part II, Column d of Schedule D (see figure 8.3). If the forester has already deducted a commission and other expenses of the sale, you must not subtract those sums again from the Form 1099-S amount to figure sale price. You may have other expenses, though, such as phone charges or attorney fees, to subtract from gross sale income.

If you receive stumpage payments directly from the buyer, every time you receive a payment of more than six hundred dollars, the buyer is required to file a Form 1099-S. This is especially true for Section 631-type sales. The sum of those payments is used to figure the sale price on Schedule D. When you make payments to the consulting forester (if that is the arrangement you have) or to others for services, you are required to file a Form 1099-MISC.

It is important to keep these forms straight. IRS computer programs that scan taxpayer returns look for 1099 income in certain places. The 1099-S is for "Gross proceeds from real estate transactions" (IRS language), so the program "looks" on the taxpayer's Schedule D—just where you want it to look. The 1099-MISC is for nonemployee compensation, which is exactly what your payment to the forester is. The program will look for this income on the forester's Schedule C. Also, don't be surprised if the timber buyers and foresters you work with do not issue 1099s. Even though it is the law, compliance is low. Don't rely on 1099s from people you do business with for record-keeping purposes. It is not unreasonable, though, to request 1099s of the buyer or forester—in writing—before the sale begins or as a condition of the contract.

Handling an Audit. Many forest owners believe that reporting the income from a timber sale as a long-term capital gain will trigger an audit. This is not true. Although in a particular year the IRS may screen returns using capital gains or losses and other parameters as flags, Schedule D is used so commonly by most taxpayers it is automatically included in the Form 1040 package. Your chances of an audit are no greater than almost anyone else's, probably less than 2 percent in any tax year.

In the unlikely event that your return might be examined, keep meticulous notes and records pertaining to the timber sale. Maintain a diary of management activities and the time devoted to each. The IRS is usually two to three years behind, so the only way to survive an examination is with good records. Another reason for good records: so the examination can be handled by mail. The burden of proof is on the taxpayer not the IRS (although this appears likely to change eventually). Even though the revenue agent will come across as an expert on timber sales, he or she probably knows very little about forests and timber. Appropriate forms and procedures aside, the agent is looking to see if you have been reasonable and fair. If you have stretched interpretations of IRS rules so they are always in your favor, your return will be questioned.

Always request that an IRS forester is present during the audit (if the main subject of the audit is timber related). The forester, of which there is at least one in each IRS region, will act as an interpreter for the auditor, since IRS auditors know very little about expenses and income from timber sales.

The most expensive aspect of settling a dispute with the IRS that goes against you is the interest penalty on the tax, figured from the date the tax was due. You can either pay the tax and penalty or make a deposit with the IRS until the matter is settled. The IRS will refund excess tax and penalties or deduct from your deposit only the amount you owe. A deposit may be withdrawn anytime during the settlement proceedings, but a disadvantage is that the principal does not accrue interest.

If an examination cannot be settled by mail, request the audit be held on or near your forest land if questions about the return are mostly related to the forest. That way, you can easily visit the property if necessary to help explain a point. The location of the audit is the prerogative of IRS, but inviting the revenue agent to your woodlands is a good way to garner home court advantage and to show exactly what goes on when forest lands are managed.

The Potential Tax Advantages of Giving Timber

One of the provisions of the JGTRRA will allow taxpayers in the lowest brackets to completely avoid tax on profits from the sale of capital assets in 2008. This aspect of the law was a sidelight to the overall effect of lower taxes. The big story when the law passed was that tax cuts favored the wealthy and this overshadowed possibly one of the most fantastic windfalls in the history of income taxation in the United States. Best of all, it is a potential windfall especially well suited to families that own marketable timber.

As noted earlier, under JGTRRA, both the holding periods and tax rates fall, effective May 6, 2003. A "long-term" capital asset is now defined by a holding period of 366 days, versus a complicated table that offered different tax rates for holding periods of from eighteen months to five years under the old law. Capital gains rates generally drop from 20 percent to 15 percent for those in the highest brackets, and from 10 percent to 5 percent for all others, except in 2008—the last year JGTRRA changes remain in effect—when the capital gains rate evaporates to zero for those in the lowest brackets.

In 2009, capital gains rates in these lowest brackets jump from zero to 10 percent; that is, of course, unless Congress votes to retain changes. The "zero-rate-in-2008" applies to married couples who make less than fourteen thousand dollars (less than seven thousand dollars for single taxpayers) from other sources of income.

The Bush administration was able to pass this tax cut, and cuts in the estate tax as well, during a weak, wartime economy because both laws come with "sunset" provisions. When a law has a sunset provision it means that unless Congress takes action before the sun sets, so to speak, the law is revoked just as though it had never existed in the first place. Controversial changes in tax law often come with sunset provisions because without them there are few supporters. Sunsetting is a sort of legislative fail safe; if a change proves detrimental, it is not necessary for Congress to revisit its mistakes; the law simply expires and things go back to the way they were. On the other hand, sunsetting a law allows Congress to revisit one of its successes and bask in its glory.

Forest owners with marketable timber and with children or other low-income dependents who can use a windfall of cash for things like college tuition, home purchase, or for other reasons, can begin structuring gifts of timber that are to be converted into cash in 2008. If the timber sale is structured in such a way as to allow capital gains treatment, the beneficiary can end up with a sizeable untaxed gift.

Generally, when a donor makes a gift of timber, he or she also gives the recipient whatever cost basis applies to that timber. For example, the parent who paid one hundred dollars per acre for forest land in the early 1960s has a total cost basis of one hundred dollars per acre in both bare land and timber. When this same parent gives a current gift of forest land (or timber) worth a few thousand dollars per acre to a son or daughter, the original cost basis is so small in proportion to current values that when the gift recipient sells timber virtually all of the income is taxed because there is so little cost basis to offset income. The zero-rate-in-2008 eliminates this gift penalty. When the tax rate is zero, the difference between cost and current values does not matter.

Gift and estate tax rules allow taxpayers to give up to eleven thousand dollars in tax-free gifts each year to as many different people as they choose. A married couple can give twenty-two thousand dollars—half from each spouse—and the gift is tax-free to both donors and recipients. Furthermore, if the gift is restricted, the donors are allowed to discount the value of gifts. For example, if the gift is timber and conditions on the gift require the recipient to sell timber in 2008 in a manner that allows income from the sale to qualify as a long-term capital gain, the restriction may allow the gift to be discounted. And if another condition requires a recipient to use cash for a specified purpose, such as tuition or health care, the gift may be discounted further. In other words, donors can give, say, twenty-five thousand dollars in timber to create a twenty-two thousand dollar gift for tax purposes. The gift is discounted because of restrictions that affect marketability. In this case, the restrictions are fairly minor so the discount rates are small. Generally, the more restrictions placed on a gift and the more those restrictions affect marketability, the greater the discount rate. For example, gifts of an undivided interest in woodlands for the purpose of vesting children into a family forest are often discounted by as much as 30 to 50 percent. The subject of using gifts of an undivided interest in forest land as an estate planning tool is discussed in greater detail below and in chapter 9.

Here are some other considerations when giving timber to children, or other low-income dependents, to take advantage of the zero-rate-in-2008:

1. Special rules apply when the gift recipient is a young child, so you should review IRS rules on gifts to minors.

2. Remember, the zero-rate-in-2008 applies only to taxpayers in the lowest brackets. In other words, if you have been reporting a dependent's income with your own, you need to let the dependent report as a single taxpayer in 2008. If the sum of income from other sources is less than $7,000, the zero-rate on income from long-term capital gains applies. You will, however, lose the dependent as an exemption on your own return.

3. If income from the sale of long-term capital assets is too great, it may trigger an Alternative Minimum Tax (AMT). If the long-term capital gain is less than the AMT exemption, there should be no

extra tax. In 2005, the AMT exemptions are $40,250 for single taxpayers and $58,000 for married couples.

4. The current holding period for long-term capital gains is twelve months plus one day. In other words, plan to make the final gift of timber at least one day more than a year before you expect the timber sale to commence in 2008.

5. Have the recipient structure the timber sale in 2008 so that it is considered a sale of capital assets and not ordinary assets. In other words, sell timber as a lump-sum so that all payments are received in 2008, or use the mill-tally sale method. As discussed in chapter 6, the lump-sum method sells the right to cut standing trees, and the mill tally method sells standing timber that the owner retains rights to until the timber is measured at the mill. Of the two, the lump-sum method is the most risk-free for the seller, but both methods will qualify so long as the holding period is met and payments are received before the end of 2008.

6. The woodland-owning donor can use tree-marking paint to designate and differentiate gifts to more than one recipient. In other words, an orange slash marks a 2004 gift to recipient A; yellow marks a gift in the same year to B. In 2005, an orange dot marks recipient A's gift, a yellow dot marks B's gift, and so on. This type of system will require extra bookkeeping for the consulting forester, but it avoids having to designate specific sale areas for each gift.

7. Plan to sell primary-order branches in hardwood tops for fuelwood as part of the timber sale, even if the sale involves a different buyer. Income from products already on the ground is considered ordinary income not subject to capital gains rules. Only trees connected to land are considered capital.

8. It is tempting to include the spouse of your son or daughter in this type of gifting arrangement. Nevertheless, it is almost always a bad idea to include spouses in family gifts. The risk of divorce is too great, and a gift that you had intended for one of your children may end up at the center of bitter dispute over marital assets even before 2008 rolls around.

9. If you decide to discount the annual gifts, keep the rate low (less than 20 percent) and be sure to document each gift with a paper trail. Remember also that the value of gifts will appreciate between now and 2008 (due to timber growth, changes in value, and inflation) so structure gifts to avoid triggering an alternative minimum tax.

10. Finally, make sure to arrange a contract for services with a logging contractor or come up with some other way to commit both a stumpage buyer and a logger to fulfill the terms of a timber sale contract in 2008. Depending on the contract, it is probably not necessary to have all timber cut and hauled in 2008, but it is necessary that the contract is fully executed during that year to take advantage of the zero rate.

In January 2009, long-term capital gains rates go back to 10 and 20 percent and the holding period rules revert from eighteen months to five years. Only drastically positive changes in the outlook for the United States will compel Congress to revisit the Jobs and Growth Tax Relief Reconciliation Act of 2003 with a vote to retain these changes. And so the zero-rate-in-2008 is probably a once in a lifetime opportunity to give timber to children, or other low income dependents, who can completely avoid taxation when it is sold.

Estate Taxation

Recent changes in the gift, estate, and generation skipping trust (GST) tax rules, in 1997 and again in 2001, have obviated a succinct discussion in a book such as this of the effects of these taxes on the long-term decisions of woodland owners. In general these changes have allowed taxpayers to pass—by gift and by bequest—larger amounts not subject to taxation, and this is good news for most woodland owners. But the cost of lower gift and estate taxes is greater complexity, so much so that even a relatively minor taxable estate requires the expertise of an attorney who is well versed in both the laws and their current interpretations. Whether or not any given forest owner requires these services is a question of the extent of an owner's holdings, the location of those holdings relative to more developed uses of land (such as for housing), any conservation easements the owner may have passed to a qualified organization, the value of other assets, marital status, and the owner's general plans for dispersing the estate upon his or her demise. Exemption limits under current law are so generous that most woodland owners will be able to pass their entire estate untaxed. And, as of 2004, the exemption limits on the GST tax will equal the estate tax exemption. The GST tax is intended to prevent a decedent from avoiding estate taxes altogether by passing assets in trust for the benefit of grandchildren (in other words, skipping a generation). But the law that defines exemption limits on both estate and GST taxes, which gradually increases to the point of no estate or GST tax in 2010, is set to expire in 2011 unless Congress votes to retain elimination of these taxes (table 8.4).

Estate and gift taxation have been a feature of tax law in the United States since 1916, probably first promulgated to prevent the formation and continued growth of fabulously wealthy dynasties.

Table 8.4. Estate tax exemption limits and rates paid on taxable estates based on the Economic Growth and Tax Relief Reconciliation Act of 2001.

Year	Estate and Generation Skipping Transfer (GST) Tax Exemption	Highest Estate (and gift)[1] Tax Rates
2004–2005	$1.5 million	48 to 47 percent
2006–2008	$2 million	46 to 45 percent
2009	$3.5 million	45 percent
2010	Estate & GST Tax repealed	Gift tax equal to top individual tax rate of 35 percent
2011[2]	$1 million (plus inflation adjustment)	55 percent (plus 5 percent surtax)

[1] In 2002 the gift tax exemption was increased to $1.0 million where it will remain—under current law—until 2009. The estate and GST exemption is reduced by the amount of the gift tax exemption used.

[2] If Congress does not act to continue the repeal of the estate and GST tax before the end of tax year 2010, the rules revert back to those passed in 1997.

In the later half of the twentieth century appreciation of assets due to inflation resulted in more families being subject to the estate tax, a fate often discovered only after a surviving parent passed away. Since spouses have always been allowed to inherit tax-free the value of a husband or wife's share of the total estate, the heavy burden of estate tax was felt only after the surviving spouse died. With little or no planning a married couple of modest means, but owners of extensive forest holdings, could end up paying twice the amount of estate tax due or miss the opportunity to avoid estate tax altogether. Why? Because the IRS views a husband and wife as separate taxpayers when it comes to figuring taxes due on gifts and on the final estate. Thus a couple that puts the bulk of their assets into trusts, one in the name of each spouse, can shelter twice the exemption amounts listed in table 8.4. Lowering taxable estate value is discussed in chapter 9.

Another very significant aspect of gift and estate tax law not changed in 2001 are the rules that apply to tax exempt gifts. A taxpayer can make an unlimited number of gifts of up to eleven thousand dollars per recipient per year that are not subject to the gift tax. Since spouses are viewed as two taxpayers, a husband and wife can give up to twenty-two thousand per year absolutely tax free to as many different recipients as they please. These nontaxable gifts are discussed further in chapter 9 as a way to pass an undivided interest in forest land to children and grandchildren.

Under current law when a decedent passes assets to an heir the cost basis of those assets are stepped-up to their fair market value on the date the decedent passed away. This rule is especially significant when the asset is forest land and timber since a stepped-up cost basis means lower taxes on capital gains when timber is sold. In 2010, when both the GST and estate taxes are repealed, the step-up provision for inherited assets is also repealed, but with the following exception: a step-up is available for the first $1.3 million per decedent, and an additional $3 million for property passing to a spouse. Thus a spouse can have up to $4.3 million of half of jointly held assets stepped-up in basis to the fair market value on the date a decedent passed away.

Beginning in 1997, Congress allowed family-owned businesses the option to pass up to $1.3 million of business assets free of estate tax so long as the business accounted for at least 50 percent of the total estate and surviving family members agreed to keep the business going. This provision was repealed in 2004 when the personal exemption of $1.5 million exceeded the family-business exemption limits allowed under the old law.

Also under the 1997 law, an executor could elect to exclude up to 40 percent of the value of land from which a conservation easement had been donated to a qualified charitable organization. But a condition of this allowance was that the land must be located "within a 25-mile radius of a metropolitan area, a national park or a wilderness area, or within 10 miles of an urban national forest" (IRS language). The 2001 law eliminated such restrictions, thus allowing the executor of any woodland owning family to lower the taxable estate after parents have passed away, provided the other heirs agree.

Since the 1980s many woodland owning families have been surprised—usually after a surviving parent has passed away—to discover that the estate of parents of modest means turns out to be valued far in excess of expectations. These deceased "land rich, cash poor" parents often leave their children with the problems of paying estate taxes—both federal and state. With little cash on hand, the executor is forced to sell timber or land—usually to the highest bidder—and productive forest land is converted to condominiums. Repealing the estate tax will lessen the burden on forest owning families that want to keep managed lands intact, but don't expect the estate tax to disappear altogether after 2010. Tax experts estimate that raising the exemption from $2 million (in each of tax years 2006, 2007 and 2008) to $3.5 million in 2009 will lower revenue by $23 billion per year. Elimination of the tax in 2010 is expected to cost in excess of $53 billion, a hefty sum of revenue that Congress is not likely to give up. Thus, it is highly probable the estate tax will return in 2011.

Chapter 9

Planning for Woodlands in Your Estate

No one likes to think about dying so the most difficult aspect of estate planning is contemplating one's mortality. It is hard enough to effect good planning over just a few years of one's lifetime (for some of us, a few weeks). How then can one expect to plan for an indefinite future of which he or she is not even a part? Estate planning is tough business so most people put it off till the last minute or until it is too late. Mixed feelings about children, an unstable marriage, or a belief that the estate is so small as to not warrant planning are other reasons people procrastinate. Even valid excuses aside, if you own woodlands and it is your intention to keep forests intact and well managed, an estate plan is essential.

Estate planning literature commonly deals with conservation of wealth: how best to pass assets so as to avoid taxation, lower transfer costs, and divide wealth in an equitable manner. To most estate planners, forest lands are just another asset. An individual's estate is the sum of what he or she owns: cash, personal belongings, intellectual property (copyrights, patents, etc.), retirement plans, life insurance, investments, and real estate. In its simplest form the estate plan describes what happens to your property when you're no longer around to make decisions.

What makes the need for estate planning of woodlands more important than for other assets? Plenty of reasons, but foremost among them is that a reasonable planning horizon for most forest types typically exceeds a lifetime. From the perspective of decisions that are strictly good for the forest, this more than any other reason is why forest planning should always look beyond the current owner's tenure (figure 9.1). Another reason, from a strictly financial perspective: woodland values have appreciated at rates that far exceed inflation in many parts of the country. It is not uncommon for a family that always thought of itself as poor to discover an enormous equity in forest land and in some cases an estate tax is due. Often, the only way to settle an estate (pay any taxes that might be due and divvy the estate among heirs) is to sell timber before its time, or even divide the land into saleable parcels.

Estate planning is a primary issue of our times, as baby boomers watch their parents age, and parents wonder, "What do we do with our property?" Much has been written on the subject, and many excellent books cover all the angles. There are even some do-it-yourself books for people who hate to pay for legal advice. (See the references for books on estate planning that are readily accessible in local bookstores.) Forest owners who have not yet done any estate planning are encouraged to follow up this chapter with one or more other books that delve into the subject in a way that is far beyond the scope of this book. However, as much as I advocate woodland owners being actively involved in managing their lands, estate planning is not a do-it-yourself proposition. To effect a good estate plan, you need solid legal advice from someone who has experience with that body of law. Even a small, seemingly inconsequential mistake in documentation can void the entire effort, leaving the family more confused and distraught than if you had done nothing at all.

Since a surviving spouse can inherit a decedent's estate tax free, and settling an estate whose principal asset is forest can be complicated, many forest owners assume the way to avoid the hassles of estate planning is to leave everything to a spouse. The problem with that strategy is, even though a spouse can inherit free of tax an estate of "unlimited" value, eventually the surviving spouse will die, and IRS rules allow only one exemption, the amount of which depends on the year a surviving spouse dies (see table 8.4). Thus tax on the estate portion attributable to the first spouse to die is deferred until the surviving spouse passes. Even though the

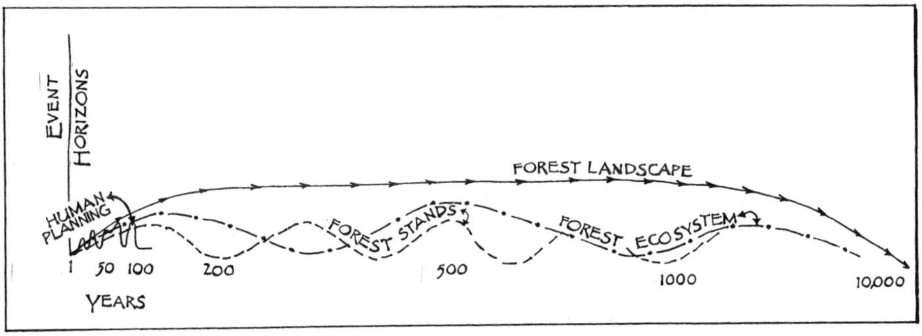

Figure 9.1. People, forest stands, ecosystems, and whole landscapes exist in different event frequencies. Human circumstances can change, month to month or year to year, while ecosystem changes—in the absence of human intervention—take place over a much longer timeframe. Good forest-management planning should exceed a single generation and recognize events at least at an ecosystem level.

exemption limits in table 8.4 are generous and cover most forest owners, it is very easy to double the exemption with planning no more sophisticated than that which goes into a good forest management plan. Why? Because when it comes to gift and estate taxation, the IRS looks upon a husband and wife as two taxpayers, not one in the form of a married couple. For this reason a husband and wife have two exemptions, one in the name of each spouse.

One of the goals of an estate plan is to arrange the assets of a family (i.e., usually the combined assets of a married couple) so as to avoid paying death taxes on amounts up to the maximum exemption of the first spouse to die, as well as on the maximum exemption available to the surviving spouse. If the total estate is worth more than the maximum exemptions available to each spouse, additional strategies can be employed to further minimize estate taxes. Gifts, donations to qualified organizations, and other methods can be used to make the estate tax as low as possible. Finally, a proper estate plan anticipates the taxes and other expenses that might be due when the surviving spouse dies and ensures a ready source of cash to pay taxes and other expenses without having to liquidate assets.

Estate transfer costs include all the expenses the family will sustain to settle the affairs of the final estate. These include federal and state death taxes, and administrative expenses such as the cost of probate to settle with creditors and to disperse the estate to heirs. Probate is the legal process of proving the validity of a will, securing authority from a court to represent the deceased and to carry out the will's provisions. A will is a properly executed legal document in which a person declares to whom his or her assets are to go after death. When a person dies without a will, the decedent's estate is said to be *intestate*. Possessions usually go to the surviving spouse and to children based on a formula defined by state law. If there is no surviving spouse and no will, the probate court resolves questions of who gets what, again by formula. Probate can take six months to three years or more, depending on the complexity of the estate and arguments raised by people who make claims against the estate. The probate process is speeded up, or avoided altogether, with good estate planning. Although probate is almost always presented in a negative context, it does have poitive attributes. For example, since the nature of probate is to settle the affairs of a decedent it is a very public process and thus a great way to keep people honest.

Precisely what is estate planning and what is the connection to forest-management planning? It is a process to consider the value and disposition of all real and personal property and property rights owned by a person, a married couple, or a family. When forests are a principal asset, estate planning is usually done in anticipation of passing the land to others, but with three things in mind: (1) to continue a forest-management legacy and to keep land intact and in the family, (2) to minimize the cost of transferring ownership when the estate is dispersed, and (3) to provide for dependents and heirs. Item 1 is usually the victim of item 3.

Continuing a forest-management legacy means providing guidance to those who will make management decisions in the future. It is their job to ensure wildlife habitats are protected, roads are maintained, timber grows to rotation, and stands are adequately regenerated. As planner, it is your job to provide leadership, direction, and continuity with clear statements about how the land is to be managed. It is easy to do this without being dictatorial, but you also want to avoid tying the hands of your heirs. They must be able to react to conditions in the future that you cannot predict. The idea is to keep woodlands in the family, to inspire your children to work with and enjoy the forest as much as you do, and to give them a course to follow with latitude to make their own decisions. You probably also want to prevent them from drastically changing the use of the land, or selling it to someone who has no intention of managing the forest. This is accomplished by putting covenants into the title, or by separating the bundle of rights through the use of easements (see chapter 3). Many forest owners are reluctant to do this, reasoning the restrictions on use will decrease the marketability of the land. It is true—all other things equal, a buyer will pay less for a title with restrictions than one without. Many experts in this field, however, believe we will see strong markets for protected lands in the future. This means your forest could actually increase in value as a result of restricting its title in your estate, so that if your children decide to sell, they will have no problem locating a buyer who wants to continue managing the woodlands. Also, more often than not the tax benefits of giving an easement for conservation purposes to a local land trust are attractive. (This is discussed in detail in the section on charitable contributions.) If there are no local land trusts, seek out like-minded people in your community and form your own. The process of forming a local land trust is discussed later in this chapter.

Aside from providing a long-term plan for forest resources, estate planning is a means of providing for dependents and heirs after you pass away. The plan identifies who will make decisions in your absence. It also provides a means for a ready source of cash to pay day-to-day expenses, outstanding medical bills, and any other expenses needed to settle affairs. A common strategy is to purchase life insurance and name a spouse, a trust, or your heirs as beneficiaries. Life insurance is not subject to probate and it is usually paid within weeks or even days after death. Do not, however, make the mistake of naming your estate as the beneficiary. Doing so assigns the insurance benefit as part of your probated estate. An insurance agent can offer more information on life insurance policies and payout options that cover expenses immediately after you die. Another ready source of cash is a jointly held savings or checking account. If you specify that the co-owner of the account has rights of survivorship, the funds in the account belong to—and are accessible by—the joint owner when you pass away.

It is often a good idea to grant a general durable power of attorney for financial matters (see chapter 6) to a spouse or family member. This will allow someone to act in your behalf if you become incapacitated. A common legal error among spouses is to execute a power of attorney that has no "durable" provisions and is not recognized as valid after the principal becomes incapacitated, although state laws on this are changing. Even with a durable power of attorney, it is a good idea to provide a copy to people with whom you do business so there is no question if something happens to you. A word of caution: a durable power of attorney is an extremely powerful legal document that authorizes another individual to act in your behalf. You must trust that person implicitly. The document creating a durable power of attorney can be drawn up, signed, and held by your lawyer with specific instructions about the circumstances under which you want to have the document passed to your designee. A durable power of attorney expires when you do, so the person who holds it must be cautioned not to try to use it after you have passed away.

As a woodland owner, it is very important to involve your children in the estate-planning process. To a large extent, the success of your efforts will depend on their interests in following your forest-management plans when your estate is dispersed to them. However, in many instances, the owner assumes a son or a daughter will take over the tree farm, but the children have no interest. This is not a problem as long as you know their feelings before leaving them the land, and they in turn understand and respect your commitment to the woodlands and will honor your plans. Even if your children do not want to be directly involved in the continued management of the family forest, you can still keep the land intact and devise a means for them to benefit from woodland income.

When it comes to estate planning, families do not communicate well. Yet it is extremely important that your heirs understand and accept your plans. Sometimes the best way to bring up the subject of estate planning with children is to ask them outright what they would like to see. You may be surprised to learn they have already given much thought to the final disposition of your assets. This is one of the reasons children do not bring up the subject—it appears as if they are waiting for you to die.

To have a meaningful conversation with children about these matters, it is important to make them feel comfortable so they speak their mind. Do not focus on the dying and loss. Rather, think about what you are leaving behind. Remember, as paraphrased from Aristotle, "A whole [life] is that which has beginning, middle, and end." Dying is as much a part of life as living. To die well is to do so in consideration of the people you leave behind. And it is an enormous responsibility to die without having given careful consideration to the long-term disposition of your forests.

The Estate-Planning Process

The first step in planning your estate is to learn more about the subject. There are many excellent resources, and workshops on estate planning for woodland owners are common in all parts of the country. Because you will need to assemble a team of experts to pull the plan together, your job is to become a well-informed consumer. Most of the current literature on estate planning assumes the reason for your interest is to shelter assets from taxation. Although this is a valid concern, there are other reasons for planning. The discussion that follows emphasizes reasons for estate planning that have to do with keeping forest lands intact, productive, and in the family.

Once you know a little more about estate planning, generate a wish list of things you would like to see happen after you are gone, just as though you were going to live indefinitely. For instance, there may be a stretch of stream on your land you have always wanted to improve for brook trout habitat. You realize now you will never get to that project in your lifetime, but you still want to see it done. Write it down.

Consider what the future might hold for forests in your area. If you believe surrounding lands may be developed in the future and important habitats destroyed, you may want to dedicate your forests, or a portion of them, to providing critical habitat for species that might be threatened. Write it down.

Perhaps you have a favorite stand of trees that you had hoped would one day become large, very highly valued, veneer-quality logs. Although the stand could be harvested now for a substantial profit, you think it best to wait. Write it down. And what about other favorite places—where you like to hunt, or ski, or picnic, or special places you find spiritually fulfilling? There may be areas of historical significance that you want to see protected, such as caves or other special habitats—anything you think is important that you would like to see managed, protected, or used after you die, write it down.

Next, assemble a list of your assets. Include everything of value to you and your family, whether it has any monetary value or not. You would be surprised to learn that something you regard as a worthless bauble is a treasure to one of your children. For the assets that have titles, find out how the property is held (see chapter 3). When you hire an estate-planning attorney, these are some of the first questions he or she will ask. If you can, try to estimate the current fair market value of each asset. Even a rough estimate will help when it comes time to partition the estate for tax purposes. Estimate the rate at which your estate is appreciating.

Meet with your children or other heirs. Tell them about your planning efforts, with special emphasis on the woodlands. The importance of this discussion is to ascertain their interest in carrying on as managers. It will also give you a sense of how to balance the value of assets to proportionally disperse your estate. For instance, if your daughter is interested in the forest (even without the development rights), you may want to offset this with a bequest of stock, bonds, or other assets to her siblings. Also, if your children express interest in specific items, such as antiques, furniture, art, or other objects, you may want to affix a note or label to the piece with the child's name on it, besides making a bequest of the object in your will. This can avoid confusion, bad feelings, or dissention among children when they divvy up your possessions. Also, do not be offended if something particularly special to you is not requested by one of your children. Try to be as objective as possible.

The estate-planning team should include your consulting forester, accountant, an estate-planning attorney, an insurance underwriter, your personal representative or executor, and, possibly, one of your children. Estate planning is a relatively new and somewhat specialized type of law practice. Chances are good that the local attorney who has always handled your work will not have the expertise to draw up and execute the necessary documents. If the attorney is also a friend, there may be bad feelings when you hire someone else for the estate plan. Under no circumstances should you feel obligated to provide legal work to anyone for reasons other than competency. In this area, even small errors are costly, and you will not be around to help clear things up. Ascertain that the attorney you work with has extensive experience in estate planning, preferably where woodland assets are involved. A good way to obtain a reference to an attorney is to inquire at your state or local land trust. Attorneys who have worked with land trusts usually have had experience with estate planning involving forests.

A good source to help locate a qualified estate planner is the American College of Trust and Estate Counsel (3415 S. Sepulveda Boulevard, Suite 330, Los Angeles, CA 90034, 310-398-1888). The college requires members to have a minimum ten years' experience in estate planning and sound local and national references. Not every qualified estate planner is a member of the college, but the college can be a good place to start your search.

An executor is the person named in your will whom you trust to handle business decisions, pay bills, and disperse your belongings to the people you have designated in your will. Anyone can serve as executor, even your attorney. Often, surviving spouses or children are appointed to represent the deceased. There are many points to consider in picking an executor that are beyond the scope of this book, but you definitely want someone who understands your commitment to the forest and is willing to ensure your requests are fulfilled—at least during his or her time of appointment. If you decide to avoid probate through the formation of a living trust (discussed later), you need to appoint a trustee, who can also serve as your personal representative.

Assuming that keeping forest lands healthy, productive, and intact is a priority, you need to locate a consulting forester who understands your goals and is capable of achieving them. This may or may not be the person with whom you have worked in the past.

The consultant must be someone you believe in and trust as much as you trust your personal representative or trustee. If you have any misgivings about consultants you have worked with in the past, it is time to shop for a new advisor. If your heirs are not apt to be up to speed about making management decisions after you have died, develop an agency relationship with the consultant, and create the necessary documentation that allows the consultant to act for your trust or your estate when you are gone. Because it is legally impossible to act as an agent of a recently dead person, it is essential the consulting forester is identified as an agent to your estate, much as you will appoint someone to be your personal representative or executor to handle your personal and financial affairs and to disperse your estate.

One of the first things the consultant will do is update the management plan, complete an appraisal of the woodlands, and document your ideas for the future forest. The woodland appraisal will probably need to be accepted and certified by a state-licensed appraiser. This is usually not a problem if the numbers in the appraisal seem reasonable.

Perhaps one of the most difficult decisions will be designating a family member through whom the consulting forester communicates with others who have an interest in the forest—at least until your affairs are settled and the estate has been dispersed. You may opt to have the consultant communicate through the executor. Or you may want to appoint one of your children or another trusted heir to work directly with the consultant to implement your plans; he or she may well also be the person who will inherit the land (less any rights you might have sold, donated, or bequeathed for conservation purposes).

Lowering Estate Value

Under current law, the estate and generation skipping trust taxes are eliminated in 2010, but no one expects that Congress will allow this source of revenue to evaporate permanently. A slight consensus believes Congress will bring these taxes back with a $2 million exemption adjusted each year to account for inflation. Even though it would make perfect sense to allow well-managed farm and forest lands to pass untaxed from one generation to the next, the chances of such a dispensation are not worth betting on. Given the long-term nature of forest investments, woodland owners should always know the approximate value of their holdings and the current laws that affect estate taxation. Beyond this, it is all guesswork.

Estate planning to most people means avoiding estate taxation. If the value of your assets exceeds the gift and estate tax exemption limits discussed in chapter 8, your estate will owe a tax. An important part of the estate-planning process is figuring out the fair market value of your estate, or approximately what you think it might be worth on the date you (or your surviving spouse) will pass away. Obviously, it is impossible to be precise, and no one expects you to die as "planned." Make a good guess, though, because if the value exceeds whatever exemption limits are in place a tax may be due.

If you know the total estate value (plus taxable gifts) exceeds the exemption limits in table 8.4, you can begin lowering your estate's value by making tax-exempt gifts, charitable contributions, giving or willing certain rights to conservation organizations, and by other means. You and your spouse can also establish the special tax-saving forms of a living trust to avoid taxation on the portion of the surviving spouse's estate that exceeds the maximum exemption. Remember, the surviving spouse can inherit an estate of unlimited size; but when that spouse dies, only one exemption is available. If the exemption available to the first spouse to die is not used to set up a trust, it is permanently lost to the family's estate.

A living trust can be designated to divide the family's assets into two trusts, thereby taking advantage of the exemptions available to husband and wife. It is an excellent way to beat the estate tax (or at least lower taxes), avoid probate, and keep forest land in the family. (Trusts are discussed in more detail later.)

Sharing Property with Children. When title to property is held between two or more people as "joint tenants with rights of survivorship" (often abbreviated on documents as JTRS or JTROS), the surviving joint owners automatically own 100 percent of the property when one owner dies. An interest that someone has in a JTROS property title is not part of the person's probate estate. Whatever interest the decedent had in the property automatically reverts to the survivors. Consequently, many families mistakenly use this strategy to remove assets from a parent's estate to avoid estate taxes on the property. Unless the children can prove they contributed to the formation of the joint tenancy, or the joint tenancy was formed as a result of a long-term, tax-exempt gifting strategy, the full value of the JTROS title is included in the decedent's estate for estate tax purposes, even though ownership has automatically passed to the surviving children. In other words, simply changing the property title to include children is not a valid strategy to lower estate value. Also, when you share title as joint tenants, you give up control of the property, and a joint tenant cannot sell his interests without consent of the others (state laws vary in this matter). Fortunately, a joint tenant's share is usually not very marketable.

Another, more acceptable way to share title with children and lower estate values at the same time is discussed in the sections on family partnerships and limited liability companies.

Personal Gifts. The IRS allows a single taxpayer (donor) to make annual, tax-exempt gifts of up to eleven thousand dollars per individual (donee) to an unlimited number of donees. A married couple (considered to be two taxpayers by the IRS) can give twenty-two thousand dollars in tax-exempt gifts per donee. So long as the gift is less than these amounts, no federal gift tax is due (although a state gift tax may be due). Also, the gifts do not reduce or consume the exemption on lifetime gifts; they are entirely exempt from federal taxation (so long as the gifts meet the conditions described above). A gift can be cash or anything of value, but it must be given unconditionally and be immediately negotiable for its fair market value on the date of the gift. In other words, the gift must be worth the amount claimed when the gift was made.

Conceivably, a married couple owning forest land could give undivided interests in woodlands to their children in the amount of twenty-two thousand dollars per child per year. If those children are married, the gift can be as high as forty-four thousand dollars to each married couple (that is, twenty-two thousand dollars per donor spouse to each donee son and his wife, who is also a donee). However, since the gift must be unconditional, this may not be the best way to handle forest assets. A cash-strapped son might be forced to sell his gift despite your wishes. There is also the possibility of divorce, and remember that the gift carries with it whatever basis you have in the property (at least until 2010, see chapter 8). If your cost basis in forest land is small in proportion to current fair market value, your family may be better off to inherit forest land rather than receive it as annual gifts. Before making this determination, however, review the section on estate taxes in chapter 8 and seek the advice of a qualified estate planner. Also, regardless of a gift's basis there are ways to make annual tax-exempt gifts of forest land to children while maintaining control over the assets, a concept discussed in greater detail later in this chapter.

Charitable Contributions. Another way to lower estate value is to make charitable contributions to qualified organizations. There are three types of qualified organizations: (1) public charities, such as universities; (2) semipublic charities, which are not controlled by state charter; and (3) private charities.

Most charitable organizations, public and private, can accept gifts and ensure tax benefits to the donor. Private charities must meet the requirements of IRS Code Section 501(c)(3)—basically a not-for-profit, charitable, educational organization—to offer tax-savings benefits to donors. The fair market value of gifts to qualified public charities can offset up to 50 percent of the donor's adjusted gross income (AGI) in any single tax year. The value of gifts that exceed 50 percent of AGI can be carried over into succeeding tax years for up to five additional years. The deduction can be limited to 20 or 30 percent of AGI per year for certain gifts, but the carryover rules are the same. See IRS Publication 526 for more information on charitable contributions.

Gifts can take the form of cash, art, jewelry, stocks and bonds—anything of value. Although the strategy for a forest owner might be to lower estate value by giving nonforest assets to keep the woodland resources intact, it is not uncommon to give an easement "for conservation purposes." The "benefactor" of the donation is usually a land trust. Any qualified conservation organization, however, can accept the donation of an easement. Private easements given to a neighbor do not qualify as a charitable contribution. (The details of qualified charitable contributions are discussed later in this chapter.)

Some of the advantages of giving an easement to a land trust are the following:

- Estate values are dramatically lowered because the easement eliminates the proportion of fair market value of land that is attributable to its potential value for development.
- Because the easement is usually a transfer of development rights, the land is protected from development but is still owned by the family and can be sold or passed to new owners (with the easement still intact).
- The donor can use the value of the gift to offset up to 50 percent of income in the current year with the opportunity to carryover unused benefits for up to an additional five years.

The tax advantages of giving an easement are thus twofold: it lowers income tax liability while you are alive, and it can lower or eliminate estate tax liability after you are gone. Because the fair market value of the property has been lowered by the value of the easement, property taxes should be lower. This is not often the case, though, and the point has not been argued enough in courts to have established precedence. Still, if you have given an easement that encompasses development rights, your property assessment should be substantially lower. Local taxing authorities are reluctant to lower the assessment on protected lands because land trusts do not pay taxes on easements they hold. (And why should they since the easement in their hands is a liability because of the promises they made to the donor?) The nature of easements means they have no market value, since the trust cannot sell the easement. From the town's perspective, it is as though a portion of its grand list has evaporated. Most authorities on the subject agree, the dilemma of how to tax protected lands will be resolved as more and more communities address the question of fair taxation on farm and forest lands.

The valuation and purpose of easement gifts for conservation is being scrutinized by congressional committees that believe some charitable contributions are nothing more than tax loopholes for the wealthy. Legislators are contemplating limitations on gifts for conservation purposes so that only easements that "benefit a specific government conservation program" will allow donors to deduct 100 percent of the gift's value. The changes are intended to raise revenue while putting an end to a developer's ability to "finance the building of subdivisions and golf courses with the tax savings of a conservation easement." Such changes will most likely have little or no impact on woodland-owning families whose intentions are to keep productive forests intact.

Deferred Gift. A gift to a qualified charitable organization can also be deferred. The deferment can be specified many different ways. For instance, the gift can be effected immediately but with a provision that you (and your survivors, if you wish) receive income from the property even though the title of the property has passed. A gift of a remainder interest means you continue to own and enjoy the benefits of the property while you are alive. When you die, whatever is left of the property (i.e., the remainder) goes to a charitable organization. A testamentary gift is any gift effective on death. When made to a qualified charitable organization, the value of the gift is fully deductible when figuring the total taxable estate. The testamentary gift has estate tax advantages but does not have current income tax savings (table 9.1). This is because the donor can change his or her mind (rewrite the will) before death. A gift of a remainder interest does have income tax advantages as well as estate tax savings. Figuring the income tax advantages of a remainder interest, however, is very complicated and requires the services of a qualified estate planner or accountant.

A variation on the gift of a remainder interest is a present gift of a future interest in property. This is an especially useful technique when the gift involves real property, such as woodlands. The charitable organization that accepts the gift usually wants to have a large degree of control as to how the property is used during the lifetime of the donor (or the other beneficiaries if the future interest extends beyond the lifetime of the donor). In exchange for control, the charitable organization—usually a land trust—will hold the property in trust and pay the donor an annual fixed or variable annuity that is based on a percentage of the fair market value of the assets. When the donor or designated beneficiaries pass away, the property belongs to the charitable organization. These types of gifts must be irrevocable, so they require careful thought and planning. Gifts of a remainder interest are often used when the donor does not have any direct descendants and he or she is concerned about the cost of elder care and/or a protracted illness. Organizations that

Table 9.1.Tax implications of different gift and bequest strategies to lower estate value.

Option	Income Tax Effects	Estate Tax Effects
Easement gift	Savings	Savings
Remainder interest gift	Savings	Savings
Testamentary gift	No Savings	Savings
Gift to children	No Savings	Savings
Will to children	No Savings	No Savings
Testamentary gift of retirement assets* (IRAs, 401ks, etc.)	Savings	Savings

* So long as the gift is an irrevocable gift to a qualified charitable organization it can create immediate saving on income tax.

accept present gifts of future interests are usually very flexible about the terms of the annuity. They are more than willing to design support arrangements that ensure the donor that costs will be met during his or her lifetime, and will usually also accept the donor's conditions about how the land is to be managed and used by future owners. This type of arrangement—usually with a land trust—is very appealing to single woodland owners with no children. In exchange for a future interest in well-managed forest lands, the trust will agree to bear the responsibility of elder care and also sees to it that the donor dies with the dignity he or she deserves.

Special Valuation. IRS rules allow farm and forest lands to be evaluated for estate tax purposes using special valuation procedures, discussed in chapter 8. These procedures allow lands to be assessed at current-use values rather than fair market value, at the discretion of the executor but only if family members agree. If it is the family's intention to keep forest lands intact, but the parents never got around to doing the necessary paperwork, special valuation may be an option. Recapture rules apply, however, if the land is used for purposes other than what was specified in the special valuation. The services of a qualified estate planner and an independent appraiser are necessary to claim special valuation of forest resources.

Living Trusts

A trust is an arrangement that divides legal and beneficial interests in property among two or more people (Prestopino 1989). All trusts have four parts:

1. The *grantor*, also known as the *settlor, donor, creator*, or *trustor.* This is the person with the property who initiates the trust and establishes the directions governing the administration of all trust property.
2. The *corpus*, or body of the trust, also known as the *principal.* This is the property the grantor has transferred to the trust.
3. The *trustee* is a person or other entity agreeing to hold legal title to the property for the benefit of others.
4. The *beneficiaries* are those who benefit from the trust without having any legal ownership.

Trusts are usually formed as a means of avoiding probate upon incapacity and death, and to provide for individuals who may not be capable of managing property themselves. It is also a way to conserve property so it is not squandered by beneficiaries who might otherwise be compelled to do so.

A living trust is created during your lifetime. Like a will, it includes directions for the disposition of assets in the trust both during your lifetime and upon your death (Bove 1991). In a living trust, the grantor is also the trustee and the beneficiary. In other words, income from property held in the living trust is paid to the grantor, and all the property remains in the grantor's complete control. When the grantor passes away, trust income is paid to survivors, or the property in the trust is dispersed to heirs. Because the trust involves a legal transfer of a person's property to the trust, and the trust spells out what is to happen to those assets, there is no need for probate. When the grantor is also the trustee, a *cotrustee* and/or *successor trustee* is usually appointed. That way when the grantor dies, the trust is not left without a trustee.

So what is the benefit of a living trust to a forest owner? A living trust can be designated to double the amount that can pass free of estate tax to the children of a married couple. This type of trust is referred to as a *unified credit trust*, an *A/B trust*, a *credit-shelter trust*, or a *family trust*. See Tab. 9.2

Consider the case of a married couple who own forest land, and the 2005 value of their land and all other assets is $2.1 million. Assume, further, that the estate is appreciating at an annual rate of 7 percent. Current rules allow a surviving spouse to inherit the entire estate without paying any taxes. But when that survivor passes away, the portion of the estate value that exceeds the exemption amount that year is taxed. Under current law, the exemption is $1.5 million in 2005, $2 million in years 2006 through 2008, $3.5 million in 2009, and in 2010 the estate tax is repealed.

If the husband in the example above passes away in 2006, the wife inherits the entire estate tax free. But is the wife dies a year later in 2007, her $2.4 million estate is subject to a $2 million exemption leaving a taxable estate of $400,000. Within nine months her executor must pay an estate tax of $180,000 on this amount. If the wife lives until 2009, the available exemption will shelter her entire estate. And if she dies in 2010 the exemption is irrelevant because the estate tax is suspended, but for one year only. If she manages to live until 2011—and Congress has not acted to continue the repeal of the estate tax—her estate would be subject to the rules promulgated in 1997. Under those rules the estate tax exemption is $1 million (plus an adjustment for inflation), leaving a taxable estate of approximately $2 million (remember, the 2005 estate equal to $2.1 million is growing at an average annual rate of 7 percent, so the value in 2011 is about $3.15 million). The tax rate on a $2 million taxable estate in 2011 (under the 1997 rules) is 55 percent plus a 5 percent surtax.

If this same couple had transferred their assets to an A/B trust—which is really two trusts, one in the name of the husband and the other in the name of the wife—the family could have avoided federal estate tax altogether (table 9.2). By dividing their combined assets into two trusts, they can take full advantage of estate tax rules, doubling the allowable exemption amounts. So, for example, in 2005 they can shelter $3 million; in 2006, 2007, and 2008 the amount increases to $4 million; and in 2009 they can shelter up to

Table 9.2. Formation of a family trust and projection of its effects on estate taxes.

Year	Event	Status	
2005	A/B trusts formed	Husband and wife estate = $2.1 million	
		Husband trust	Wife trust
		$1.05 million	$1.05 million
		(Assets appreciate at 7% compounded per annum.)	
2006	Husband dies*	Husband trust	Wife trust
		$1.12 million	$1.12 million
		(Both trusts are lower than exemption amount and income is available to the surviving spouse.)	
2009	Wife dies	Husband trust	Wife trust
		$1.38 million	$1.38 million
		(The wife's trust is lower than exemption amount so no estate tax is due.)	
2010	If the wife dies this year, the entire estate is exempt from taxation.		
2011	If wife dies this year—and Congress fails to retain changes—the estate tax exemption drops back to $1 million, allowing the wife to shelter $1 million of estate value. An estate tax will be due, but it is much less than would have been the case without formation of the A/B trusts in 2005.		

* When the husband passes away his trust becomes irrevocable, and both the corpus and subsequent growth are sheltered from estate tax.

$7 million of assets. And, if Congress does fail to retain the estate tax exemption after 2010, they still take full advantage of whatever the exemption amounts are in the future. Another huge advantage of the unified credit trust is that while either or both spouses are alive all income from property held in the trust is paid to them or to the surviving spouse. When the surviving spouse dies, the trust is dispersed to heirs, or it can continue with the children or others who are designated to benefit from the income.

The particulars of living trusts are far beyond the scope of this book. Many excellent references have been written on the subject (see the references section). A word of caution: although it is possible to create your own living trust, it is tricky business and best left to a qualified estate-planning attorney. Properties need to be retitled to the trusts, and you must follow IRS rules to the letter. It may cost from a few hundred to a few thousand dollars in legal fees to set up the trusts (expect to pay between $1,200 and $2,000), but the tax savings can be astronomical (depending on the circumstances, estate tax savings in excess of a few hundred thousand dollars). Also, a trust avoids probate expenses of three to ten thousand dollars.

Strategies for Passing Woodlands

Take a look at your forest management plan. It is almost a sure bet there are stands that will not fully mature until long after you have passed away. Even if you are the healthiest person in the world, there is nothing like a long-term forest management plan to trigger uneasy contemplation of one's longevity. And the facts are some—perhaps most—of the benefits you managed for will not mature in your lifetime. Woodland owners who work with their lands eventually develop a close affinity to the forest. Cashing in on the expense and effort of thinning and other precommercial treatments is no longer as important as figuring out who will carry on in the next generation.

If this dilemma rings true you may have begun to think about who will take over in your stead. A son or daughter? A grandchild? Perhaps you have had conversations with potential heirs to ascertain their willingness to carry on your management plans. You may have some ideas about who will take your place, but you're not completely comfortable with turning everything over even to the closest son or daughter. Your heart says it's OK, but your instincts tell you something else leaving you discomforted with the thought of just bequeathing the forest to your children.

Unfortunately, your instincts are correct: most children will end up selling the family forest to settle the estate. You like to think your children won't quibble about money after you're gone, but the fact is that they do. Leaving well-managed forest land to children in the hope that they will carry on your forest management ideals is more often than not a prescription for failure. I have seen more than a few instances where the best laid plans of Mom and Dad were discarded the first time the children argued about their shares. Soon after, loggers are invited onto the property to look at the timber or the land is sold outright to the highest bidder.

It is possible to keep forest lands intact while passing them through generations of your family even in circumstances where your children don't care about the forest. Although it can be a tough decision to make, forest owners who want to keep ecosystems intact and in the family have four options: a family partnership, a closely held S corporation, a limited liability company (LLC), or a qualified trust for conservation purposes. A fifth alternative not discussed here is a multi-generational trust. The goal of any one or a combination of these options is to maintain a forest management legacy, predicated on the idea that the forest values important to you are timeless. Your children may not appreciate your efforts, but future generations will.

Family Partnerships. A partnership is a noncorporate association of two or more people, each of whom owns a share of an undivided interest in property. An undivided interest is similar to the shares of a corporation. When you buy stock, you are buying shares of the corporate assets, not any one part of the company. The concept of undivided interests as it relates to family partnerships involving forest land is perfect because it does not require a specific designation of woodlands to any one of the partners: it avoids the need to split up the land among the children.

A family partnership can be a form of limited partnership where there are two types of partners: (1) general partners who make all decisions—you and your spouse—and are responsible for day-to-day affairs and (2) limited partners—your children. Although limited partners own an undivided interest in the assets, they have no authority to make decisions. Also, the children are usually asked to sign agreements that allow the other partners to buy out an individual's interests should he or she decide to leave the partnership. Children obtain an undivided interest in forest land through annual, tax-exempt gifts from parents described earlier in this chapter. Or, parents can pass the land as a single gift so long as the amount is less than the lifetime exclusion for taxable gifts. For the period 2005 through 2009, the lifetime gift exclusion is $1 million per taxpayer, or $2 million per married couple, plus any discounts for lack of marketability as discussed in chapter 8. Also, the estate and generation skipping transfer exemption is reduced by the amount of the gift tax exemption used.

It is significant to note that IRS gives careful scrutiny to family partnerships designed solely (and obviously) to avoid estate taxes. Another thing to remember is that excessively high discount rates on gifts are the flag, so special care and good, sound legal advice is essential.

The primary benefit of a family partnership is that it allows parents to disperse the estate but keep forest assets intact. Because the estate (or a large share of the estate) has been dispersed to the partnership, little or no estate tax is due. And the parents maintain control—even if their share of the partnership is small compared to the children's shares—until new general partners are appointed. The new general partner(s) is the child or children who have the greatest interest (intellectual, not financial) in the forest and the best ability to carry on in the parents' traditions. The other children share income and other benefits of owning forests, but they make no decisions. Only the general partners are responsible for activities on the forest.

In addition to those advantages already mentioned, family partnerships are easy to set up and they pass tax savings and credits directly to the partners. A major disadvantage of the partnership structure is that the general partners are liable for the actions of the partnership. This exposure to liability is one of the primary reasons that family partnerships are little used anymore for passing forest land within the family. The parents forming a partnership are willing to accept liability, but the distribution of liability becomes a problem for subsequent generations. Another disadvantage is that the family partnership can usually pass lands successfully from parents to children, but the complications of future generations are often too much for the partnership to handle. A relatively new variation on the theme of the family partnership is the *limited liability company* (LLC) described later in this chapter. It offers the corporate benefits of protection from personal liability and all the benefits of a family partnership.

Closely Held S Corporation. A corporation is an entity set up under four primary conditions:

1. Limited liability for the owners
2. Centralized management
3. No restrictions on ownership interests (anyone can hold stock)
4. Continuity of existence (a corporation exists in its own right)

As a separate entity, it is taxed as such and this is one of the primary disadvantages of the corporate structure: profits are taxed twice; first as corporate income, then as income when profits are dispersed to the owners. Congress created the S corporation to allow small businesses and nonprofits to incorporate providing owners protection from liability while eliminating double taxation. But—as is the case with most things involving the IRS—it is not as simple as that. There are many rules an S corporation must abide by in order to maintain its status. For example, an S corporation cannot have more than one hundred shareholders (increased from seventy-five as of January 2005) and it can have only one class of stock. In 2004, the American Jobs Creation Act allowed family members—representing up to six generations—to be treated as one shareholder but only United States citizens can hold stock. Also, when a shareholder is sued for personal reasons (not related to the business of the S-corporation), his or her shares are viewed as assets that can be seized by court action.

A closely held or *closed* S corporation is a special variation that allows the corporation to restrict ownership (contrary to the third condition of a corporation mentioned above). For this reason, the closely held S corporation is a favorite of small family businesses even though ownership interest is limited to thirty shares. Being able to control ownership, along with all the other advantages of a corporation, make the closely held S corporation a popular method for keeping well-managed forest lands in the family. It still is, but the limited liability company (LLC) is proving to be a far more flexible alternative.

Limited Liability Companies (LLC). Even though the concept of a limited liability company (LLC) has been in existence for more than a hundred years, first in Germany then throughout Europe spreading in the 1900s to Latin America, it has only been in the last few years that every state in the United States has developed a statute that allows this form of organization. Vermont was the last state to adopt an LLC statute in 1996.

One of the useful features of an LLC structure—especially as it relates to long-term management of forests—is that profit motive is irrelevant. Thus, the family forest LLC can be dedicated to any purpose: investment, business, conservation, or—best of all—any combination of motives. LLCs provide the liability protection of a corporation, pass-through taxation aspects of a partnership, and the essential ability to restrict ownership in the family forest that a closely held S corporation provides. Plus, an essential added benefit, crucial to an entity that must add members at the same rate that families grow: there are no limitations on the number of members an LLC can have. The individuals that form the LLC, also known as *founders*, have the choice of restricting the number of members (the concept of *members* to an LLC is exactly the same as *shares* to a corporation), allowing fractional membership, forming more than one class of membership, or allowing membership to grow with the family.

The LLC structure assumes that at least two of the four conditions of a corporation (listed above) are *not* true. In other words, IRS will tax the LLC in the same manner that a partnership is taxed if it lacks at least two of the conditions of a corporation. Most often those two are items 3 (no ownership restrictions) and 4 (continuity of existence), since an LLC by nature is intended to protect owners from liability (item 1 is always true), and there is usually (but not necessarily always) a centralized management (item 2 is true). Although it would be to the advantage of the founders of a family woodlands LLC to have it exist irrespective of the current owners (i.e., continuity of existence, just like a corporation), to meet the conditions of an LLC (that no more than two of four conditions of a corporation are false) item 4 must be false. Thus, the family woodlands LLC cannot have a continuity of existence. It must either exist at the will of the owners (which is a problem for a long-term, intergenerational enterprise) or have a finite existence. On the surface, this condition appears to be a problem for an intergenerational family woodlands enterprise, but it need not be. Even though it might be possible to demonstrate that a family forest LLC lacks centralized management (in other words, item 2 is false, which means the LLC could have a *continuity of existence*), it would be exceedingly difficult, perhaps impossible, for the company to do business if all decisions were handled by committee.

As to form, the LLC is composed of two parts, one public, the other private. The founders of an LLC must file Articles of Organization, usually with the secretary of State (which does not have to be the state where woodlands are located or the residence of any of the owners). The *articles*, in their most basic form, are simple answers to a series of questions; the state law that governs the few statutory requirements of the LLC, the physical location of it's offices, the name and location for the agent of process (if the LLC is ever *served* with legal papers, who is the lucky person willing to accept them?), and the LLC's fiscal year. The name of the company must include LLC, or LC, indicating that it is a limited liability company. The owners or principals are called *members*, and one of the questions has to do with whether the company is to be managed by members or by a *manager*, who may or may not also be a member. Another question has to do with the issue of continuity of existence. The founder must choose whether the company exists at the will of its members, or has a fixed term after which the LLC expires.

Good legal advice is necessary to choose the state where the LLC will reside, since state statutes vary, and how to deal with the question of continuity of existence. If the founders designate an *at-will* LLC, the company can be easily dissolved by vote of the members in subsequent generations. To avoid a premature disbanding of the company, the founders can form a *term* LLC. Given the long-term nature of forests and forest investments, founders can easily argue that a reasonable duration is 120 years or more by tying the term into the amount of time it takes to grow timber. Although this may sound somewhat drastic, the operating agreement, discussed below, can specify conditions the members can use to shorten the LLC if absolutely necessary, and/or to establish a new term upon expiration of the old one. When a term LLC expires it automatically becomes an at-will LLC until the current members decide to dissolve the company or establish a new term.

The second—private—part of an LLC is the *operating agreement*. It sets forth in detail the purpose of the LLC, who its members are, and all the conditions of the company. The operating agreement regulates all the company's affairs, including how it conducts business. It also spells out important matters of governance. For a family woodland owning business, it should also include the founder's management plan and describe how management decisions are to be made in the future. The operating agreement also describes how members will handle the *expiration* of the term (presumably by specifying a new term) and how managers or the member-management team will operate. Since the operating agreement is a proprietary document of the LLC, it is not filed with the secretary of State but each member should have a copy.

The process for creating a family forest LLC might look something like this (assuming the founders have done their homework on LLCs and they are working with an attorney who has experience setting up family businesses using this form of organization):

- A husband and wife set up a member-managed, term LLC by filing the Articles of Organization in the name of the family. There are a number ways to transfer forest assets into the LLC, and this is where solid legal assistance is invaluable.

- Next, they develop the operating agreement, which is like a contract between the members as to the purpose and operation of the company. The parents—or founders—as managers, retain control over the land but the agreement describes how management control is passed on to future generations.

- Forest land is appraised so the founders can use the annual IRS gift exclusion to vest children in undivided interests (shares) in the LLC. Using the annual gift exclusion is described later in this chapter.
- The founders amend the operating agreement as necessary to account for unforeseen events, since one of the benefits of LLCs is that they are easily amended. They must also locate a new manager or members willing and able to serve in a management capacity. Depending on how the operating agreement is written, managers may be selected from family or they can select a non-member, such as a forestry consultant. One of the most important functions of the operating agreement is helping members identify new managers. A hypothetical operating agreement is described later in this chapter.
- Income from the family woodlands LLC can be distributed to the members (or in trust for children), much as a dividend is paid by a corporation. If a future family member wants out of the LLC, the operating agreement describes how that member's shares are purchased, and if the member's offspring are eligible to buy back in to the LLC.
- When the family forest LLC term expires the operating agreement describes how members are to proceed to set up a new term if they so desire.

The LLC is perfectly suited to passing forest lands and carefully considered forest management plans to family members. It is easy and cost-effective to set up, can be easily amended, and the manager controls the property and decision-making, whether or not the manager is also a member. The primary disadvantage is that it may be difficult to effect continuity without sacrificing the pass-through tax benefits. If the IRS determines that an LLC exists independent of its members, it may view the arrangement as a corporation resulting in back taxes and penalties. Good legal advice can help prevent this from happening.

A Family Forest LLC Operating Agreement. A long-term LLC can allow family members—now and well into the future—to be the recipients of both tangible and intangible forest benefits, but without forcing any one family member to dedicate his or her life to carrying on Dad's legacy. It is this perception that often causes current owners to rethink the wisdom of dedicating one child with the "golden brick," who must then sink or swim while attempting to keep the forest afloat. And when a forest is the principal asset, other children are apt to feel cheated, even though the son or daughter who accepted the responsibility would gladly pass it off. By forming an LLC, the golden brick resides with the company leaving children to enjoy the benefits of forests without the hassles; or to get involved if they are so inclined. It sounds too good to be true, but it is not, so long as the founders give careful thought to language in the LLC's operating agreement.

As discussed earlier, the operating agreement is a proprietary document of the LLC, which means that it is private to all except members and it does not need to be filed with the state. There are, however, some necessary requirements implicit to the LLC that the operating agreement cannot obviate. For example, members have rights to see the books and records of the company; all members have a duty of loyalty and care to one another and to the purpose of the LLC, and they are obliged to act in good faith and deal fairly. Statutory requirements vary by state, and some allow more freedom than others. For this reason, prospective founders will want to read up on LLCs and choose to organize in a state that offers the best set of conditions for a company whose purpose is to manage forest lands and keep them intact for many, many years. As of this writing, there are more than three hundred books in print on limited liability companies.

When the purpose of an LLC is to pass forest lands within the family, and to create a management structure that allows goals and objectives established under the current forest management plan to be maintained until the plan says it is time to act, organization and wording of the operating agreement are crucial to long-term success. Here are some of the elements founders will want to include in an operating agreement:

- A strong opening paragraph that clearly describes the purpose of the LLC: to pass forest lands within the family—intact—for the LLC's term and longer; to manage long-term timber investment values; to create and maintain wildlife habitats (for named species); to provide opportunity for recreational purposes (either reserved for the family, or for townspeople). The opening paragraph sets the tone for the rest of the agreement and so it is essential that it explain why the founders set up the LLC in the first place.

- The operating agreement should describe an organizational structure that puts most of the decision-making power into the hands of a relatively few members, or into the hands of a manager. For example, any child or grandchild is automatically a member of the LLC, but their ability to vote is vested to them as they acquire a financial interest in the company. It is the equivalent of having more than one class of stock; and the highest class has voting rights to select a board, and then the board appoints a set of directors, who are actually charged with making decisions.

- Governing members can be divided into three functions: administrative, judicial, and legislative (modeled after the U.S. Constitution). The administrative committee makes day-to-day management decisions. But for some decisions that require drastic measures (such as effecting a timber harvest or installation of an expensive road), there must be a vote of the entire membership. Discrepancies are sent to the judicial committee charged with making a decision that the members agree to accept. The judicial committee is acting like an arbitration panel, and its decisions become precedence for future decisions. There are many different alternatives to create a reasonable management structure for a member-managed LLC, but the goal of any structure should be to further the original cause of the LLC while installing necessary checks and balances. Carrying the balance of power analogy further, a legislative committee might be charged with interpreting the original founders' operating agreement, and any subsequent changes, to help establish policy for future decision-making.

- If the operating agreement is amended to put a manager in charge (a consulting forester, for example), the manager is a fiduciary of the LLC; the equivalent of a trustee to a trust. Even with a manager-managed structure, the members should retain the power to impeach a manager, as described above. In fact, the operating agreement can spell out conditions that cause an automatic impeachment. And the agreement should also describe the process of appointing a new manager.

- Generally, the members of an LLC are the owners and income and expenses are passed directly to them for tax purposes, unless the operating agreement describes a different method. Given the marginal return on forest investments, the agreement may want to specify periodic payouts of profits rather than annual payouts. Income can be distributed to members (or in trust for children), in much the same way dividends are paid by a corporation. Given a choice, people will choose simplicity over almost any alternative, allowing them more time to enjoy forests, and less effort spent worrying about the business.
- The operating agreement should restrict membership to children who are direct descendants of the founders (including adopted children). In fact, prospective spouses (those who are marrying into the family) should agree to waive any rights to the family LLC as a potential marital asset in the case of divorce. If a future family member wants out of the LLC, the agreement describes how that member's shares are purchased and if the member's offspring are eligible to buy back in to the LLC. The operating agreement can also grant a nonvoting membership to any direct descendent, but each generation must choose one family member to obtain a voting interest.

At the end of a term, the operating agreement should spell out the process voting members will use to establish a new term, or to dissolve the LLC for cause. Since dissolution of the LLC involves land, legal advice is absolutely essential. The founders may want to think about local conditions 150 years from now that might prompt them to encourage members to dissolve, or to create a new term. If members should decide to dissolve the LLC, the founders can specify that the land—or development rights—are given to a local land trust. Finally, the operating agreement should also include a copy of the forest management plan and make reference to it in virtually every clause. Future LLC members should never lose sight of the original purpose that prompted the founders to take the steps they did to ensure that forests are kept intact and in the family.

Vesting Heirs in the Family Forest

Probably the easiest way to vest heirs into the family forest is by using the annual gift exclusion discussed in chapter 8. It makes no difference if the organizational structure is a closely held S corporation, a family partnership or a limited liability company, structuring of the gift is the same. A donor can give up to eleven thousand dollars each year to as many people as he or she desires and the gifts are completely excluded from taxation. Thus a husband and wife can give a combined twenty-two thousand dollars to each person they want to bring into the family forest. And if the shareholder or operating agreement puts restrictions on how the recipient can use the gift, the IRS allows the gift to be discounted. Since the IRS has consistently accepted a 30 percent discount rate on assets transferred from parents to children—who must accept the assets according to the terms of the agreement—the parents can annually transfer, say, $28,000 to each child for a tax-exempt gift of $19,600 ($28,000 less 30 percent is $19,600). With such tax-exempt gifts to each of four children, the parents can pass up to $112,000 in forest value each year. It is important to note, however, that the discount rate cannot be assigned arbitrarily. A qualified appraisal is essential to support valuations and discount rates for IRS purposes.

Parents can also use the lifetime exclusion on taxable gifts, which is currently set at $1 million per taxpayer or $2 million for a married couple, to pass all or a significant portion of the land to heirs in a single transaction. With discounting—at 30 percent—the parents can pass up to approximately $2.85 million of an undivided interest in forest land to create a $2 million gift. As discussed in chapter 8, under current law the lifetime gift exclusion has been decoupled from the estate exemption, but the estate exemption is reduced by the amount of the gift tax exemption used. Although expert opinions vary, most believe the lifetime gift and estate exemptions will be unified once again after 2010, with a combined exemption of $1.5 to $2 million—but this is only a guess.

It is absolutely essential to obtain reliable legal advice before making gifts of an undivided interest in forest land. The process used to create shares or membership interests, restrictions on how the recipient can use the gift, and other important tax-related and legal issues must be resolved in such a way that forest is not divided or ends up in the hands of the wrong person. For example, it is almost always a good idea to not include spouses of your children (or heirs) in the gift because a divorce could leave an interest in the forest in the hands of someone who is no longer family. Generally, it is easier to protect a gift of a membership interest in an LLC than it is to protect the shares of an S corporation. You will also want to leave open a way for shareholders or members to sell their interest, usually back to the organization and according to the terms of the agreement. When you have realized the goal of maintaining a long-term forest management strategy—while also keeping land in the family—your children (and their children) will applaud your genius.

Land Trusts

Over the past forty years, hundreds of mostly local, private, nonprofit conservation organizations have emerged to protect important forest and farmlands from development. Land trusts, as these organizations have come to be known, grew out of a need to provide donors with assurances that lands could be protected long after they had died. The word *trust* has the same meaning here as applied elsewhere: an arrangement that divides legal and beneficial interests in property. The word *protection* usually means from development into nonforest or nonfarm uses. The purpose of land trusts is to give individuals a choice about how lands will be used when passed by sale, gift, or bequest. The land trust, with respect to your forest land, is the equivalent of the personal representative of your estate, with one important difference: a land trust is a legal entity that has been carefully designed and formed to exist in perpetuity. Even if the organization you work with goes out of business fifty or one hundred years from now, a carefully crafted chain of successors will take on the obligation of always and forever protecting the property's title and your legacy to the land.

The most common method of protecting forest land is to give an easement (see chapter 3) to a state or local land trust. Also known as a transfer of development rights, the easement is designed by the donor or grantor to specifically allow certain activities while disallowing others. Although the easement may disallow development, it can specify certain areas where family members (present and future generations) are allowed to build if they so desire. The easement can be as general or as specific as you—the grantor or donor—require, within the limits imposed by the IRS. The more specific the easement, however, the more difficult and expensive it is to enforce.

A land trust will sometimes buy an easement to protect an especially significant tract, but usually it will only accept gifts. A donor is expected to pay the costs of appraising the easement's value and the legal costs of drafting and recording the easement. Most land trusts try to recover the costs of staff involved in the transaction. Donors are usually also asked to provide an endowment, a lump sum of money that the trust invests to help cover the cost of enforcing the easement in the future. Wealthy donors are also asked to make gifts of the type described in table 9.1. For some people, the income and estate tax advantages of gifts to a land trust are very appealing. IRS rules regarding charitable contributions generally apply to the gift of an easement and any endowments.

A common misconception of land trusts is that they buy up land and lock it away. Nothing could be further from the truth. A land trust only rarely becomes involved in outright land purchase, and then briefly—only just until it can find another buyer who is willing to purchase the property with an easement. Land trusts mostly accept gifts of easements (which are of no value to the trust, since it cannot resell the easement). They exist on membership dues and contributions, foundation grants, special state appropriations, and outright gifts of land and other assets. When a land trust accepts an easement from a woodland owner, it expects the owner to help draft the easement and to have clear plans as to how the land is to be used. Family descendants can inherit the land, and they can carry on the original forest-management plans. They can also sell the land to a buyer who is willing to accept the title with easements. And a family can reserve areas for house lots if doing so is acceptable to the land trust.

Generally, land trusts do not dictate how forest lands are to be managed. Rather, they negotiate an appropriate and acceptable management strategy with each owner and design an easement that ensures those practices are followed. It is the current owner's responsibility to follow the plan, and if he or she strays from the plan, the land trust will intervene. What constitutes straying from the plan is spelled out in the easement. Most trusts will not quibble over small changes in management. But severe alterations to the landscape, houses going up, or any drastic and obvious violation of the easement will cause the land trust to investigate. An owner of protected forest lands should seek guidance from the land trust that holds the easement before implementing management practices that alter the landscape. Also, as part of the land trust's perpetual monitoring responsibility, a representative from the trust periodically will visit to ensure the easement is intact.

After working with a local land trust, some owners decide to leave a remainder interest in their land to the trust (as described above in the section on charitable contributions). The tax advantages—both income tax savings and lower estate taxes—are often very attractive. This is especially true for owners without children, or for those with children who are not interested in owning the land. When a land trust accepts land as an outright gift, or a gift of a remainder interest, it will usually separate the development rights and then sell the land (either during the life of the donor or after, depending on the circumstances) to someone who is willing to honor and protect the easement. Any profits from the sale are used to continue its good work. Under certain circumstances the land trust will set up an annuity, the beneficiary of which is the donor until he or she dies. The trust will also make arrangements for elder care and other expenses the owners are apt to sustain during the balance of their lives. Most land trusts are highly flexible in the design of easements and financial arrangements as long as their primary concern is met: to protect land from development.

Like-Kind Exchanges

Land trusts often identify parcels that are important for connecting wildlife travel corridors, for protecting water resources or prominent vistas, or for adding to an existing block of protected land. When owners of these lands are approached, often they are unwilling or financially unable to donate an easement. For instance, even a willing owner may not have enough current income to take full advantage of the tax savings when an easement is donated, and may be expecting profits from a sale of the land at retirement. An unwilling potential donor may not want to lose the economic potential of the land for crops, timber, or future development. For both willing and unwilling potential donors, a like-kind exchange with a land trust may prove acceptable.

A *like-kind exchange* is a tax-free transaction, usually initiated by a land trust but not necessarily, whereby an owner exchanges his or her property for qualified, like-kind property. As long as the like-kind property qualifies under IRS rules, there is no taxable gain. The advantage to a landowner is the ability to defer the capital gain that would otherwise be due with an outright sale, and to obtain property of like-kind that allows fulfillment of financial goals with minimal impacts on important landscape features. The advantage to the land trust—and society—is protection of significant lands from development. For more information on like-kind exchanges, contact your local land trust.

Like-kind exchanges are not unique to land trusts even though they are a common method that trusts use to protect land. Any taxpayer has the right to exchange property held for investment or for other productive purposes under Title 26, subsection 1031 of the Internal Revenue Code. By following the rules of such an exchange, the taxpayer avoids having to pay capital gains on the theory that the gain from the sale of one property is being used to purchase another property of equal or greater value and for similar purposes. Thus an owner of forest land in Connecticut can sell the land and use the proceeds to purchase forest land in Idaho. To qualify, the purchaser must use an intermediary, such as a lawyer, to handle the exchange. Within forty-five days of the sale of the property in Connecticut, for example, the owner must locate a property of similar value in Idaho and notify the intermediary. Then the purchase of the Idaho property must be consummated within 180 days of the sale of the Connecticut forest. If handled properly, there are no capital gains on income from the Connecticut land. A like-kind exchange is the perfect tool for a family that is forced to relocate. Or in situations where development pressures have dramatically inflated forest land values for a family that has no intentions of developing land. They simply sell the land that is doomed for development and use the proceeds to acquire productive forest lands in an area that is less threatened.

Forming a Local Land Trust

Creating a land trust requires three things: people, money, and land—usually in that order. Locating like-minded people in a community who are willing to invest time in the significant effort required to form a land trust is probably the easiest of the three. But locating financial support and convincing local farm and forest owners that it is a good idea to donate easements from their lands is more challenging.

In order to meet IRS standards that maximize the amounts donors can deduct when they make gifts (of cash, easements, or of land outright), the trust must achieve status as a public charity. It must also obtain status as a private operating foundation, which means no (or limited) political lobbying among other things, and it must obtain status as a *supporting organization*, meaning that it is contributing to the efforts of one or more parent organizations. It is also critical for a land trust to obtain—and protect—a tax-exempt status with the IRS. Doing so triggers a host of IRS requirements having to do with where it gets its money, recordkeeping and—once again—restrictions on lobbying.

The initial leg work to form a local land trust is considerable and without question requires the service of an attorney, preferably one who is well versed in IRS rules that govern nonprofits. Nevertheless, it is possible to form a land trust that suits the needs of local people. An excellent source on the subject is: *Starting a Land Trust—A Guide to Forming a Land Conservation Organization*, published by the Land Trust Alliance. To obtain a copy, or for more information on land trusts in your area, contact The Land Trust Alliance (1319 F Street NW, Suite 501, Washington, DC 20004-1106, 202-638-4725, www.lta.org).

The Forest Legacy Program

The Forest Legacy program was introduced in the 1990 Farm Bill to "protect environmentally sensitive forest lands." It represented a first attempt to use federal dollars to purchase conservation easements on private lands. Generally, the purpose of easements is to restrict development on productive forest lands and to protect forest ecosystems while also requiring owners to employ sustainable practices. First funded in 1992, the program now encompasses conservation easements in twenty-six states and territories. To date the U.S. Forest Service has spent $132 million to obtain conservation easements on more than six hundred thousand acres of forest land with a market value of nearly $270 million. In addition to the states and territories where Legacy lands are located, sixteen additional states have either been authorized to establish Forest Legacy projects or authorization is pending.

Decisions are made by a state forester–appointed Forest Legacy committee in authorized states. Although specific criteria vary between states, decisions are usually based on a combination of: local needs, the degree to which proposed forest lands are threatened, public support for projects, and how well any given project complements other nearby conservation efforts. The U.S. Forest Service and state Forest Legacy committees underscore that the program is intended to support private ownership of forest lands and participation is completely voluntary. As with conservation easements that are sold or given to local land trusts, the owner still owns the forest and can sell or bequeath the land to prospective owners who agree to abide by the terms of the easement. The program is open to any private forest owner in authorized states. Contact your state extension forester or the state forester to find out if your land is in a Forest Legacy authorized area, and if so, how to apply.

Locating an Estate Planner

The best way to locate a suitable estate-planning attorney is to make inquiries about his or her practice. The state bar association is a good place to start. You want someone who devotes at least half-time to estate planning, which may entail preparation of five or more estate plans (not just simple wills) each month. Ask if they are involved in continuing education seminars. Because estate planning is constantly changing, active involvement in professional development in this area is essential, at least to the extent of ten or more hours per year.

Find out if the attorney has given presentations to groups on the subject and, if so, can provide you with a copy of the materials used. Most estate-planning attorneys are asked to speak a few times each year. A copy of the teaching materials will give you hints as to their focus and how well organized and experienced they are. The attorney may be able to provide references, but is bound by rules of confidentiality from revealing the identity of a client, let alone discussing the specifics of another client's estate plan. However, you can ask for permission to speak with at least one recent client, who has authorized the attorney to use them as a reference.

Another key question: Does the attorney prepare his or her own standard forms for wills and trusts or obtain them from another source? How often are the forms revised or updated? Obviously, the attorney should have his or her own forms, and updates should be continuous to reflect changes in the tax law or changes in local probate procedures or statutes. Finally, ask if the attorney has had any experience working with forest owners, especially where the disposition of forest assets was a major consideration. Have they ever worked with a forester and, if so, on what types of projects? Finding a qualified estate planner will be a relatively easy task compared to finding one who has also had the experience of working with forest owning families that want to keep lands intact. Yes, forests are assets that may contribute to a person's wealth, but the analogy between forests and other types of wealth ends there. More often than not productive forests and healthy forest ecosystems require at least two generations to become sustainable and so good stewardship is the job of families not individuals.

Summary

People who own forest land have a special responsibility that extends beyond a lifetime. It is this responsibility, more than short-term financial gains, that make estate planning an essential exercise for all families owning and tending forest ecosystems.

Following are some points to remember about planning for forests in your estate:

- Do not rely on Congress to abolish the estate tax in 2010. Although it affects relatively few families, it is a significant source of revenue.
- Do not be fooled into thinking the best way to avoid estate tax is to leave everything to your spouse. Eventually, the estate of one or the other may have to pay a tax.
- Obtain advice from a qualified estate planner on when to use joint tenancy with rights of survivorship for personal property, such as automobiles and bank accounts. Use JTROS to share woodland ownership only with the advice of an estate planner.
- Know the value of forest land in your area. It may be higher than you think—high enough to trigger an estate tax your family will not be able to pay.
- There are lawyers, and then there are lawyers who know estate planning, and then there are lawyers who know how to plan for woodlands in the estate. Choose the latter.
- Involve your children in estate planning; find out who is interested in maintaining the forest and who can carry on your traditions.
- Learn more about every angle of estate planning but don't do it by yourself. Hire an experienced estate-planning attorney (preferably one who has experience with forests) to draw up the necessary documents.
- Assemble a team that includes a consulting forester, an attorney, an accountant, an insurance underwriter, and interested family members.
- If your total estate exceeds current estate tax credit limits, investigate ways to lower the estate value.
- Consider the advantages of living trusts as a way to hold assets to avoid probate and to minimize estate taxes.
- Think about giving an easement to a local land trust to gain immediate income tax advantages, lower estate value, and ensure woodlands are protected from development.
- Finally, consider a like-kind exchange of land with a local land trust to forever protect an important feature of your forest.

Your forest estate plan should emphasize descriptive phrases and ideas you believe are important about forest values that should be recognized, managed for, protected, or celebrated in the future. This is your chance to create a living legacy by which people will remember you long after you have passed away. The plan should acknowledge uncertainty and be flexible. It should describe your visions, the principles behind decisions you have made in the past, and the conditions you believe are desirable for the future. Finally, the forest estate plan is your chance to leave behind something truly important for many generations to come.

Chapter 10

Settling Disputes

Occasionally, a forest owner is faced with a dispute of one sort or another. Unless you are an especially litigious person, your goal should be to avoid disputes. When a dispute is unavoidable, try to settle as reasonably, quickly, and amicably as possible. This may sound like a simplistic approach to what could prove to be an otherwise complex and vexing problem you share with difficult people, but using an attorney and court proceedings to solve a dispute should be viewed as a last resort. Aside from the expense and uncertainty of asking a court to help settle a dispute, most people are highly discomforted by this type of encounter with the law. Anxiety, sleepless nights, distraction, and unease are common complaints of people who find themselves party to a lawsuit. Former litigants often describe a protracted court battle as the worst experience of their lives. Even if you are certain your claims will prevail in court, the emotional expense of the battle may not be worth vindication. Sometimes it is easier and cheaper to give in than to fight.

The best way to resolve a dispute over forest lands is to avoid it in the first place. And the only way to elude disputes altogether is to shun human contact. But neither of these ideas is very reasonable since disputes sometimes find you rather than the other way around. Some people are itching for a fight—they're easy to spot—and your best bet is to avoid them like the plague. But occasionally a valid dispute arises that is unavoidable. Knowing what to expect in a woodland dispute is half the battle.

The purpose of this chapter is to describe common circumstances around which woodland-related disputes occur, and to discuss various means of resolving disputes—from attempting to resolve the problem yourself to hiring an attorney and going to court. The emphasis is on resolving disputes without a fight, and avoiding court.

Whenever two or more people cannot resolve their differences and a resolution of some sort is important, it is a dispute. In other words, people can disagree on something that is a matter of opinion and walk away with the issue unresolved—they can "agree to disagree." The outcome is not a matter of consequence. The word dispute is used here in the context of a disagreement where the resolution is important.

Common Areas of Dispute Involving Forests

Some areas where disputes involving forest lands are common (and important) follow.

Boundaries, Surveys, Rights-of-Way, and Deeds

Disputes involving these areas almost always require the services of a licensed surveyor and an attorney. Any dispute regarding a deed should be handled by an attorney. Unless you know what you are doing, you should not attempt to resolve questions about a deed by yourself. A boundary dispute may be easily resolved with respect to the concerns of the current titleholders, but when one of the owners attempts to pass title, the dispute requires formal resolution. A dispute may arise as to who will pay for professional services to help resolve the question. State laws may prescribe remedies for these types of disputes, so it is probably well worth the money to get a legal opinion.

An owner may grant a temporary right-of-way to allow a neighbor easier access to his or her lands. In some states, an owner is required to grant a temporary right-of-way specifically for forestry purposes. Sometimes the location, duration, and other relevant aspects of the right-of-way cause a dispute. The owners can usually resolve these disputes without further assistance. However, if you are asked to give a right-of-way and you are reluctant to do so—for any reason—it is best to seek legal advice.

Trespass

Trespass is a dispute with someone who is using (or has used) your land without your prior approval. It can usually be handled without the assistance of an attorney. Be sure your land is properly posted (see chapter 3), and—if necessary—follow up a personal conversation with a letter to the trespasser. As a concession, consider allowing access but limiting the scope or period of access. If the trespass has resulted in damage or loss, unless you know the laws in your state, it is best to seek legal advice. In some states, damages are automatically awarded a woodland owner for timber trespass, for example, a logger who knowingly crosses your boundary and cuts timber. Getting the errant logger to pay up is another matter. In cases of trespass, or suspected trespass, speak with the trespasser—get the story—before having threatening letters sent from your attorney.

Liability and Personal Injury

These types of claims must be handled by an attorney. When people perform work for you, they should provide evidence of general liability and workmen's compensation insurance as discussed in chapter 6.

Timber Sale Terms and Professional Service Contracts

Disputes involving these types of contracts often end up in court needlessly. As discussed in chapter 6, it easy to build provisions into these types of agreements that allow for alternative dispute resolution methods, such as arbitration or mediation, described later. The best way to avoid these types of disputes is to use clear, written communication. Also, do not view the contract as a means of forcing someone to do something not provided in the contract. That simply sets the stage for a dispute. If you do not trust the person, don't sign the contract—find someone else to do the work.

Divorce

When forest land is one of the assets in a divorce settlement, too often the land suffers a quick sale at bargain prices to a buyer who cares little for sustaining long-term forest benefits. Although resolving the larger disputes that spawn divorce are far beyond the scope of this book, spouses who care for the land can at least agree to protect it when they split up. For instance, one spouse can agree to buy the other out over time; or they may agree to give the development rights to a local land trust (and split the tax benefits). Or they may want to create a trust for their children (see chapters 8 and 9). Generally, it is better to resolve issues about the forest before one partner sues the other for divorce. A happily married couple can execute an agreement about the disposition of woodlands "in the event of a divorce." Although this may sound like anticipating divorce, at least the partners agree: the importance of forests transcend any future disputes that might come between them as a couple.

Resolving the issue of forest assets in the event of a divorce requires clear, written communication between spouses, and—since the resolutions proposed here are somewhat unusual—may require the services of an attorney to draw up the agreement.

When one prospective spouse is bringing forest land to the marriage, the parties should have a prenuptial agreement. This is especially important in the common-law states (which is every state except the following community-property states: Arizona, California, Idaho, Louisiana, Nevada, New Mexico, Texas, Washington, and Wisconsin). In a common-law state, a family court judge decides who gets what based on a wide range of factors, such as length of marriage, earning capacity of the individuals, fault, and other issues. Without a prenuptial agreement, all assets of the couple—even those brought to the marriage—may be considered joint assets. In a community-property state, the assets a spouse brings to a marriage are usually not part of the marital property. However, assets acquired during the marriage may be divided fifty-fifty, unless there is a prior agreement that specifies some other distribution. An agreement drawn up after the marriage is called a postnuptial agreement.

Taxes

A dispute over taxes usually pits you against the system. In the case of property taxes, as noted in chapter 8, you must demonstrate a mistake in your assessment or an error in calculating the tax. Forget about arguing the larger issue of fair taxation. If you do have a valid dispute, you may be able to argue it successfully without professional assistance.

Sometimes a well-informed taxpayer can handle a state or federal audit regarding income and expenses from forest lands without the services of an attorney or an accountant. If the audit involves a much broader examination—if the income from a timber sale is incidental and not the main issue—you may want to at least have your figures checked by an accountant for the year in question before going into the audit.

Solving Disputes on Your Own

As a forest owner, there will be more instances where you should attempt to resolve a dispute on your own than instances that will require professional services. The trick is in knowing when to ask for help. If you are the type of person who avoids conflict at all costs, you may want to ask someone to represent you. If you are a person who enjoys arguing and never gives up a good fight, you, too, should ask someone to represent you. The biggest mistake an individual makes in confronting others is letting his or her ego get in the way. Never, under any circumstances, should a valid dispute between individuals be taken to a personal level. That only causes the parties to lose sight of the issue, which gets lost in the fray. Animosity builds rapidly, all reason is lost, and there is no hope of reaching an easy solution. In fact, the objective often shifts from resolving the dispute to destroying the other person. It is impossible to negotiate with someone you detest.

If you know yourself well enough to admit you might be closer to one extreme or the other, you can best serve your cause by hiring a consulting forester, or some other appropriate professional advisor, to serve as your personal representative. Be wary, though, of legal advice from someone who is not qualified to give it.

Assuming you are of a mind to negotiate your own resolution to a dispute, the first objective is to identify the problem three different ways: (1) from your own perspective, (2) from the perspective of your adversary, and (3) from the perspective of a third party who knows only the facts (and not the personalities of the adversaries). This exercise is not as simple as it sounds, but you may discover that it is easier to understand the problem and resolve it than you first imagined.

Decide what you are willing to concede to resolve the dispute. This may include something you are willing to give even though you do not believe you should be required to do so. Remember, the alternative is an escalating battle, expensive attorneys, sleepless nights, lost work time, ill will, and the chance you might lose.

When you meet with your adversary, state your position on the issue(s) clearly and concisely. Listen to the opposing viewpoint, and allow ample time for the other side to state his points. Ignore any careless references that may begin to take things to a personal level. Now, restate the opposing position as you understand it. Give your adversary a chance to clarify, if necessary, and to restate the position again. Keep doing this until you can make a statement about your adversary's position that you understand and with which he agrees. Then offer a proposal to solve the problem. Or, if the dispute does not lend itself to an immediate solution, agree that both of you at least understand each other's positions.

Follow up the meeting with a letter summarizing the situation from both perspectives. Offer a proposal to solve the problem and try to set another date to meet. You may need to negotiate among proposals and counterproposals, and it may begin to appear too complicated to solve on your own. Do not despair—this is when you turn to alternative dispute resolution methods, described below.

If you do obtain an agreement, draft a letter describing the problem from both perspectives and the resolution of the items on which you have agreed. Send two copies, and have the other person sign one and return it to you. Signatures may need to be witnessed and/or notarized on this type of agreement in your state. Ask your attorney, or call your attorney's general office (appendix B). If the settlement involves more than a few thousand dollars, you may want to have an attorney review the agreement before signing it.

Alternative Dispute Resolution

A term coined by trial attorneys, alternative dispute resolution, describes a process that attempts to keep disputes out of court. Though attorneys usually represent the parties who agree to this form of resolution, the parties can do it on their own. The result is usually a faster, more comfortable, and cheaper alternative to using the courts. Alternative dispute resolution methods are relatively new, and states view the proceedings differently. If you have a question as to whether a dispute can be satisfactorily resolved out of court, check with your lawyer or the attorney general.

Mediation

The purpose of mediation is to bring the parties of a dispute together and, through the assistance of a third party—the mediator—develop the terms of an agreement that resolves the problem. It is the mediator's job to focus on the problem and its resolution, to keep tempers cool, and to negotiate a solution that is mutually acceptable. However, the parties are usually not bound to the results of mediation unless the product is a properly executed and signed agreement.

The mediator can be anyone, but preferably it is someone with proper training and previous experience. It should be someone with an excellent capacity to listen, to interpret and articulate the exact nature of the dispute, and to help the parties craft their own resolution to the problem. A good mediator is nonjudgmental; it is not the mediator's position to say what is right and what is wrong. A successful mediation is when the parties to the dispute do all the work, and the mediator just keeps the discussion on course.

Arbitration

In arbitration, the parties to a dispute usually agree to accept—before the process begins—the findings of an arbitrator, or an arbitration panel. It is akin to a private court proceedings and may be handled in much the same way. One obvious advantage of arbitration is this: unlike court proceedings, which are a matter of public record, the arbitration record is private.

Although it is not necessary to have an attorney or other representation in arbitration, depending on the nature of the dispute (and the rules regarding arbitration proceedings in your state), you may want to have an attorney present. Anyone can serve as an arbitrator, and it is not uncommon to include a clause in a timber sale contract to resolve disputes using an arbitration panel (see chapter 6).

The results of arbitration are usually binding on the parties, who are required to sign an arbitration agreement before the process begins. A disadvantage of arbitration is there are usually very few grounds for appealing the arbitrator's decision. Although state laws in this matter vary, a court judge will usually accept the decision of an arbitrator as though it were his or her own decision. It is not

A Case Study in Arbitration

This case involves Mr. A, a timber buyer and logger, and Ms. K. a local woodland owner who has contracted to sell timber to Mr. A using a mill-tally sale method (see chapter 6). The contract specifies stumpage rates, varying by species and product groups, to be paid Ms. K based on Mr. A's representations of the actual tally. In other words, Ms. K has agreed to accept the buyer's word on harvest volumes and log grades regardless of who provides the tally, so long as Mr. A assures her that the tally is correct. Among other conditions, the contract also stipulates that any disputes that might arise will be resolved by an arbitration panel of three individuals, and they will split the cost. Both parties agree to be bound by the majority decision of that panel composed of one person selected by Ms. K, another selected by Mr. A, and the third party selected by mutual agreement of the first two arbiters. A vote of two to one will settle the matter. But if such an outcome is not possible, the parties agree to empanel at least three arbitration boards before "agreeing to disagree" and settling the matter in court.

Midway through the sale, Ms K has seen a dozen tally slips from three different mills, and two checks from Mr. A's business account. She compares the total check amounts to the tally slips and discovers that she has been paid for all timber that has left her land.

Six weeks later, upon returning from town one afternoon, she sees the logger on the landing visiting with a well-dressed, European-looking man. They are standing before a pile of what appear to be extremely high-value logs.

A few days later, Ms. K receives eight tally slips from the same three mills, plus a tally slip that has been prepared by Mr. K for six thousand board feet (Mbf) of logs paid for at the very highest stumpage rates in the contract. Just as before, everything adds up. But she wonders why one of the tally slips for high-value logs was tallied on the logger's stationery. The next day she visits the logger and asks about the separate tally. After confessing that he does not understand what she is asking, the logger becomes defensive and tells her she has been paid—exactly according to the terms of the contract—for all logs removed from the property. Getting no where, Ms. K decides to drop the matter and do a little research before confronting the logger again.

A call to the local county forester confirms her suspicions: a German veneer buyer has been visiting timber sales in the area and offering top-dollar for only the finest logs. Although the forester confesses to having no direct knowledge of prices—and it is really outside the bounds of his position to quote timber prices—he reluctantly confirms that the buyer may have been paying up to five times the highest rates listed in her contract.

The next evening she calls the logger at home and confronts him with this information. Mr. A admits to selling logs to the German buyer, but also insists that he has not violated the terms of their contract. He paid the agreed-upon stumpage rates (which Ms. K had verified) and any amounts he received over and above the contract rates were his business. Ms. K disagrees claiming she had been cheated. She tells the logger that she is suspending their contract for cause (as is her right to do), and she wants to assemble an arbitration panel to decide the matter.

It takes three days to locate an arbitration panel. After each person signs an affidavit confirming no recent connections to the buyer or seller (in fact, the third party actually resides in an adjoining state), they are given copies of all the pertinent documents. On the morning of the fourth day, the panel comes together for the first time to take testimony from both parties and any expert witnesses they wish to include. The panel adjourns at lunchtime, agreeing to meet that afternoon to reach a decision. In less than two hours, they unanimously reach a conclusion.

Since the contract clearly states that all tallies are to be verified by Mr. A—regardless of their source, presumably even from the logger himself—Mr. A had not violated any terms of the contract. The panel did, however, decide that the contract terms also provided the logger an unfair advantage, one that would not have prevailed if Ms. K had been advised by a private consulting forester. Furthermore, the panel decided that even though the contract did not restrict the logger's rights to market logs to any buyer—even his own company—the logger should have negotiated his log sale to the German buyer somewhere other than on Ms. K's land. If Mr. A had done so, the panel would have found completely in his favor.

Given the circumstances, however, the panel decided that the only fair solution was to suggest that Mr. A split the profits from the veneer sale with Ms. K. and in the future the logger is to either broker logs at another location or ask the woodland owner's permission to do so from the landing, but with the risk that the owner will ask to share profits.

Late in the afternoon of the fourth day, both Mr. A and Ms. K signed the arbitration decision indicating their willingness to accept the panel's decision and to abide by its terms. In the last batch of tally slips (from the same three mills) was a separate sheet that reconciled the profit sharing from the veneer sale, and a final check with all amounts accounted for.

Note:The facts of this case-study, although intended to be realistic, are completely fictitious. Also, if an arbitration panel is intended to substitute a court proceedings to settle a dispute, it must conform with state statutes on arbitration. Expecting to complete an arbitration proceeding such as this in only four days is probably unrealistic.

surprising that many people who offer arbitration services are former judges. Arbitration is an excellent way to settle a dispute. But if you believe you cannot live with a decision that goes against you, you probably need to hire an attorney and prepare for court.

Hiring and Working with an Attorney

Few people make it through life without at some time requiring the services of an attorney. Fortunately, most encounters with attorneys are benign, such as when closing on a real estate purchase. For relatively simple, procedural tasks like that, almost any local attorney will do. But when a dispute is brewing, the person who handled your closing may not be the best person to hire as your advocate. Some lawyers specialize in litigation, and for a problem that is apt to end up in court, you want someone who knows the process. The same advice applies to any type of specialized legal need. Beyond title searches, there are many circumstances where any available lawyer simply will not due.

Also, if you are going to court (other than small claims court, where a judge is asked to give a verdict on only monetary settlements of a few thousand dollars or less, dollar limits varying by state), forget about trying to represent yourself. Consider the words of Abraham Lincoln: “The attorney who represents himself has a fool for a client.” Unless you are thoroughly familiar with courtroom procedures and the rules of evidence in your state, it is money well spent to hire an attorney if there is even a slight chance you will end up in court. Without proper representation, it is all too easy to lose a foolproof case on a technicality. This is especially true if you are the defendant, the one against whom claims are being made. There is no sympathy for the litigant who represents himself. A judge applies the same standards whether you know the rules or not.

The best time to shop for an attorney is before trouble starts. Not that you need to go through life anticipating court battles at every turn. Your sense of urgency, though, will get in the way of a careful, well-informed selection process if you begin shopping after you have a problem. It is a good idea to become familiar with attorneys in your area who have experience working with woodland issues. Ask around to obtain a list of the names of a few prospective candidates. Most attorneys do not charge for an initial consultation, which is a good opportunity to learn if they have any experience with cases involving woodlands. If you do not have a specific legal problem pending, a lawyer may be reluctant to take time to meet you. Nevertheless, you can learn a great deal about someone during the course of even a brief phone conversation. You just need to know the right questions to ask.

Shop for an attorney the same way you would a consulting

forester (see chapter 5). Competency should be at the top of your list, and you also want someone with whom you can communicate easily. If you end up in a dispute, the attorney will become your confidant and your advocate. He or she will speak for you in all negotiations with the other party and in court. You need someone who is easy to talk to, and who can quickly assimilate the legal aspects of your case.

Assuming you have called on your attorney to represent you in a lawsuit, you should reveal everything—including information that might be detrimental to your case. You must be absolutely truthful regarding the facts of the case. If you disclose information that you later change to improve (or alter) your story, your lawyer may be forced to resign. As an officer of the court, a lawyer cannot knowingly allow lies to be presented as fact, especially when stated under oath. Nor can your lawyer protect you from a lie.

Lying under oath is known as *perjury* and is a serious offense, punishable at the discretion of the judge. You are better off telling the truth, sticking to it, and letting your attorney work the angles in court that will turn circumstances in your favor without having to deceive. Also, remember that when you go to court, your life becomes an open and very public book. Your adversary can request permission to search anywhere a judge deems reasonable for the purposes of gathering information pertinent to the case—files from the hard drive on your computer, phone records, contents of safety deposit boxes—anywhere supporting information is apt to be found. Often the discovery period of a lawsuit is used to intimidate a litigant into settling out of court. Judges expect attorneys to try to settle suits out of court. If you cannot stand the heat, negotiating a settlement is an acceptable alternative to having your life explored in a public forum.

The procedural aspects of court are too vast to describe here. Suffice to say, it can take months or years in some jurisdictions to achieve a court verdict. All the while your lawyer's clock is ticking, and every month you receive a bill that at first blush seems ridiculously too high to be true. Lawyers are expensive. This fact alone is one of the main reasons to avoid court if at all possible.

Attorneys charge for their time in the following three ways:

1. *Flat fee*, similar to the "contract for services" discussed in chapter 6. This type of fee may be used for rote tasks, like title searching or drawing up a will.

2. *Fee on contingency*. When a client is suing another and a monetary award is expected, the lawyer will usually accept a fee contingent on the amount of the award. Thirty percent is common, but the amount is negotiable. Expect to pay office expenses and agreed-upon fees that are independent of the award.

3. *Hourly fee*. In the absence of a contingency-fee agreement, most attorneys charge for their time on an hourly basis. Billing is monthly and itemizes office expenses pertinent to your file, including the number of hours (and fractional hours) the lawyer has devoted to your case. If you call your attorney on the phone and engage in a five-minute call, you should be charged for one-tenth of an hour, although attorneys vary in how they treat fractions of hours. At two hundred dollars per hour a three-minute call to check on the progress of your case will cost twenty dollars. So call only when absolutely necessary and be sure to understand billing arrangements from the outset, especially hourly rates and fractional hours.

As in forestry, there are no standard contracts. For instance, you might get your attorney to agree to a cap on fees for services, costs that he or she should be able to reasonably estimate. Setting up a living trust, preparing a timber sale agreement, or negotiating a settlement are situations where it might be beneficial to set a cap. Lawyers like to be paid on a regular basis. They do not like to carry large outstanding balances on clients. Aside from the obvious reasons for this, clients have been known to not pay up when decisions go against them.

When you receive the final bill, be aware that sometimes grounds exist for offering a payment that is less than the total. Let's say you owe your attorney $6,500, a much higher balance than most law offices will carry. Perhaps you can recall incidents during your meetings when the discussion strayed from your problems to something else, or when your attorney felt compelled to carry on at length about a related experience—any other reason to justify paying less than the total bill. You might offer three thousand dollars. The attorney will consider your offer, maybe take it to the partners then counter with a final bill of $4,750. The attorney split the difference, and you saved $1,850. Your attorney accepts the lower payment on the strength of your arguments and on the reasonable assumption that it may take an inordinate effort to get you to pay the full bill. The settlement is the business equivalent of "a bird in the hand." However, if you owe $6,500, pay it. Do not use the methods described above to cheat your lawyer out of fees owed. You might have a difficult time finding an attorney the next time you need one.

Following are some legitimate ways to save money when working with an attorney:

- Ask if there are documents you can prepare to help save costs. Offer to do legwork, delivering documents to courts and elsewhere. Do not ask the attorney to perform rote tasks that you could handle.
- Always have an agenda prepared when you visit the attorney. Never allow the discussion to veer too far from it. Have your questions prepared in advance.
- Take notes to avoid asking the same question at a subsequent meeting. Ask for (by specifying in your retainer agreement) copies of all correspondence, memos, pleadings, and other documents related to your case.
- Follow your attorney's advice. Others (friends and family) will offer their opinions, possibly on similar cases. But your case is unique and you are paying for advice, so you should use it. Once a case is under way, it is unethical for your opponent's attorney to contact you. In matters related to the case, all information flows through your attorney.
- Your lawyer has an obligation to try to settle your case out of court. He or she is also obligated to communicate any reasonable offers from the opposition to you, and to make only offers that you have authorized. Clearly state your bottom line and prepare to go below it if necessary.

- Finally, regard a good lawyer on your side as an insurance policy —something you hope never to use, but if you need it someday, it's there. You can do many things to avoid disputes or resolve them before they escalate into courtroom battles. But when all else fails, there is no better advocate than an attorney who understands your circumstances and your commitment to the forest.

Appendix A. Extension Forestry Specialists in the United States

Alabama	334-844-1038	brinker@forestry.auburn.edu
Alaska	907-474-6356	ffraw@uaf.edu
Arizona	520-621-7255	cppr@ag.arizona.edu
Arkansas	870-777-9702	froth@uaexsun.uaex.edu
California	510-643-5428	standifo@nature.berkley.edu
Colorado	970-491-7780	craigs@cnr.colostate.edu
Connecticut	860-774-9600	sbroderi@canr1.cag.uconn.edu
Delaware	302-739-4811	austin@smtp.dda.state.de.us
Florida	352-846-0883	mgj@gnv.ifas.ufl.edu
Georgia	706-542-7602	cdanger@uga.cc.uga.edu
Hawaii	808-956-8708	elswaify@hawaii.edu
Idaho	208-885-6356	mahoney@uidaho.edu
Illinois	217-333-2778	m-bolin@uiuc.edu
Indiana	765-494-3580	billh@fnr.purdue.edu
Iowa	515-294-1168	phw@iastate.edu
Kansas	785-532-1444	cbarden@oz.oznet.ksu.edu
Kentucky	606-257-7596	jstringer@ca.uky.edu
Louisiana	504-388-4087	fowler@agctr.lsu.edu
Maine	207-581-2892	tnelson@umce.umext.maine.edu
Maryland	301-432-2767	jk87@umail.umd.edu
Massachusetts	413-545-2943	dbk@forwild.umass.edu
Michigan	517-355-0096	koelling@pilot.msu.edu
Minnesota	612-624-3020	mbaughma@forestry.umn.edu
Mississippi	601-325-3150	tomm@ces.msstate.edu
Missouri	573-882-4444	No e-mail address
Montana	406-243-2773	efrsl@forestry.umt.edu
Nebraska	402-472-5822	fofw093@unlvm.unl.edu
Nevada	702-784-4039	walker@scs.unr.edu
New Hampshire	603-862-4861	karen.bennett@unh.edu
New Jersey	732-932-8993	vodak@aesop.rutgers.edu
New Mexico	505-827-5830	frossbach@state.nm.us

New York	607-255-4696	pjs23@cornell.edu
North Carolina	919-515-5574	hamilton@cfr.cfr.ncsu.edu
North Dakota	701-231-8478	mjackson@ndsuext.nodak.edu
Ohio	614-292-9838	heiligmann.1@osu.edu
Oklahoma	405-744-6432	cgreen@okway.okstate.edu
Oregon	541-737-3700	forestre@ccmail.orst.edu
Pennsylvania	814-863-0401	fj4@psu.edu
Rhode Island	401-874-2912	tom@uriacc.uri.edu
South Carolina	864-656-4851	gsabin@clemson.edu
South Dakota	605-688-4737	jball@doa.state.sd.us
Tennessee	423-974-7346	wclatterbuck@utk.edu
Texas	409-273-2120	a-dreesen@tamu.edu
Utah	801-797-4056	mikek@ext.usu.edu
Vermont	802-656-2913	thomas.mcevoy@uvm.edu
Virginia	540-231-7679	jej@vt.edu
Washington	509-335-2963	baumgtnr@wsu.edu
West Virginia	304-293-2941	tpahl@wvu.edu
Wisconsin	608-262-0134	ajmartin@facstaff.wisc.edu
Wyoming	307-235-9400	ivory@coffey.com

Appendix B. Attorney General Offices in the United States

Alabama	334-242-7300	No website available
Alaska	907-465-3600	www.law.state.ak.us
Arizona	602-542-4266	www.azag.gov
Arkansas	501-682-2007	www.state.ar.us/ag/ag.html
California	916-324-5437	www.caag.state.ca.us
Colorado	303-866-3052	www.ago.state.co.us
Connecticut	860-566-2026	No website available
Delaware	302-577-3838	www.state.de.us/attgen/index.htm
Florida	904-487-1963	No website available
Georgia	404-656-4585	www.ganet.org/ago
Hawaii	808-586-1282	www.state.hi.us/ag
Idaho	208-334-2400	No website available
Illinois	312-814-2503	No website available
Indiana	317-233-4386	www.ai.org/hoosieradvocate/index.html
Iowa	515-281-3053	www.state.ia.us/government/ag/index.html
Kansas	913-296-2215	No website available
Kentucky	502-564-7600	http://ag.ky.gov
Louisiana	504-342-7013	No website available
Maine	207-626-8800	No website available
Maryland	410-576-6300	www.oag.state.md.us
Massachusetts	617-727-2200	www.magnet.state.ma.us/ag
Michigan	517-373-1110	No website available
Minnesota	612-296-6196	www.ag.state.mn.us
Mississippi	601-359-3692	www.ago.state.ms.us
Missouri	573-751-3321	No website available
Montana	406-444-2026	No website available
Nebraska	402-471-2682	No website available
Nevada	702-687-4170	No website available

New Hampshire	603-271-3658	No website available
New Jersey	609-292-4925	www.state.nj.us/lps
New Mexico	505-827-6000	No website available
New York	518-474-7330	www.oag.state.ny.us
North Carolina	919-716-6400	www.ncdoj.com/default.jsp
North Dakota	701-328-2210	No website available
Ohio	614-466-3376	No website available
Oklahoma	405-521-3921	No website available
Oregon	503-378-6002	www.doj.state.or.us
Pennsylvania	717-787-3391	www.attorneygeneral.gov
Rhode Island	401-274-4400	No website available
South Carolina	803-734-3970	www.scattorneygeneral.org
South Dakota	605-773-3215	www.state.sd.us/attorney/attorney.html
Tennessee	615-741-6474	No website available
Texas	512-463-2191	www.oag.state.tx.us
Utah	801-538-1326	No website available
Vermont	802-828-3171	No website available
Virginia	804-786-2071	No website available
Washington	360-753-6200	www.atg.wa.gov
West Virginia	304-558-2021	No website available
Wisconsin	608-266-1221	www.doj.state.wi.us
Wyoming	307-777-7841	No website available

Appendix C. Internet Resources

The websites listed here are not intended as proxies for or to act as forms of legal advice, but rather to serve as starting points for information about local, regional, and national codes and statutes. Consider, too, that many legal situations require the counsel of a lawyer.

Federal Internet Resources

USFS Forest Landowner's Guide to Internet Resources
http://na.fs.fed.us/pubs/misc/flg
USFS Stewardship and Landowner Assistance
www.na.fs.fed.us/spfo/stewardship/index.htm
USFS Main Site
www.fs.fed.us
Federal Tax Information
www.fs.fed.us/spf/coop, www.irs.gov
USFS Landowner Assistance Programs: (Includes current protocol for the Forest Legacy Program, Forest Stewardship Program, and Forest Land Enhancement Program)
www.fs.fed.us/spf/coop/programs/loa/index.shtml
Estate Planning USFS Pub (1993)
www.srs.fs.usda.gov/pubs/gtr/gtr_so097.pdf
USFS posting of Bush administration's "Healthy Forests Initiative"
www.fs.fed.us/projects/hfi/field-guide
Environmental Protection Agency Forestry Laws/Regulations
www.epa.gov/agriculture/forestry.html

State-by-State Statutes

State Legislative Websites (provided for research of regional statutes and codes; many sites listed here have searchable statute databases):

Alabama
http://alisdb.legislature.state.al.us/acas/ACASLogin.asp
Alaska
www.legis.state.ak.us/folhome.htm

Arizona
www.azleg.state.az.us/ArizonaRevisedStatutes.asp
Arkansas
www.arkleg.state.ar.us/NXT/gateway.dll?f=templates&fn=default.htm&vid=blr:code
California
www.legislature.ca.gov/research_and_publications/laws_and_constitution/laws_and_constitution.html
Colorado
www.state.co.us/gov_dir/leg_dir
Connecticut
http://search.cga.state.ct.us/dtsearch_pub_statutes.html
Delaware
www.legis.state.de.us/Legislature.nsf/fsOnlinePub?openframeset&Frame=Main&Src=/Legislature.nsf/Lookup/OnlinePub_Home?open
District of Columbia
http://dccode.westgroup.com/home/dccodes/default.wl
Florida
www.flsenate.gov/Statutes/index.cfm?Mode=View%20Statutes&Submenu=1&Tab=statutes
Georgia
www.legis.state.ga.us/cgi-bin/gl_codes_detail.pl?code=1-1-1
Hawaii
www.capitol.hawaii.gov/site1/search/search.asp?press1=search
Idaho
www3.state.id.us/idstat/TOC/idstTOC.html
Illinois
www.ilga.gov
Indiana
www.in.gov/legislative/ic/code
Iowa
www.legis.state.ia.us/IACODE
Kansas
www.kslegislature.org/cgi-bin/statutes/index.cgi
Kentucky
http://lrc.ky.gov/statrev/frontpg.htm
Louisiana
www.legis.state.la.us/lss/tsrssearch.htm
Maine
http://janus.state.me.us/legis/statutes
Maryland
http://mgasearch.state.md.us/verity.asp
Massachusetts
www.mass.gov/legis/laws/mgl/index.htm
Michigan
http://michiganlegislature.org/mileg.asp?page=ChapterIndex

Minnesota
www.leg.state.mn.us/leg/statutes.asp
Mississippi
http://index.ls.state.ms.us
Missouri
www.moga.state.mo.us/statutesearch
Montana
http://data.opi.state.mt.us/bills/mca_toc/index.htm
Nebraska
http://statutes.unicam.state.ne.us
Nevada
www.leg.state.nv.us/NRS/search/NRSQuery.cfm
New Hampshire
http://gencourt.state.nh.us/rsa/html/indexes/default.html
New Jersey
www.njleg.state.nj.us
New Mexico
http://legis.state.nm.us/newsite/default.asp
New York
http://assembly.state.ny.us/leg/?cl=0
North Carolina
www.ncleg.net/homePage.pl
North Dakota
www.state.nd.us/lr/information/statutes/cent-code.html
Ohio
www.legislature.state.oh.us/search.cfm##orc
Oklahoma
www2.lsb.state.ok.us/tsrs/os_oc.htm
Oregon
www.leg.state.or.us/ors/home.html
Pennsylvania
www.pacode.com/secure/search.asp
Rhode Island
www.rilin.state.ri.us/Statutes/Statutes.html
South Carolina
www.scstatehouse.net
South Dakota
http://legis.state.sd.us/statutes/index.cfm?FuseAction=StatutesTitleList
Tennessee
http://tennessee.gov/sos/acts/index.htm
Texas
www.capitol.state.tx.us/statutes/statutes.html
Utah
http://le.utah.gov/%7Ecode/code.htm
Vermont
www.leg.state.vt.us/statutes/statutes2.htm

Virginia
http://leg1.state.va.us/000/src.htm
Washington
http://search.leg.wa.gov/pub/textsearch
W. Virginia
www.legis.state.wv.us
Wisconsin
http://folio.legis.state.wi.us/cgi-bin/om_isapi.dll?clientID=73493&infobase=stats.nfo&softpage=Browse_Frame_Pg
Wyoming
http://legisweb.state.wy.us/statutes/statutes.htm

Various Reliable Sources of Legal Information

The leading internet source on forest and forest products taxation
www.timbertax.org
Free glossary of legal terms
www.wvu.edu/~exten/depts/af/ahc/glossprp.pdf
Free information on Living Trusts sponsored by the state of Ohio
www.co.franklin.oh.us/probate/departments/trusts.htm
Free legal information on estate law, trusts, etc. from the American Bar Association
www.abanet.org/rppt/public/home.html
University of Pittsburg School of Law Online Law Center (free searchable legal database)
http://jurist.law.pitt.edu/sg_prop.htm
Cornell University Law School—The Legal Information Institute (free searchable database of legal information)
www.law.cornell.edu
Yale University Law School—The Avalon Project (free searchable database of historical law documents and more)
www.yale.edu/lawweb/avalon/avalon.htm

Sustainable Forest Management and Green Certification Systems

Forest Stewardship Council
www.fscus.org
Smartwood (an example of one such certification system in practice)
www.rainforest-alliance.org/programs/forestry/smartwood/index.html
Scientific Certification Systems
www.scscertified.com/forestry
National Forestry Association
www.greentag.org

Family Forests, Forest/Land Trusts, and Forest Cooperatives

Washington state
www.familyforestfoundation.org/index.html

The West Coast
 www.pacificforest.org
Wisconsin
 www.wisconsinfamilyforests.org
Community Forestry Research Center
 www.forestrycenter.org
New England Forestry Foundation
 www.newenglandforestry.org/home/index.asp
Private Landowner Network (national conservation resource)
 www.privatelandownernetwork.org
Vermont Land Trust
 www.vlt.org
Land Trust Alliance
 www.lta.org
The Trust for Public Land
 www.tpl.org
Maine Land Trust Network
 www.mltn.org
The Wilderness Society (estate planning information)
 www.giftlegacy.com/plgive_main.jsp?WebID=GL2004-0109
Gathering Waters Conservancy (Wisconsin)
 www.gatheringwaters.org
Center for Wildlife Law
 http://ipl.unm.edu/cwl
Land Trust of Virginia (easement information)
 www.landtrustva.org/easement_what.asp
Piedmont Environmental Council's "All about Easements"
 www.pecva.org/conservation/allabouteasements.asp
Southern Regional Extension Publication Site
 http://sref.info/publications/online_pubs
Georgia Environmental Policy Institute (Searchable publication about easements)
 www.p2pays.org/ref/14/13632.htm
Idaho sponsored glossary of legal terms
 www.id.uscourts.gov/glossary.htm
Free business law website sponsored by the Fed (laws of running a business, consideration of arbitration/alternative dispute resolution)
 www.business.gov
Vermont Coverts–Woodlands for Wildlife, Inc.
 www.vtcoverts.org

State Forestry Divisions

These primary state-based web resources are valuable starting points for regional landowner technical advice and assistance.

Alabama
 www.forestry.state.al.us

Alaska
www.dnr.state.ak.us/forestry
Arizona
www.land.state.az.us/programs/fire.htm
Arkansas
www.forestry.state.ar.us
California
www.fire.ca.gov/php
Colorado
http://forestry.state.co.us
Connecticut
http://dep.state.ct.us/burnatr/forestry
Delaware
www.state.de.us/deptagri/forestry
District of Columbia
www.ddot.dc.gov/ufa/site/default.asp?ufaNav_GID=1621
Florida
www.fl-dof.com
Georgia
www.gfc.state.ga.us
Hawaii
www.hawaii.gov/hfciforest
Idaho
www2.state.id.us/lands
Illinois
http://dnr.state.il.us/conservation/forestry/index.htm
Indiana
www.in.gov/dnr/forestry
Iowa
www.iowadnr.com/forestry/index.html
Kansas
www.kansasforests.org
Kentucky
www.forestry.ky.gov
Louisiana
www.ldaf.state.la.us/default.asp
Maine
www.state.me.us/doc/mfs/mfshome.htm
Maryland
www.dnr.state.md.us/forests
Massachusetts
www.mass.gov/dcr/stewardship/forestry
Michigan
www.michigan.gov/dnr/0,1607,7-153-30301_30505—,00.html
Minnesota
www.dnr.state.mn.us/forestry/index.html

Mississippi
www.mfc.state.ms.us
Missouri
www.conservation.state.mo.us/forest
Montana
http://dnrc.state.mt.us/forestry
Nebraska
www.nfs.unl.edu
Nevada
www.forestry.nv.gov
New Hampshire
www.nhdfl.org/index.htm
New Jersey
www.state.nj.us/dep/parksandforests
New Mexico
www.emnrd.state.nm.us/forestry
New York
www.dec.state.ny.us/website/dlf
North Carolina
www.dfr.state.nc.us
North Dakota
www.ndsu.nodak.edu/ndsu/lbakken/forest
Ohio
www.ohiodnr.com/forestry/default.htm
Oklahoma
www.oda.state.ok.us/forestry-home.htm
Oregon
www.odf.state.or.us
Pennsylvania
www.dcnr.state.pa.us/forestry
Rhode Island
www.state.ri.us/dem/programs/bnatres/forest
South Carolina
www.state.sc.us/forest
South Dakota
http://legis.state.sd.us/index.cfm
Tennessee
www.state.tn.us/agriculture/forestry
Texas
http://txforestservice.tamu.edu
Utah
www.ffsl.utah.gov
Vermont
www.vtfpr.org/htm/forestry.cfm
Virginia
www.dof.virginia.gov

Washington
 www.dnr.wa.gov/forestpractices
West Virginia
 www.wvforestry.com/index.cfm
Wisconsin
 www.dnr.state.wi.us/org/land/forestry/index.htm
Wyoming
 http://slf-web.state.wy.us/ami/forestry.htm

Glossary

Abstract of title. A historic summary of property title transfers, with evidence of a current, proper title and an opinion on any encumbrances that may impair or restrict title, usually prepared by an attorney or title company.

Acre. An area of land containing 43,560 square feet, approximately equal to the playing area of an American football field.

Adaptive management. A process based on the idea that continual improvement is possible when applying practices and policies that are observed and learned over time.

Addendum. A written statement, memorandum, change, or endorsement to the original terms of a document. An addendum to a will is known as a *codicil*, and an addendum to an insurance policy is known as a *rider*.

Administrator. A person appointed by the probate court to handle the affairs of a decedent who has died *intestate* (without a will).

Ad valorem. A Latin term that literally means "at value." It applies to property assessments that are based on current fair market value of an asset and not necessarily on its potential to produce value.

Adverse possession. When an owner's claim to property is passed to another against his or her will by action of a public entity, through *eminent domain*, by action of a court judgment, or through some other process whereby another individual stakes a claim against an owner's property. State statutes define the conditions under which an individual can claim the property of another through adverse possession.

Affidavit. A written statement that the author claims is the truth. In most states, the author must also swear an oath before a *notary public* affirming the statement is true.

Agent. A person who acts at the behest of another who is the sole beneficiary of those actions. An agent has a fiduciary responsibility to the person (or entity) he or she represents.

Alienation. The process whereby a property owner passes title to another.

Amortization. A schedule (usually monthly) for repaying debt in equal amounts that includes interest paid on the outstanding balance. As the debt is repaid, more and more of each monthly payment is attributed to the original loan amount. Early payments are mostly interest on the principal sum.

Annuity. A series of equal payments to be paid over a period as specified by a contract. A life insurance annuity is an investment where the insured pays a sum of money to an insurer who agrees to provide an *annuity* beginning at some point in the future, as specified in a contract. The person who receives the annuity (which can usually also be paid as a single lump sum) is called the *annuitant*. The annuitant may be the insured, or someone the insured has appointed as beneficiary.

Arbitration. A process whereby differences are settled between two or more parties based on the decisions of one or more persons who know the facts of the dispute. In arbitration, the disputants usually agree to accept and live by the decision of the arbitrator(s) even before the process begins.

Assignment. A transfer of rights from one party (*assignor*) to another (*assignee*).

Attractive nuisance. A feature of private property, such as a pond, that holds danger for children but attracts them nevertheless.

Balloon note. A loan agreement whereby the lender agrees to a long loan period to make monthly payments more affordable for the borrower, with the condition that the borrower repay the entire loan usually long before the period expires. A note or loan balloons on the date the borrower agrees to repay the full balance.

Basal area. A measure of tree density. It is determined by estimating the total cross-sectional area of all trees measured at breast height (4.5 feet above the ground) and expressed in square feet per acre.

Beneficiary. A person who is legally entitled to benefit from a trust, life insurance annuities, or the profits of an estate, without having control over the assets.

Biodiversity conservation. An approach to managing land that espouses practices that maintain or enhance diversity of plants and animals.

Bond. Something of value, usually money, that is offered to secure a promise to fulfill an obligation. A *performance bond* is a common element of a timber sale contract.

Breach. Failure to fulfill the terms of a contract.

Capital. Any asset that can be used to generate more capital, income, or wealth.

Capital gains. Profits obtained from the sale of capital.

Capital improvement. An expenditure that increases the value or extends the useful life of a capital asset.

Capital loss. When a capital asset is sold for less than its original cost plus capital improvements less allowable depreciation.

Capitalization. A method of determining property value that considers potential net income and a rate of return on investment over a fixed period.

Caveat emptor. A Latin term that means buyer beware. Caveat venditor, "seller beware."

Chattel. Any personal property.

Closing. The event where legal title is transferred and all financial matters and other conditions of a purchase agreement are finally resolved.

Clouded title. An encumbrance created by a lien, claim, or document that casts doubt on the current title.

Codicil. See *addendum*.

Collateral. Something of value that is offered to secure the repayment of a debt.

Collusion. An illegal agreement between two or more people to defraud someone else.

Color of title. A deed that appears to be valid but in fact is not, usually due to fraud, such as forgery.

Compensatory damages. A monetary award in a judgment that compensates the injured party for actual losses.

Condemnation. The result of a government's right of *eminent domain* to take property when it is deemed in the public's best interest to do so. A condemnation requires "just compensation" to the owner whose interests have been condemned. See *eminent domain*.

Consequential damages. A monetary award in a judgment that is equal to the loss the breaching party could have foreseen as a result of his or her nonperformance.

Consideration. Value that is offered to someone in exchange for a promise or set of promises.

Conveyance. The transfer of an interest in real estate.

Covenant. A promise or a binding agreement that can pass from one property owner to the next when written into a deed. A *Covenant Running with the Land* binds future owners to maintain the covenant, irrespective of when it was created.

Covenant of seizen. The grantor's promise and warranty (in a deed) that he or she does own the property and has full and exclusive rights to convey a clear and marketable title to the grantee.

Cruise. A survey of forest stands to determine the number, size, and species of trees, as well as terrain, soil conditions, access, and any other factors relevant to forest-management planning.

Curtesy. (From common law, an antiquated concept that is now governed by state statute.) A husband's preemptive rights to his decedent wife's estate. It is most apt to apply to the couple's domicile.

Damages. Money awarded by a court for injuries sustained as a result of the actions or inactions of another. See *compensatory damages*, *consequential damages*, *liquidated damages*, and *punitive damages*.

Deed. A legal document that describes the rights a person has to real property.

Deed restriction. Also known as *restrictive covenant.* Any condition set forth in a deed that defines or limits the extent of a deed holder's rights.

Defamation. An attempt to injure another person's reputation by making false statements.

Defendant. A person against whom a *plaintiff* has filed a suit.

Deposition. Sworn testimony given outside of court, usually in preparation for trial.

Depreciation. As applies to IRS rules, the annual cost of an asset used for business purposes, which can also be deducted from gross income. Business equipment depreciates according to schedules established by the IRS.

Devise. A testamentary gift of real estate from a *devisor* to the person receiving the gift, the *devisee.*

Diameter (or DBH). Tree diameter at breast height, taken at 4.5 feet above average ground level at the base of the tree.

Discovery. The process of obtaining facts in connection with a lawsuit, usually in preparation for trial. Depositions are part of the discovery process.

Dominant estate. When the rights to real estate have been separated, the *estate* created by the separation of rights is the dominant estate. It is the property that benefits from an easement. The estate from which the rights have been separated is the servient estate. The holder of an easement has the dominant estate, while the holder of the property from which the easement evolved has the servient estate.

Dower. (From common law, an antiquated concept that is now governed by state statute.) A wife's preemptive rights to her decedent husband's estate. It is most apt to apply to the couple's domicile.

Durable power of attorney. An extreme type of agency relationship that gives someone the power to make decisions for another person even after that person has become incapacitated (but is not dead).

Duress. A person who is compelled or forced to do something against his or her will is acting under duress.

Easement. A separation (commonly irrevocable) of the rights an owner normally has in real estate that vests a portion of those rights to another person or entity is known as an easement.

Easement appurtenant. Also known as an *appurtenant easement*, it is a right to use another's land that is attached to and benefits the title of, most commonly, an adjacent property. For instance, an easement to a neighbor for a driveway is noted as an easement appurtenant in the neighbor's property title.

Easement by necessity. Usually a temporary right to use another's land for access to otherwise landlocked properties. Some states require this type of easement (from a *servient estate*) for defined uses, such as farming or forest management. See *dominant estate*.

Ecosystem health. A somewhat controversial term among foresters when applied to forests; as used here it implies that a healthy forest ecosystem is one where the essential ecosystem integrity is maintained largely within the limits imposed by nature. The term also implies that careless or excessive human use can lead to a degradation of ecosystem integrity.

Ecosystem management. A new approach to managing forests that "attempts to meet human needs without disrupting the integrity of the ecological processes by which forest ecosystems sustain themselves" (David Brynn, Middlebury, Vermont).

Eminent domain. A right of government (local, state, and federal) to take private property for public use. See *condemnation*.

Equitable title. An interest in property held by someone other than the deed holder, usually created by a contract. A timber sale creates an equitable title to gain access to woodlands and harvest timber as specified in the contract.

Escheat. A right of state government to claim private property of a decedent who has died intestate and without legal heirs.

Escrow. The holding of money or property by a disinterested party until the conditions of a contract are met. By state law, some types of escrow accounts are non–interest bearing.

Even-aged. A situation in a forest stand where the difference in age between trees forming the main canopy usually does not exceed 20 percent of the age of the stand at *rotation*.

Exclusionary. A clause in a contact that states, in effect, "If it is not listed here, assume the act or practice is excluded from the agreement."

Exculpatory clause. Although not fully recognized in all states, it is a clause in a contract that releases someone, usually a landowner, from personal liability.

Executed contract. When all of the conditions of a contract have been met by all parties, the contract is said to be *executed*.

Executor. A person named in a will to act as the personal representative of a *decedent.*

Express contract. A contractual agreement specifically stated, either oral or written.

Fiduciary. A person with a legal duty to act for the benefit of another. An agent has a fiduciary responsibility to his or her *principal.*

Finder's fee. In forestry, an amount paid by a timber buyer to a third party for information that leads to a purchase of standing timber.

Foreclosure. A court-ordered process where property is sold to repay a debt on which the property holder has defaulted.

Forest type. A natural group or association of different species of trees that commonly occur together over a large area. Forest types are defined and named after one or more dominant species of trees in the type, such as the spruce-fir and oak-hickory types.

Fraud. Any illegal act or misrepresentation of facts intended to deceive or cheat another person.

General partnership. All members of the partnership share in management, profits, and liabilities.

Grant. In realty, a conveyance of interests in land by deed.

Grantee. The person to whom grant of a deed is made. Usually the purchaser.

Grantor. The person who is passing or alienating title. Usually the seller.

Habitat. The place where a plant or animal can live and maintain itself.

Haul road. An interior forest road that connects the log landing with public roads, usually constructed with gravel and designed to support the weight of fully loaded log trucks.

High grading. An exploitive logging practice that removes only the best, most accessible, and marketable trees in a stand.

Holding period. As it relates to IRS rules, it is the minimum period that a taxpayer must own a capital asset before selling it with the advantage of lower tax rates on income from long-term capital gains.

Holographic will. A handwritten will that is signed by the testator, but not witnessed.

Implied contract. A contractual obligation implied by the actions (or inactions) of the parties.

Indemnification. To protect against injury, loss, or damages due to the actions of another. In a timber sale contract, the buyer will usually agree to "indemnify and save harmless the seller from any injuries, losses, or damages resulting from the harvesting and transportation of timber."

Injunction. A court order to stop someone from doing something.

Intestate. A person who dies without a will leaves an estate that is intestate.

Involuntary lien. A lien imposed on property for back taxes, or for other reasons, without the consent of the owner.

Interrogatories. Written questions, the answers to which are also written by a person who swears the answers are complete and truthful. A pretrial method of *discovery*.

Irrevocable. Immutable, or incapable of being changed in any way.

Joint and several liability. When two or more people agree to the terms of a contract, it should specify that they are all liable together (*jointly*), as well as independently (*severally*), if one or more of the parties refuses to hold up their end of the bargain.

Judgment. A decision rendered by a court.

Landing. A cleared area varying in size from a quarter acre to two or more acres, usually near a public road, where logs from the woodlands are skidded and sorted, then loaded onto trucks for transport to various markets.

Libel. A defamatory statement in writing that cannot be proven by facts.

Lien. A claim imposed against the title of a property as security, such as for repayment of a debt.

Limited partnership. A union of individuals usually for business purposes, where some individuals share profits and losses but do not make decisions for the partnership (*limited partners*), while other partners run the business (*general partners*).

Limited power of attorney. A legal instrument that authorizes an individual to act as an agent of another person but with limitations on the time or scope of authority. See *durable power of attorney* and *power of attorney*.

Liquidated damages. A monetary amount agreed to by the parties of a contract that represents reasonable compensation for damages that might result if one of the parties fails to perform.

Living will. A properly executed and witnessed document that outlines the extent to which medical personnel should use life-support and other heroic measures to sustain the life of the person named in the will.

Log. A section of the main stem (trunk) of a tree, varying in length and minimum diameters according to local market standards, that is usually sawn into lumber. As a verb, log refers to the process of harvesting, extracting, and transporting logs to a mill.

Marking guidelines. The rules used to mark a forest stand to implement a prescription.

Maturity. In forest trees, it is usually expressed in two ways: (1) financial maturity—when a tree has reached the point where it has maximized value growth from the market's perspective; and (2) biological maturity—when a tree has reached the point where the energy costs of maintaining itself exceeds the energy input from photosynthesis.

Biologically mature trees are usually much older than the age of financial maturity.

Mbf. An abbreviation for "one thousand board feet."

Merchantable. A standing tree that has a net value when processed and delivered to a mill or some other market after all harvesting costs, transportation costs, and profit are considered.

Mineral rights. A portion of the bundle of rights that allows the holder to explore and extract any minerals (or specific minerals) at any time in the future.

Monument. A fixed object identified by a surveyor, usually for the purposes of marking property corners.

Motion. A formal request of the court during a legal proceeding.

Notary (or Notary Public). A public official who will witness a signature and verify that the person is, in fact, who he or she claims to be. When a document is notarized, it includes an imprint of the notary's seal.

Partnership. An agreement between two or more people, usually for the purposes of doing business together. See *general partnership* and *limited partnership.*

Per capita. A Latin term used in trusts and wills that literally means "by heads." A division of property per capita means equal shares to all.

Per stirpes. A Latin term used in trusts and wills that means "by stocks, or by roots." A division of property per stirpes means a parent's share of an estate is divided among his or her children. If Mom dies before Grandpa, Mom's share of Grandpa's estate is divided among her children.

Perjury. Lying under oath.

Personal representative. See *executor.*

Plaintiff. The person who initiates a lawsuit against a *defendant.*

Power of attorney. A legal instrument that authorizes an individual to act as an agent of another person. See *limited power of attorney* and *durable power of attorney.*

Prescription. A course of action to effect change in a forest stand.

Principal. In an agency, the principal is a person who has authorized an agent to act on his or her behalf. In finance, principal is an amount originally invested or the outstanding balance (excluding interest) of a loan.

Probate. The legal process of proving the validity of a decedent's will and dispersing the estate to legal heirs.

Punitive damages. A monetary award in a court judgment that is in addition to compensatory and consequential damages, for the purposes of punishing the defendant.

Ratify. To accept or approve of the acts of another person after the fact.

Recording. The process of filing documents with the town or county clerk for the purpose of giving public notice of claims, and establishing priority over subsequent claims.

Regeneration. The natural or artificial (by planting) renewal of trees in a stand.

Restrictive covenants. Written conditions imposed on a deed that prohibit or restrict certain activities or uses of the land. Any condition that reduces the full bundle of rights is a restrictive covenant that a grantee agrees to honor and maintain. See *covenants that run with the land*.

Retainer. A fee paid to a service provider that is an advance on the cost of future services. In forestry, a retainer can be identified as *consideration* from the *principal* in a contract that establishes an agency relationship with a consulting forester. A retainer paid to a lawyer is usually an advance on the cost of future services.

Rider. An amendment to a document that applies especially to property insurance. See *addendum*.

Right of first refusal. A form of *consideration* in a contract, where one party agrees to consider a future offer from the other party before soliciting other offers. A right of first refusal is often an element in a timber sale contract where the buyer, or the buyer's agent, also provides services.

Right-of-way. A type of easement where a titleholder gives or sells (or leases) the right to cross over a portion of his or her land. The term is used commonly for roadways; gas and water mains; and sewer, power, and telephone lines.

Riparian rights. Rights and obligations that relate to land abutting water, water courses, and the use of water, especially in states west of the Mississippi.

Rotation. Usually considered to be the length of time it takes to grow an even-aged stand to the point of financial maturity. See *maturity*.

Royalty. A share of profits claimed by the owner of property who allows another to harvest, recover, or use assets from the property.

Sawlog. See *log*.

Sawtimber. Trees that have obtained a minimum diameter at breast height that can be felled and processed into *sawlogs*.

Servient estate. The property from which an easement has been granted. See *dominant estate*.

Severance damages. Usually a sum of money paid to a property owner when a condemnation by *eminent domain* of a portion of his or her property causes the remaining property to lose value.

Silviculture. The "art and science" of growing forests for timber and other values.

Skidder. A four-wheel-drive tractorlike vehicle, articulated in the middle for maneuverability, with a cable or grapple on the back end for hauling logs from stump to a landing area, where they are loaded onto trucks.

Skid trail. Any path in the woods over which multiple loads of logs have been hauled. A trail that enters a main log landing area is called a *primary skid trail.*

Slander. A defamatory oral statement that cannot be proven by facts.

Stand. A community of trees occupying a specific area and "sufficiently uniform in composition, age, arrangement, and condition as to be distinguishable from the forest on adjacent areas."

Statute of limitations. A state law that sets limits on the amount of time a plaintiff has to file suit against a defendant.

Stipulation. An agreement, promise, or guarantee. Also a condition or requirement of a legal document. In court, it is a mutual agreement as to the source and validity of information presented during a legal proceeding.

Stumpage. The value of timber as it stands in the woods just before harvest (on the stump). In some parts of the country it is considered to be a residual sum; that is, the market value of rough lumber minus all the costs of production back to the stump. Whatever is leftover is *stumpage,* the value of a standing tree.

Sublease. An assignment of a lessee's rights and responsibilities to another person.

Subpoena. A written order from a court requiring an individual to appear and testify.

Sustainability. The capacity of an ecosystem to provide benefits in perpetuity without substantially compromising ecosystem integrity.

Sustained yield. A continuous and even flow of wood products available from well-managed forests.

Title. The body of facts or events that support a claim of ownership in real or personal property. In real estate, a deed, if unclouded and proper, is evidence of title. See *deed.*

Title insurance. A type of insurance policy that is fully paid for when title passes to a new owner. It warrants and guarantees the title is valid, unclouded, and marketable.

Tort. A noncontractual, civil wrong that results in injury to another person. Stealing from someone is a tort.

Trespass. An uninvited use or encroachment of a person's rights to private property.

Trust. An agreement or contract where the legal and beneficial interests in property are separated according to the terms of the document.

Trustee. The person or entity that holds and manages property (i.e., controls the legal interests of the property) for the exclusive benefit of another, known as the *beneficiary*.

Trustor (or Settlor). The person who created a trust and whose property is deeded to the trust.

Usury. Extracting a rate of interest on a loan that is excessive, as defined by state statute.

Variance. An exception to current rules for good cause. In real estate, variances apply to zoning regulations.

Vest. To grant or endow with rights, authority, or property. A properly alienated deed to forest land vests the rights and obligations of ownership to the grantee.

Voidable. A contract that appears valid but is not because of errors or other flaws that cause injury to one of the parties. The injured party's claim of a *voidable* contract may cause a court to find the contract (or parts of it) void.

Will. A properly executed and witnessed document drawn up by an individual providing for the disposition of real and personal property upon the person's death.

Yield. Total forest growth over a specified period of time, less mortality, unmarketable fiber, and cull.

Zoning. Local ordinances that control how land is used in a municipality, especially as it relates to building. See *variance*.

References

Ambrose, S. E. 1996. *Undaunted Courage.* New York: Simon and Schuster.

American Forest and Paper Association. 1994. *Federal Laws and Regulations Affecting Private Forestry: What Foresters and Landowners Need to Know to Be in Compliance.* American Forest and Paper Association, 1111 19th St., N.W., Washington, D.C. 20036.

Barlowe, Raleigh. 1990. *Who Owns Your Land?* Publication No. 126. Southern Rural Development Center, Mississippi State, MS 39762.

Barry, Vincent. 1994. "Moral Issues in Business." In Lloyd C. Irland, ed., *Ethics in Forestry.* Portland, OR: Timber Press.

Birch, T. W. 1994. T*he Private Forest: Land Owners of the United States, 1994* (Preliminary Findings). White paper. USDA Forest Service, Northeastern Forest Experiment Station.

Boorstin, Daniel J. 1983. *The Discovers*, 2 vols. New York: Harry N. Abrams, Inc.

Bove, Alexander A., Jr. 1991. *The Complete Book of Wills and Estates.* New York: Henry Holt and Co.

Brodsky, S. L. 1991. *Testifying in Court: Guidelines and Maxims for the Expert Witness.* American Psychological Association, Washington, D.C.

Brown, Curtis. M., Walter G. Robillard, and Donald A. Wilson. *Brown's Boundary Control and Legal Principles*, 5th ed. New York: John Wiley and Sons.

Davenport, F. G. 1917. *European Treaties Bearing on the History of the United States and Its Dependencies to 1648*, 4 vols. Washington, D.C.: Carnegie Institution.

Frascona, Joseph L., Edward J. Conry, Gerald R. Ferra, Terry L. Lantry, Bill M. Shaw, George J. Siedel, George W. Spiro, and Arthur D. Wolfe. 1984. *Business Law Text and Cases: The Legal Environment*, 2nd ed. Dubuque, IA: W. C. Brown.

Freese, F. 1974. *A Collection of Log Rules.* USDA-FS General Technical Report. FPL. Online at: www.fpl.fs.fed.us/documnts/FPLGTR/fplgtr01.pdf.

Gorte, Ross W. 2004. *Forestry Assistance Programs.* Congressional Research Service, Library of Congress. Order Code: RL 31065.

Gregory, G. R. 1972. *Forest Resource Economics.* New York: The Ronald Press.

Haney, Harry L., W. L. Hoover, W. C. Siegel, and J. L. Greene. 2001. *Forest Landowners' Guide to the Federal Income Tax.* USDA Forest Service, Agricultural Handbook No. 71B. Available online at www.fs.fed.uspublications/2001.

Hazard, G. C. and M. Taruffo. 1993. *American Civil Procedure.* New Haven, CT: Yale University Press.

Irland, Lloyd C., ed. 1994. *Ethics in Forestry.* Portland, OR: Timber Press.

Kaplan, E. J. 1979. *Evidence.* Springfield, IL: C. C. Thomas.

Kaufman, P. C. and S. H. Green. 1987. *Understanding Estate Planning and Wills*, 2nd ed. Stamford, CT: Longmeadow Press.

Lusk, Harold F., Charles M. Hewitt, John D. Donnell, and A. James Barnes. 1978. *Business Law: Principles and Cases*, 4th ed. Homewood, IL: R. D. Irwin, Inc.

Martus, C. E., Harry L. Haney, and William C. Siegel. 1995. "Local Forest Regulatory Ordinances." *Journal of Forestry* 93(6):27–31.

McEvoy, T. J., 2004. *Positive Impact Forestry—A Sustainable Approach to Managing Woodlands.* Washington, D.C.: Island Press.

McLauchlan, W. P. 1977. *American Legal Process.* New York: John Wiley and Sons.

Morison, S. E. 1971. *The European Discovery of America: The Northern Voyages—A.D. 500–1600.* New York: Oxford University Press.

———. 1978. *The Great Explorers: The European Discovery of America.* New York: Oxford University Press.

Murray, C. 2004a. *Liability of State Officials Under the Endangered Species Act.* In Proceedings—NCASI Northern Regional Meeting, Portland, ME. Western Michigan University, Kalamazoo, MI.

———. 2004b. *No Surprises Policy.* In Proceedings—NCASI Northern Regional Meeting, Portland, ME. Western Michigan University, Kalamazoo, MI.

Newcomb, Steve. 1992. "Five Hundred Years of Injustice." *Shaman's Drum* (Fall):18–20.

Parker, L. S. 1989. *Native American Estate—The Struggle over Indian and Hawaiian Lands. Honolulu: University of Hawaii Press.*

Pearson, Karl G. and Michael P. Litka. 1980. *Real Estate: Principles and Practices,* 3rd ed. Columbus, OH: Grid Publishing Co.

Phillips, D. T. and B. S. Wolfkiel. 1994. *Estate Planning Made Easy.* Chicago: Dearborn Financial Publishing.

Prestopino, C. J. 1989. *Introduction to Estate Planning.* New York: Dow Jones-Irwin, Inc.

Ring, A. A. and J. Dasso. 1977. *Real Estate Principles and Practices*, 8th ed. Englewood Cliffs, NJ: Prentice-Hall.

Robillard, Walter G. and Donald A. Wilson. 2001. *Evidence and Procedures for Boundary Location*, 4th ed. New York: John Wiley and Sons.

Schneider, Arnold E., John E. Whitcraft, R. Robert Rosenberg, and Robert Olaf Skar. 1967. *Understanding Business Law*, 4th ed. New York: McGraw-Hill

Sharpe, Grant W., Clare W. Hendee, Wenonah F. Sharpe, and John C. Hendee. 1995. *Introduction to Forest and Renewable Resources*, 6th ed. New York: McGraw-Hill.

Shumate, W. A. 1995. "Preserve Timberland and Save Taxes through Family Partnerships." *Forest Farmer* (November–December 1995):17–18.

Sigler, J. A. 1968. *An Introduction to the Legal System*. Homewood, IL: The Dorsey Press.

Small, S. J. 1992. *Preserving Family Lands: Essential Tax Strategies for the Landowner*, 2nd ed. Boston: Landowner Planning Center.

Smith, David M., Bruce C. Larson, Matthew J. Kelty, P. Mark, and S. Ashton. 1997. *The Practice of Silviculture*, 9th ed. New York: John Wiley and Sons.

Terry, Brent W. 1995. *The Complete Idiot's Guide to Protecting Yourself from Everyday Legal Hassles*. New York: Alpha Books.

Thacher, John Boyd. 1903. *Christopher Columbus: His Life, His Work, His Remains*, 3 vols. New York: AMS Press.

Wilford, John Noble. 1981. *The Mapmakers*. New York: Alfred A. Knopf.

Zhang, D. 1996. "State Property Rights: What, Where and How?" *Journal of Forestry* 94(4):10–15.

Index

Board of Directors